TECHNIQUES FOR MONITORING FEDERAL SUBAWARDS

2nd Edition

We've Moved!
Thompson Publishing Group
805 15th St., NW, 3rd floor
Washington, DC 20005
(202) 872-4000 (Editorial Offices)
1-800-677-3789 (Customer Service)

ii THOMPSON
www.thompson.com

ii THOMPSON

Insight you trust.

îî THOMPSON

Thompson Publishing Group, Inc.

Thompson Publishing Group is a trusted name in authoritative analysis of laws, regulations and business practices that helps corporate, government and other professionals develop regulatory compliance strategies. Since 1972, thousands of professionals in business, government, law and academia have relied on Thompson Publishing Group for the most authoritative, timely and practical guidance available.

Thompson offers loose leaf services, books, specialty newsletters, audio conferences and online products in a number of subject and regulatory compliance areas. These Thompson products provide insightful analysis, practical guidance and real-world solutions to the challenges facing grants professionals today and beyond. More information about Thompson's product offerings is available at http://www.thompson.com.

To order any Thompson products or additional copies of this book, please contact us:

Call: 1-800-677-3789
Online: www.thompson.com
Fax: 1-800-999-5661
Email: service@thompson.com
Mail: Thompson Publishing Group
Subscription Service Center
PO Box 26185, Tampa, FL 33623-6185

Executive Editor: Don Hoffman

Desktop Publisher: Laurie S. Clark

Techniques for Monitoring Federal Subawards, 2nd Edition, is published by Thompson Publishing Group, Inc., 1725 K St. N.W., 7th Floor, Washington, DC 20006.

Printed in the United States

ISBN: 978-1-933807-29-4

Table of Contents

Table of Contents

Part A: Subaward Requirements

Origins of Federal Rules for Monitoring Subawards

Federal agencies award billions of dollars every year to state and local governments, colleges and universities and other organizations to administer a myriad of federal assistance programs. Through hundreds of federal programs, these agencies carry out federal mandates and public policies created by executive order of the president or legislation enacted by Congress. For the most part, federal agencies rely on their grant recipients to implement these programs by adhering to program rules and governmentwide policies for administering federal grant dollars – the "strings attached." Grant recipients have to comply with a plethora of these federal rules, ranging from restrictions on how much "overhead" they can charge to a federal grant, to parameters for the types of scientific study that can be funded with federal research dollars, to the income limits of families whose children can receive subsidized meals at school. Federal agencies use various methods – financial reports, progress reports and audits – to ensure grant recipients' proper stewardship of federal funds.

In many cases, grant recipients do not administer these programs themselves. Rather, they subaward or "pass-through" some or all of their federal funds to subrecipients that often run the programs, such as when a large university receives federal grant funds to study global climate change and subawards half of the funds to a nonprofit research institute to conduct a large portion of the research program. In this scenario, the university would agree to comply with the terms of the grant agreement as a condition of receiving the federal funds. In turn, the nonprofit subrecipient must comply with the requirements of the subaward agreement that include many (if not all) of the terms of the federal agency/university agreement as well as any other conditions imposed by the university. Even though a grant recipient might pass-through federal grant dollars to subrecipients (sometimes as much as 90 percent of federal funds received), it is ultimately the primary grantee's responsibility to ensure that federal funds are spent according to the prescribed federal requirements, including any subgranted funds.

Subrecipient Monitoring: New Tool But Old Requirement

For many years, grant recipients (or "pass-through entities") have had to ensure that their subrecipients adhere to governmentwide and program-specific requirements set forth in the grant agreement. This has been especially true since the devolution of federal grant administration to the states in the early 1980s (also known as "new federalism"). At that time, many federal assistance programs (e.g., the Community Development Block Grant) were revamped so that agencies awarded more federal funds to states and other large organizations that in turn subgranted the funds to smaller recipients. A few key policies were issued to address this increase in subawarded federal funds. The U.S. Office of Management and Budget (OMB) in 1988 revised its grant administration rules for state, local and tribal governments to, among other things, incorporate provisions that reflect this shift in grant administration. OMB later revised its governmentwide rules for universities and nonprofits to include similar provisions. Currently, both the common rule for state and local grant administration and OMB Circular A-110 (grant administration rules for colleges, universities and other nonprofit organizations) specifically mandate that federal grant recipients monitor "each program, function or activity" funded with federal grant dollars – including subawards.

With passage of the Single Audit Act in 1984, federal agencies and grant recipients had a new tool – the single audit report – for monitoring and ensuring grantee and subgrantee compliance, respectively. The act required single audits of governments receiving more than $100,000 in federal funds in a year. (Universities and other nonprofit organizations were not at that time within the purview of the act or its implementing policy, OMB Circular A-128.) Governments that received between $25,000 and $100,000 could have either a single audit or an audit "in accordance with federal laws and regulations governing the programs they participate in." Here, again, these audits of smaller awards were used to review and assess compliance.

But Congress amended the act in 1996 to change the audit coverage in three key ways: by raising the single audit threshold to $500,000, by applying the act to universities and other nonprofit organizations that had been covered by a hybrid single audit policy since 1990, and by barring grantees from using federal funds to cover the cost of single audits of exempt subrecipients. OMB amended Circular A-133, *Audits of States, Local Governments and Nonprofit Organizations,* in 2003 to specifically exempt grant recipients and subrecipients that spent less than $500,000 a year in federal awards from federal audit requirements. Instead, those recipients must make their records available for review by pass-through entities and federal awarding agencies.

From a federal standpoint, the raised audit threshold was an efficient and effective way to concentrate audit coverage on the larger federal awards and subawards, but it placed more of a compliance burden on primary recipients. Recognizing that fewer recipients and subrecipients would be covered by single audit requirements, Congress specifically required pass-through entities to monitor all of their subrecipients. This is especially challenging for recipients whose subrecipients fall below the audit threshold, because there is no single audit report to review. Thus, primary grantees have to use other tools to ensure their subawarded funds are being spent properly. And it is these tools that auditors performing single audits will test (using guidance in the OMB *Circular A-133 Com-*

pliance Supplement) to determine whether primary grantees are effective in ensuring proper stewardship of federal funds.

How This Manual is Organized

Part A of *Techniques for Monitoring Federal Subawards* discusses the variety of compliance monitoring tools that grant recipients and subrecipients can use and provides practical guidance for executing them. Chapter 2 explains the role of the key participants in the subaward process, starting with the pass-through entity's responsibilities for monitoring subrecipients, as well as vendors and commercial organizations. It also addresses the subrecipient's various administrative and reporting responsibilities. The chapter concludes with a look at the resources of the federal awarding agency available to the pass-through entity and the subrecipient.

Chapter 3 describes the key provisions of an effective subaward agreement that will achieve monitoring goals. Explaining first the importance of a well-written scope of work and budget, the chapter then describes the various types of program-related and administrative laws and regulations that should be included in the agreement to ensure that subrecipients comply with the necessary requirements while carrying out federal program purposes. It also provides a brief discussion on structuring the agreement.

Chapter 4 provides an in-depth look at the monitoring techniques that pass-through entities and subrecipients have found to be useful. It discusses factors pass-through entities should consider before selecting a monitoring activity, describes and compares the various tools available, including single audits, limited-scope audits, onsite visits and document reviews, and provides tips on choosing the best ones.

Chapter 5 addresses a vital part of the monitoring process – effective communication – that is sometimes overlooked or ignored. Looking at the myriad forms communication can take, the chapter discusses everything from the importance of the subaward agreement and federal agency guidance issued at the start of the subaward to the need for ongoing, informal contact between the pass-through entity, subrecipient and federal awarding agency throughout the subaward.

Emphasizing the importance of follow-up, chapter 6 describes the best ways pass-through entities can inform subrecipients about monitoring findings and provides advice to subrecipients on taking corrective action. Chapter 7 reviews the aspects of a pass-through entity's monitoring procedures that auditors will test. It identifies the types of findings auditors might report and describes how to avoid them. It also presents a sample process that the Office of Inspector General used to review management of grant programs within the Department of Health and Human Services.

Part B of *Techniques for Monitoring Federal Subawards* presents in-depth discussion of selected grant management issues. Chapter 8 presents a detailed discussion of the important elements of a subgrant agreement and describes a method for structuring these documents. Chapter 9 explains some logical and sensible practices grantees can adopt to implement a sound subrecipient monitoring program. Chapter 10 discusses the cash management rules grantees and subgrantees must follow.

To help make the subrecipient monitoring process easier, Part C of *Techniques for Monitoring Federal Subawards* includes sample subaward agreements. Part D contains regulatory requirements, including excerpts of OMB circulars and the *Circular A-133 Compliance Supplement.* Also included is a glossary of common terms relevant to subrecipient monitoring issues.

Roles and Responsibilities of Key Participants

2

U nderstanding the relationship and responsibilities of the participants involved in the subaward process is essential to creating a successful subrecipient monitoring relationship.

Federal funds originate from a federal awarding agency that is authorized by a grant-enabling statute to develop and administer a federal assistance program. Based on the statute, the federal agency awards federal funds to grant recipients, such as state and local governments, colleges and universities or nonprofit organizations, to carry out the federal program. Some grant recipients perform all of the federal grant activities themselves, but many recipients pass through federal funds either to subrecipients that administer many of the program functions and objectives, or to vendors that provide goods and services under the program.

While the federal funds originate from a federal awarding agency, the participants most directly involved in subrecipient monitoring are the pass-through entity (or primary recipient) and the subrecipient because they are parties to a subaward agreement (see Chapter 3).

FLOW OF FEDERAL FUNDS
Federal Awarding Agency
↓
$
↓
Pass-Through Entity
↓
$
↓
Subrecipient or Vendor

Pass-Through Entity Responsibilities

A pass-through entity is responsible for ensuring that all of the federal funds it receives, including those passed through to subrecipients, are used only for program-related purposes as described in the pass-through entity's original grant agreement. But before a pass-through entity makes a subaward, it should verify that the program laws and regulations allow subawards. Some program laws prohibit subawards or limit the amount of funds that grant recipients can pass through to subrecipients. Other program laws may limit the amount of funds that primary recipients may keep for administrative costs, guaranteeing the majority of the funds are distributed to subrecipients. To determine if subawards are permitted, a pass-through entity should first review its original grant agreement, which may address the question. Beyond the agreement, a pass-through entity can review the program legislation or contact a federal agency program official to get an answer.

Even if a primary recipient is authorized to make a subaward, it should determine if a subaward is the best instrument for awarding federal funds. A subaward is defined as an award of financial assistance in the form of money, or property in lieu of money, made under a grant by a grantee to an eligible subgrantee. Generally, a primary recipient makes a subaward to provide public assistance or achieve a public purpose authorized by a federal law. For example, the Workforce Investment Act (WIA) is designed to provide job training, education and employment services to dislocated workers and other individuals. Therefore, state agencies that receive WIA funds from the U.S. Department of Labor would subaward the funds to nonprofit organizations that actually train individuals to join the workforce.

SUBRECIPIENTS VS. VENDORS

It is not always clear when the pass-through entity should award federal funds to a subrecipient or a procurement contract to a vendor.

A subrecipient is a state or local government, college, university or nonprofit organization that expends federal awards received from a pass-through entity to carry out a federal program. Under a subaward, a subrecipient generally:

- determines who is eligible to receive federal financial assistance;

- has its performance measured against whether the objectives of the federal programs are met;

- has responsibility for programmatic decision-making;

- has responsibility for adherence to applicable federal program compliance requirements; and

- uses federal funds to carry out a program of the organization as compared to providing goods or services for a program of the pass-through entity.

In contrast, a vendor is a dealer, distributor, merchant or other seller providing goods or services that are necessary for conducting a federal program. These goods or services may be for an organization's own use or for the use of beneficiaries of the federal program. Under a procurement contract, a vendor:

- provides goods or services within normal business operations;

- provides similar goods or services to many different purchasers;

- operates in a competitive environment;

- provides goods or services that are ancillary to the operation of the federal program; and

- is not subject to compliance requirements of federal programs.

Because there may be exceptions to these characteristics, pass-through entities should look at the substance of the relationship to the determine whether to award a subaward to a subrecipient or a contract to a vendor. Also, because not all of the characteristics may be present, pass-through entities must use their judgment in determining whether an entity is a subrecipient or vendor.

However, in some instances it may be more appropriate for a primary recipient to enter into a procurement contract with a vendor. A procurement contract generally is used when a primary recipient buys goods or services for its own use or benefit. For example, a state agency would award a procurement contract to a vendor to buy file cabinets to store its WIA records. While the state agency generally could charge all or part of the cost of the cabinet to the WIA program, it would not be considered a subaward. Still, another example of a contract under a grant would be an agreement between a sponsor of adult day care centers, receiving funds under the U.S. Department of Agriculture Child and Adult Care Food Program, and a food service company to provide meal service for eligible senior citizens and other adults at those day care centers.

Once a pass-through entity has determined that it can award federal money to a subrecipient, it should award the funds, usually through a competitive solicitation process, unless the program regulations require otherwise, to an eligible subrecipient. The solicitation should identify the eligibility requirements a subrecipient must satisfy, the activities to be performed, the size of the award, the duration of the program, and refer to any applicable laws, regulations and guidelines. A subrecipient should read the entire solicitation and review the applicable laws and regulations to make sure that it can meet all of the program requirements before it applies for the subgrant.

Pass-through entities should keep in mind that the solicitation process is the first step to ensuring that subrecipients carry out the program activities and requirements. The pass-through entity should review the subrecipient's proposal for completing the project, including its budget for performing the program activities to determine if the entity can properly manage the project and if its proposed costs are reasonable, allowable and allocable under the program regulations and the Office of Management and Budget (OMB) cost principles (Circulars A-21, A-87 and A-122).

State and local governments that are passing through funds to subrecipients are encouraged to use application requirements that are no more detailed or burdensome than those prescribed for federal granting agencies in the grants management common rule.

Pass-through entities should be aware that they cannot make subawards to organizations that have been suspended, debarred or otherwise deemed ineligible to participate in federal assistance programs. (The General Services Administration maintains a list of parties that are suspended or debarred, which is online at: http://www.arnet.gov/epls or is available from the Government Printing Office at (202) 512-1800.) They should require all of their subrecipients to submit certifications that they are not suspended, debarred or otherwise ineligible as part of their application.

When a pass-through entity makes the subaward, it must identify the origin of the federal assistance by informing each subrecipient of the *Catalog of Federal Domestic Assistance* (CFDA) title and number, award name and number, award year, if the award is research and development (R&D) and the name of the federal agency. When any of this information is unavailable, the pass-through entity must provide the best information available to describe the federal award. A pass-through entity also must advise subrecipients of any requirements imposed on them by federal laws, regulations and the provisions of contracts or grant agreements, as well as any additional requirements imposed by the pass-through entity. For example, many public policy laws that are included in the original grant from the federal awarding agency to the pass-through entity such as the Americans With Disabilities Act or Section 504 of the Rehabilitation Act of 1973 flow down to the pass-through entity and must be included in the subaward agreement (see Chapter 3).

A grantee that passes through funds to subrecipients is responsible for monitoring their activities to ensure that federal awards are used for authorized purposes in compliance with the federal program laws, regulations and grant agreements and that performance goals are achieved. Monitoring can include document reviews, onsite visits, training or telephone calls (for a complete discussion of monitoring tools, see Chapter 4). Pass-through entities having a single audit performed must prepare a schedule of expenditures of federal awards and, if practical, identify the amount provided to subrecipients from each award. If a pass-through entity has an adequate monitoring system in place, it should be able to identify its subawards in the schedule.

As part of their monitoring responsibilities, pass-through entities must ensure that any subrecipients spending at least $500,000 in federal awards during the subrecipient's fiscal year have an audit performed in accordance with Circular A-133.

Once monitoring is complete, pass-through entities must communicate the results to their subrecipients, including any problems that need to be corrected, recommendations for improvement and other advice. Similarly, pass-through entities must issue a management decision on audit findings disclosed in a subrecipient's single audit report within six months after receipt of the report and ensure that the subrecipient takes appropriate corrective action. In addition, a pass-through entity must consider whether it should adjust its own records as a result of any subrecipient audits.

Finally, the pass-through entity should require each subrecipient to permit the pass-through entity and its auditor to have access to the subrecipient's records and financial statements as necessary for the pass-through entity to comply with Circular A-133 and its monitoring responsibilities.

CHECKLIST OF PASS-THROUGH ENTITY RESPONSIBILITIES

✔ Identify and provide information about federal awards (e.g., CFDA information) to subrecipients.

✔ Inform subrecipients about compliance requirements.

✔ Monitor subrecipient activities.

✔ Ensure subrecipients have single audits, if required.

✔ Provide technical advice and training, if necessary and feasible.

✔ Issue management decisions within six months on subrecipient single audit findings and ensure subrecipients take corrective action.

✔ Consider whether pass-through entity records must be adjusted as a result of subrecipient audits.

✔ Require subrecipients to permit the pass-through entity and its auditors access to their records for monitoring and audit purposes.

Special Considerations for Vendors and For-Profit Subrecipients

In contrast with awards of federal funds to subrecipients, payments for goods and services to vendors using federal program money generally are not subject to Circular A-133 audit or other monitoring requirements. In most cases, the pass-through entity's compliance responsibility for vendors is only to ensure that the procurement, receipt and payment for goods and services comply with laws, regulations and the provisions of contracts or grant agreements. Program compliance requirements normally do not flow down to vendors.

However, when the vendor's performance of its contract affects the pass-through entity's ability to comply with program requirements, the pass-through entity must monitor the vendor's performance to ensure it will satisfy the affected program requirements. For example, under the student financial assistance (SFA) program, many universities contract with service centers to administer student loans. Although the service centers are vendors, they perform a function that is integral to the SFA program objectives such as disbursing SFA funds or cutting off assistance when a beneficiary is no longer eligible. Therefore, the university must ensure that the service center is disbursing funds or performing other duties in compliance with SFA regulations. When these vendor transactions relate to a major program, the scope of the pass-through entity's audit must include determining whether the vendor transactions comply with laws, regulations and the provisions of contracts or grant agreements for that program.

Like vendors, for-profit subrecipients are not subject to Circular A-133's audit requirements. However, both pass-through entities and subrecipients should be aware that the U.S. Departments of Justice and Health and Human Services (HHS) expanded the scope of Circular A-133 to apply to commercial recipients and subrecipients when they adopted the circular into their regulations. HHS permits commercial organizations to choose between a Circular A-133 audit or a financial-related audit of the HHS programs performed in accordance with *Government Auditing Standards*.

Nonetheless, pass-through entities must establish requirements to ensure that their for-profit subrecipients comply with the applicable program regulations. A pass-through entity's subaward agreement with the for-profit entity should describe the applicable compliance requirements and the subrecipient's compliance responsibilities. To ensure compliance by for-profit subrecipients, pass-through entities should consider pre-award audits, monitoring during the subaward, and post-award audits.

Primary recipients should incorporate any monitoring requirements into the grant agreement. Primary recipients that subaward a large amount of federal funds (e.g., more than $500,000) to for-profit subrecipients may want to require that those subrecipients have a Circular A-133 audit or an audit in accordance with *Government Auditing Standards* as a term of the subaward agreement. As an alternative, a primary recipient may require a for-profit subrecipient to have an agreed-upon procedures engagement performed by an independent public accountant (IPA) (see Chapter 4). The IPA would perform certain procedures to test the subrecipient's compliance with various program-related regulations. The primary recipient and subrecipient also should specify in the subaward agreement who arranges and pays for the audit or engagement. (They should also verify that the cost of such audits are chargeable to the federal award.) Additionally, primary recipients may require periodic reports from or make site visits to for-profit subrecipients.

Subrecipient Responsibilities

A subrecipient is awarded federal funds to perform the services or activities described in the subaward agreement. It must ensure that when performing those services or activities it complies with all of the requirements of the subaward agreement. A subrecipient should set up systems for managing the subaward activities. It should establish a grant accounting system to trace federal fund expenditures to show the money has been spent according to program requirements and produce required financial reports. An accounting system also should help a subrecipient maintain the necessary records that identify receipts, disbursements, assets, liabilities and balances should a pass-through entity, federal awarding agency or some other entity want to review them. Strong internal controls are vital to safeguarding its assets, ensuring the reliability of accounting data and complying with management policies and grant terms and conditions.

Beyond the grant accounting system, a subrecipient should consider establishing other grants management systems, including a procurement system for making purchases using subaward money, a property management system and a reporting and recordkeeping system that addresses not only financial records and reports, but also program income and performance requirements.

Once a subrecipient has its grants management systems in place, it should do some self-assessment to ensure that the systems are working. Are the proper records being including in the files? Have the necessary financial and progress reports been submitted to the pass-through entity? Is the subrecipient prepared for a monitoring visit or audit by the pass-through entity or an auditor?

CHECKLIST OF SUBRECIPIENT RESPONSIBILITIES

✔ Administer the grant from award to closeout.

✔ Develop internal policies and systems to ensure effective management of federal funds and compliance with public policy requirements.

✔ Ensure the organization has a financial management system and any other systems that are appropriate such as procurement and property management systems.

✔ Establish a budget of the costs required to perform the program and a method for monitoring actual costs against the budget.

✔ Keep abreast of changes in policies, procedures or requirements and advise staff of any changes.

✔ Request prior approvals when necessary.

✔ Make the most of site visits by the pass-through entity by showing organizational strengths and successes.

✔ Prepare necessary reports.

✔ Keep the pass-through entity aware and informed about subaward project progress.

In addition to setting up grants management systems, the subrecipient must ensure it complies with any public policy requirements included in the subaward. Those requirements may include federal requirements such as the Freedom of Information Act and Section 504 of the Rehabilitation Act of 1973 that flow down from the grant agreement between the pass-through entity and the federal awarding agency to the subrecipient (see Chapter 3). The agreement also may include additional requirements imposed by the pass-through entity such as accounting and reporting requirements. To ensure compliance, the subrecipient should establish internal policies (e.g., for hiring and employing individuals with disabilities) and properly train its staff.

The subrecipient also must keep up with and implement any changes in the program requirements that affect its grants administration. To learn about changes to program or agency requirements, a subrecipient can review the *Federal Register,* which is available online at http://www.access.gpo.gov/ or the CFDA, which is online at http://www.gsa.gov/fdac/. Also, the subrecipient should contact its pass-through entity about any changes to program requirements.

If a subrecipient passes through funds it receives to their own subrecipients, they should set up a plan for monitoring those subrecipients' use of the funds.

Subrecipients often must obtain prior approval from the pass-through entity when required by the subaward agreement such as when there is a change in the scope of work or an unexpected large expenditure. Otherwise, the pass-through officials might disallow the costs and the subrecipient would have to absorb the costs of any unallowable activities. Beyond obtaining prior approval, the subrecipient should have regular contact with the pass-through entity (see Chapter 5). If a subrecipient has questions or problems with a subaward, the pass-through entity may be able to provide technical advice to remedy the situation. The subrecipient should also share its successes, such as achieving program goals earlier than expected, with pass-through officials.

By communicating with the pass-through entity on a regular basis, the subrecipient can ask questions about upcoming monitoring visits or required reports and prepare the specific information that the pass-through entity has requested. And once the monitoring visit is complete, the subrecipient will be better able to follow up on any problems identified in their reports or during a visit.

Subrecipients that spend $500,000 or more in federal awards also must have a single audit performed in accordance with OMB Circular A-133. They must engage the auditor to perform the audit, prepare the necessary documentation, such as the financial statements, and submit the single audit reporting package, which includes the auditor's opinion and reports, to the pass-through entity and the Federal Audit Clearinghouse. As with monitoring visits, the subrecipient must follow up on any findings identified during the audit by describing the corrective action it plans to take and actually making the corrections.

Federal Awarding Agency Responsibilities

The federal agency that awarded the funds to the prime recipient has no direct contractual relationship with the pass-through entity's subrecipients. Nonetheless, it wants to confirm that federal funds ultimately are used for program objectives and, therefore, wants to know that the prime recipient is monitoring its subrecipients. The federal agency can rely on the pass-through entity's single audit to determine if the pass-through entity is adequately monitoring its subrecipients. A single audit report with no findings should assure the federal awarding agency that the pass-through entity's monitoring procedures are sufficient. When there are findings, the federal agency can work with the pass-through entity to improve its monitoring procedures. It can suggest additional programs and compliance areas to review. Also, the federal agency can suggest additional monitoring techniques that have been successful for other pass-through entities.

While federal agencies usually do not interact with subrecipients, most subaward agreements give the federal awarding agency the right to review the subrecipient's records and inspect its operations. Federal agencies that are concerned about the use of federal funds by subrecipients may consider performing spot checks of actual subrecipients, particularly with the increase in the single audit threshold and the number of subrecipients that do not have to have a single audit performed. Subrecipients should maintain their records and operations in compliance with the subaward agreement because the federal awarding agency, as well as the pass-through entity, can make site visits or request documents for review.

The federal awarding agency also may be a good source of information for both pass-through entities and subrecipients. Agency officials can answer questions that either a pass-through entity or a subrecipient has about program requirements. For example, they can clarify whether certain activities or costs proposed by the subrecipient are allowable under the subaward. In many instances, subrecipients must obtain prior approval before taking certain actions such as making major changes to the budget. If the pass-through entity has any question about the subrecipient's planned action, it may want to get approval from the federal awarding agency, ensuring that the activity is indeed allowable.

Federal agencies also can inform recipients and subrecipients about any programmatic changes that are made during the subaward, such as setting up a new type of accounting system or completing new reports, and help with their implementation.

A few federal agencies provide guidance on monitoring subrecipients under a particular program. For instance, the U.S. Department of Housing and Urban Development has guidance for monitoring Community Development Block Grant (CDBG) program subrecipients. The guidance emphasizes the areas that a pass-through entity should focus on when monitoring CDBG subrecipients.

In addition to answering questions about specific program requirements, federal agency officials also can help recipients and subrecipients with questions about grants administration in general. Many of the officials are familiar with OMB's grants administration and cost principle circulars and can answer questions about their requirements such as establishing a recordkeeping system or calculating indirect costs.

The Subaward Agreement

The subaward agreement potentially is a primary recipient's most important tool for monitoring subrecipient activities. In the agreement, the primary recipient should describe the services or benefits that the subrecipient must provide when administering the federal program. It also should identify the various laws and regulations that the subrecipient must comply with as a condition of the subaward. This includes program-specific requirements such as eligibility criteria and matching obligations, public policy laws for protecting civil rights and the environment, governmentwide administrative mandates affecting the subrecipient's accounting and recordkeeping systems, and state and local laws imposed by the pass-through entity.

The agreement also should describe the pass-through entity's monitoring rights and responsibilities, the areas that the pass-through will monitor, the types of monitoring activities the pass-through entity plans to use such as prior approvals, financial reports and onsite visits and, if possible, the frequency of those activities.

By drafting a clear subaward agreement, pass-through entities can prevent problems and help ensure that subrecipients carry out the requirements of the subaward, work to achieve related performance objectives and comply with the applicable program requirements or strings attached to the subgrant. Additionally, a well-drafted agreement will help subrecipients prepare for any monitoring activities because they will know the areas to be covered, the procedures the pass-through entity plans to use and when the activities will occur.

Components of a Subaward Agreement

Each subaward agreement is different because each one involves different organizations, programs and activities. Nonetheless, pass-through entities that make many subawards should consider developing a standard agreement for each of the different federal grant programs that they administer. These agreements can be used for awarding program funds to different subrecipients to provide for more uniform administration of such funds by subrecipients. Pass-through entities must include certain information in the subaward agreement: the CFDA program name and number, the award name and number, the award year, if the award is for research and development, and the name of the federal awarding agency.

If any of this information is unavailable, the subaward agreement must provide the best information available to describe the federal award. A subaward agreement should describe the federal program requirements imposed on the subrecipient by program laws, regulations and the provisions of contracts or grant agreements, as well as any supplemental requirements imposed by the pass-through entity. Auditors performing a pass-through entity's single audit must perform tests to ensure the pass-through entity provided this information to its subrecipients.

As part of the standard language, the agreements generally should incorporate additional basic information such as the names of grantee and subgrantee, the duration of the agreement, contact persons and the funding amount. Beyond this information there are several key provisions that a pass-through entity should consider including in the subaward agreement to ensure that subrecipients are aware of their responsibilities and carry out the program properly and to enable the pass-through entity to monitor the subrecipient's activities.

Scope of Work and Budget

Each subaward agreement should include a scope of work, which describes the services or benefits that the subrecipient will provide. It also should clarify where and how the subrecipient will provide the services or benefits. The pass-through entity also should include a proposed budget of the costs of providing those services and benefits.

All of the activities described in the scope of work must conform with the federal program requirements and objectives. For example, the scope of work included in a CDBG subaward for day care services must be consistent with the CDBG program objectives of helping low- and moderate-income persons and supporting community development. The scope of work, therefore, might describe the subrecipient's major tasks such as:

*   maintaining the facilities in conformance with applicable laws and regulations;

*   informing the moderate- and low-income communities of the availability of services;

*   accepting applications and making eligibility determinations for children seeking to enter day care; and

*   offering day care services.

With the passage of the Government Performance and Results Act, federal agencies must establish program performance objectives and measure their achievement. Many federal agencies are including such performance requirements in their grant awards, which in turn flow down to subrecipients. Thus, the scope of work may specify certain levels of accomplishment or goals that the subrecipient must achieve for each activity to be performed for a specific time period (e.g., monthly) and the related costs. This could include identifying the number of beneficiaries served. A subaward agreement for job training, for example, might require that the subrecipient provide:

- job training to 30 eligible individuals per month;

- counseling and job search advice to 20 eligible individuals per month; and

- job placement for 15 eligible individuals per month.

Each scope of work is unique. It must reflect the purpose of the federal program and the methods proposed by the subrecipient to administer the federal program. Thus, the scope of work in another CDBG subaward agreement would be completely different if the purpose is to build a public housing facility. It would include a detailed description of the building plans and a work schedule that identifies the major performance benchmarks, associated costs and corresponding dates in the construction process.

The scope of work may be written directly in the agreement or it may be incorporated by reference. Often, the scope of work has been proposed by the subrecipient in its application for the subaward. In such cases, the pass-through entity may incorporate the subrecipient's application, with a few modifications, into the subaward agreement as an exhibit or attachment.

Regardless of whether the scope of work is specifically included in the contract or incorporated by reference, when monitoring a subrecipient, a pass-through entity would perform procedures to ensure that the subrecipient is performing the activities described in the agreement's scope of work. For example, in the case of the subaward to build the public housing facility, the pass-through entity could request reports on the status of the construction, review documentation such as construction workers time sheets or make site visits to ensure the construction is proceeding as required.

The pass-through entity should incorporate the subrecipient's proposed budget for performing the subaward. The budget identifies various costs associated with administering the subaward such as staff salaries, utilities, supplies, materials and fringe benefits. Using both the scope of work and the budget, the pass-through entity can monitor the subrecipient's expenditures against the proposed budget and the specific performance goals or benchmarks described in the scope of work. It can identify any unanticipated spending patterns that may reflect problems that need to be addressed.

Program Authorizing Statute

The pass-through entity generally should include in the subagreement relevant portions or all of the program's authorizing statute. The authorizing statute establishes the program and describes (usually) the program's purpose and objectives, eligibility requirements, matching requirements and other requirements that are important to administering the program. The level of detail provided in authorizing legislation varies, however. Generally pass-through entities want to ensure that subrecipient's activities conform with the program legislation when performing any monitoring activities.

Program Regulations

Program regulations also flow down from the original grant between the federal awarding agency and the pass-through entity to the subaward between the pass-through entity and the subrecipient. In many instances, the program regulations describe the eligibility requirements, the allowable program activities, describe how the subrecipient should treat program income and include other program-related requirements. However, because program regulations generally are extensive, they usually are incorporated by reference into the subaward agreement. For example, a CDBG subaward agreement might state, "The subrecipient agrees to comply with the requirements of Title 24 of the *Code of Federal Regulations,* Part 570 (U.S. Department of Housing and Urban Development CDBG program regulations)." As with the authorizing legislation, the pass-through entity should give the subrecipient a copy of the relevant provisions of the regulations, and the subrecipient should be sure to review them.

In addition to referencing the program regulations, pass-through entities may incorporate certain important requirements directly into the agreement to ensure that subrecipients comply with them. For example, if a subrecipient is administering a subaward such as the TANF program, the pass-through entity may include the specific eligibility requirements in the agreement, perhaps as part of the scope of work, because of the importance of eligibility determinations to the TANF program.

Public Policy Requirements

Primary grantees should incorporate all public policy requirements in their subaward agreements. These requirements are imposed on grant recipients and their subrecipients by executive order of the president, a law enacted by Congress (either a statute that applies to all federal grantees, such as the Drug-Free Workplace Act, or a program authorizing statute such as the Elementary and Secondary Education Act), and regulations issued by federal agencies. Still, there are additional public policies that must be complied with, regardless of whether an organization receives federal funding. Examples of these are the Americans With Disabilities Act and the Civil Rights Act.

Additionally, there are public policy requirements or mandates that apply to only certain federal assistance programs or certain activities under those programs. For example, the Uniform Relocation Assistance and Real Property Acquisition Policies Act mandates that federally assisted programs or activities that displace or disturb people or buildings (by, for example, obtaining rights-of-way to construct a new road or bridge) provide for relocation assistance to displaced persons or organizations.

Regardless of the source or origin of public policy requirements, primary grantees must ensure that they themselves and their subrecipients comply with them. How should primary grantees determine which requirements apply to subrecipients? First, pass-through entities may want to require their subrecipients to submit a statement of assurance with their subgrant applications that they will compy with the public policy requirements. This statement of assurance could mirror the one organizations submit to federal agencies when applying for federal grant funds. Second, pass-through entities should review their grant agreements with federal agencies to determine the applicable public policy requirements to incorporate into their subaward agreements, as most if not all of them "flow down" to the subrecipient level. Third, primary grantees should review the program authorizing statute and regulations for any other public policy requirements that may

---

EXAMPLES OF PUBLIC POLICY REQUIREMENTS

- Title VI of the Civil Rights Act of 1964 (prohibits discrimination based on race, color or national origin)

- Section 504 of the Rehabilitation Act (prohibits discrimination against disabled individuals by recipients of federal financial assistance)

- Age Discrimination Act of 1975

- Freedom of Information Act (grants public access to federal records)

- Title IX of the Education Amendments of 1972 (prohibits gender discrimination in federally assisted education programs)

- Davis-Bacon Act (sets wage rates for laborers and construction workers working on projects funded by federal assistance)

- Work Hours Act of 1962

- Drug-Free Workplace Act of 1988

- Uniform Relocation Assistance and Real Property Acquisition Policies Act of 1970

- National Environmental Policy Act

- Safe Drinking Water Act of 1974

- The Clean Air Act and the Federal Water Pollution Control Act

- Wildlife Protection

- The Coastal Zone Management Act of 1972

- Historic Preservation Act

- Affirmative Action Requirements of Executive Order 11246

These are only a few of the many public policy requirements that could flow down to subawards. Pass-through entities preparing a subaward agreement should include all of the applicable public policy requirements identified in program legislation and regulations.

---

apply. Finally, grantees should contact federal program and other grants officials should they have questions about which requirements apply.

Administrative Requirements

The subaward agreement should describe how the subrecipient should administer the federal program. Generally, state agencies should follow state laws and procedures when administering federal subgrants. While state agencies most often are primary grantees, they can receive subawards from other organizations such as nonprofit entities. For example, the American Red Cross may receive disaster relief training funds from the Federal Emergency Management Agency that it subawards to various state emergency management agencies.

Local governments such as cities, towns and Indian tribal governments that receive subawards should follow the administrative requirements in the Office of Management and Budget's (OMB's) grants management common rule, *Uniform Administrative Requirements for Grants and Cooperative Agreements to State and Local Governments.* Similarly, colleges and universities or nonprofit organizations that are administering federal subawards must follow the administrative requirements in OMB's Circular A-110, *Uniform*

Administrative Requirements for Grants and Agreements With Institutions of Higher Education, Hospitals and Other Nonprofit Organizations.

Certain federal programs such as Medicaid, the National School Lunch program and other entitlement programs, block grants authorized by the Omnibus Budget Reconciliation Act of 1981 and certain grants to local educational agencies (LEAs), are exempt from OMB's administrative requirements. Instead, state and local governments administering such subawards must follow the administrative requirements specified in the program legislation or regulations and, in many cases, rely on state administrative requirements for such areas as accounting, budgeting, procurement and treatment of equipment.

Subaward agreements should specifically state which governmentwide grants management policies apply or even include the text of them. Some pass-through entities are content with inserting a provision in the subaward agreement that requires the subrecipient to follow the applicable federal grants management circular. For example, a nonprofit subrecipient may be required to certify that it will comply with the administrative requirements of Circular A-110 as codified by the federal awarding agency. This may be sufficient when the pass-through entity is dealing with an experienced subrecipient that is familiar with OMB's administrative requirements. However, pass-through entities that frequently have new subrecipients should consider enumerating the subrecipient's various administrative responsibilities in the subaward agreement. Subrecipients are more likely to understand and carry out their responsibilities if they are spelled out in the agreement, rather than in a document that is incorporated by reference.

There are several administrative requirements that the pass-through entity should include in the subaward agreement. For instance, the subaward agreement should describe the type of financial management system that a subrecipient should establish. Generally, pass-through entities should require their subrecipients to maintain a financial management system that provides financial information about the federal program being administered that will satisfy the reporting requirements of the subaward. Additionally, subrecipients should maintain records that adequately identify the source of federal funds and how those funds were spent. The subrecipient's financial management system also should ensure adequate internal control over cash management, consistent treatment of costs with the applicable cost principles and sufficient source documentation to support

FEDERAL COST PRINCIPLES APPLICABLE TO GRANTS	
Type of Subrecipient	**Applicable Cost Principles**
State, local or Indian tribal government	Circular A-87, *Cost Principles for State, Local and Indian Tribal Governments*
Nonprofit organizations	Circular A-122, *Cost Principles for Nonprofit Organizations*
Colleges and universities	Circular A-21, *Cost Principles for Educational Institutions*
Hospitals	U.S. Department of Health and Human Services regulations 45 C.F.R. Part 74
For-profit organizations	*Federal Acquisition Regulation* 48 C.F.R. Part 31

the accounting records. An example of a more detailed financial management provision that could be included in a subaward agreement with a college or university follows:

> The subrecipient agrees to comply with OMB Circular A-110 and agrees to adhere to the accounting principles and procedures required therein, use adequate internal controls and maintain necessary source documentation for all costs incurred.

> The subrecipient must administer its program in conformity with Circular A-21, *Cost Principles for Educational Institutions.* These principles must be applied for all costs incurred whether charged on a direct or indirect basis.

This provision could be modified for a nonprofit organization or a state or local government agency by incorporating the appropriate grants administration circular and cost principles.

By including detailed information in the subaward agreement about financial accounting, the pass-through entity can prevent confusion among subgrantees. The grants management common rule explains that states must expend and account for federal grant funds in accordance with state laws and procedures for expending and accounting for state funds. In contrast, local governments and Indian tribal organizations, which also are subject to OMB's grants management common rule, must follow the financial management standards described in the administrative circular. Pass-through entities that make awards to state and local government agencies should tailor the subaward agreement to prescribe the financial management requirements appropriate to the type of subrecipient receiving the award.

The subaward also should address how the subrecipient will be paid. OMB's grants administration circulars recommend that the pass-through entity should pay the subrecipient in advance. However, there may be instances when an alternative method of payment is appropriate such as if the subrecipient fails to minimize the time between the transfer of funds from the pass-through entity and their disbursement, or if the subrecipient is considered high-risk. The pass-through entity can insert a provision to pay the subrecipient on a cost-reimbursement basis. Also, if the subaward is for a construction contract, the pass-through entity can select a cost-reimbursement payment method. The pass-through entity may require other forms of payment if required by the type of subaward.

Pass-through entities may want to spell out in the subaward that failure by the subrecipient to comply with subaward conditions can result in the withholding of payments.

The subaward agreement should explain that the subrecipient can use the subaward money only for charges that are allowed under the applicable federal cost principles. It also should specify the applicable cost principles. For instance, nonprofit organizations are subject to Circular A-122, *Cost Principles for Nonprofit Organizations.*

The pass-through entity also may want to include provisions that address the subrecipient's procurement system. Subrecipients that are states should follow the same procedures that they use for making procurements with nonfederal funds. The state, however, must ensure that every purchase includes any clauses required by federal statutes and regulations. Local governments and Indian tribal subgrantees must use their own procurement procedures that reflect applicable state and local laws and regulations, as well as federal requirements. In addition, they should review the requirements in OMB's grants management common rule for additional guidance. Nonprofit organizations, colleges and universities also must create their own procurement procedures that prevent the purchase of unnecessary items and otherwise follow the standards in Circular A-110.

The subaward should specify the types of reports that the subrecipient must submit to the recipient, including both financial and progress reports. The agreement should specify when the reports are due and the types of information that they should contain because the pass-through entity will rely on these reports to monitor subrecipient activities and ensure their compliance with the subaward agreement and relevant federal laws and regulations.

The agreement should specify the programmatic records that a subrecipient must maintain and how long those records must be retained. For example, a CDBG subaward agreement between a city and a nonprofit subrecipient may require the recipient to maintain the following:

*   records providing a full description of each activity undertaken;

*   records demonstrating that each activity undertaken meets the national objectives of the CDBG program;

*   records required to determine the eligibility of activities;

*   records required to document the acquisition, improvement, use or disposition of real property acquired or improved with CDBG assistance;

*   records documenting compliance with the fair housing and equal opportunity components of the CDBG program; and

*   financial records required by CDBG program regulations and Circular A-110.

Generally, the agreement should specify that a subrecipient should retain records for a period of three years, unless litigation or audit findings require the subrecipient to keep them for a longer period of time. An example of a record retention provision follows:

> The subrecipient shall retain all records pertinent to expenditure incurred under this contract for a period of three years after the termination of all activities funded under this agreement. Records for any displaced person must be kept three years after he/she has received final payment. Notwithstanding the above, if there are litigation, claims, audits, negotiations or other actions that involve any of the records cited and that have started before the expiration of the three-year period, then such records must be retained until completion of the actions and resolutions of all issues, or the expiration of the three-year period, whichever occurs later.

In addition to describing the reports and records that the subrecipient should maintain, the pass-through entity should require the subrecipient provide access to any program books and records to not only the pass-through entity but also auditors and federal awarding agency officials.

The pass-through entity should specify in the agreement when the subrecipient must obtain prior approval from the pass-through entity to take certain actions. OMB's grants administration circulars require that subrecipients obtain prior approval for certain activities such as when there is a change in the scope or objective of the project or a transfer of training funds to pay for other expenses. While the pass-through entity can waive certain prior approval requirements, they should consider requiring such prior approvals as a method of monitoring their subrecipients. In fact, subrecipients that are considered high-risk could be required to obtain additional prior approvals. OMB's grants management circulars both authorize pass-through entities to require additional prior approvals when awarding funds to high-risk subrecipients.

> ### ADMINISTRATIVE REQUIREMENTS CHECKLIST
>
> The subaward agreement should specify the pass-through entity's and subrecipient's responsibilities for the following administrative requirements:
>
> ✔ Financial management standards
>
> ✔ Payment
>
> ✔ Matching
>
> ✔ Reporting and recordkeeping
>
> ✔ Cost principles
>
> ✔ Period of availability
>
> ✔ Procurement
>
> ✔ Program income
>
> ✔ Real property
>
> ✔ Equipment
>
> ✔ Supplies
>
> ✔ Monitoring
>
> ✔ Audits

The pass-through entity should include a provision giving it the right to monitor subrecipient activities. The provision should describe the areas the pass-through entity will monitor, which generally are the subrecipient's provision of required services or benefits and its compliance with applicable laws and regulations referenced in the agreement. The primary recipient may want to specify in the agreement how many monitoring visits will be required and when those visits will take place, or it may negotiate the details during the subaward period. The subaward agreement also should specify that the subrecipient will have a Circular A-133 audit, if necessary. Only subrecipients that spend $500,000 or more in federal awards in a year are required to have a single audit.

The pass-through entity should include the period of time that the federal money is available for the subrecipient's use. Often funds are available only for a limited amount of time, and a subrecipient can charge to the subaward only those costs that are incurred during that period of time. Another administrative area that the pass-through entity should address is the subrecipient's responsibility to obtain matching funds from non-federal sources. Many federal programs require grant recipients and subrecipients to obtain matching funds from state agencies, nonprofit entities or other private sources.

Other areas that the pass-through entity should consider addressing include the subrecipient's treatment of program income, real property and equipment, patents and copyrights, supplies, and the right of either party to terminate the agreement. Not all of these areas may need to be included in the subaward agreement, however. For example, if the subrecipient is performing a research and development project, it probably will not need to purchase, use or dispose of real property.

Pass-Through Entity Requirements

In addition to incorporating certain federal requirements into the subaward agreement, pass-through entities may impose additional state laws and regulations that the subrecipient must fulfill as part of the subaward process. For instance, subrecipients may have to comply with state environmental laws as well as federal requirements. Also, a state may impose a shorter single audit report submission deadline than is required by Circular A-133 to comply with a state law (e.g., many states have enacted their own single audit requirements and deadlines). The pass-through entity may address other issues in the subaward, including arbitration of disputes, insurance and indemnification requirements. Pass-through entities also may impose special conditions on select subrecipients. For example, a subrecipient may have had findings in a certain area such as eligibility determinations on previous audits. In response, the pass-through entity may require as a condition of the new subaward that the subrecipient submit additional documentation regarding its eligibility procedures.

KEY PROVISIONS OF A SUBAWARD AGREEMENT

- Subaward identification, including CFDA name and number, award year and awarding agency

- Scope of work and budget

- Program authorizing statute

- Program authorizing legislation

- Administrative requirements

- Requirements and conditions imposed by the pass-through entity

---

Structuring the Agreement

Pass-through entities can structure subaward agreements several ways to incorporate the federal program and cross-cutting requirements. Some pass-through entities might choose to reference all of the federal and state laws and regulations directly in the agreement. In such a case, the subaward agreement is the subrecipient's main source of information regarding the laws, regulations and requirements with which it must comply. The subrecipient is responsible for finding, reviewing and complying with the requirements that are incorporated in and apply to its subaward.

Other pass-through entities require their subrecipients to sign a statement certifying that it will comply with applicable federal (and state) laws and regulations such as the Single Audit Act Amendments of 1996 and Circular A-133, the Civil Rights Act of 1964 or the Davis-Bacon Act. The certification statement, not the subaward agreement, identifies the specific laws and regulations that apply to the subaward. The pass-through entity then incorporates by reference the certifications as part of the overall subaward agreement. (For an illustrative certification statement, see Fig. C-2 in Part C of this manual.)

To assist subrecipients with complying with their subgrant agreements, pass-through entities should consider incorporating additional guidance as part of the subaward agreement. Some pass-through entities develop guidance, in the form of either an attachment to the subaward agreement or a separate handbook that is referenced in the agreement, that explains the applicable compliance requirements in understandable language. The guidance may also provide recipients with techniques on how to comply, illustrative examples or sample forms that recipients may have to complete. Pass-through entities may find it more effective and less costly to provide added guidance at the beginning of a subaward to help their subrecipients carry out the program requirements rather than providing the advice as follow-up to audits or monitoring reviews that require corrective action by one or more subrecipients.

Chapter 8, How to Write Subgrant Agreements, presents a detailed discussion of the important elements of a subgrant agreement and describes a method for structuring these documents.

Effective Monitoring Procedures

4

There are a variety of methods primary grantees can use to oversee their subrecipients' compliance and performance. Many of these tools are already part of the grant award and management process, while others are common (but not so obvious) actions that can be taken to effectively monitor subawards. Pass-through entities need to determine which ones will work best for their subrecipients. However, what will work for one particular organization may not be the best tool for each and every subrecipient or subaward.

Pass-through entities can look at many of the federal grants management and audit policies as a starting point for developing and choosing monitoring tools. For example, OMB's *Circular A-133 Compliance Supplement* suggests that primary grantees can review financial and progress reports submitted by subrecipients or schedule site visits to review records and observe operations (both of which are chargeable to federal awards). Moreover, primary grantees can review subrecipients' single audit reports or arrange for limited-scope audits of certain areas (e.g., eligibility determinations) of subrecipients that are exempt from having single audits.

Still, there are other tools that are not specifically mentioned (or mandated) in federal rules and policies, but are quite effective. By providing training and technical assistance to subrecipients, for example, primary grantees can work with subrecipients to review operations and records, ultimately to identify and correct any problems early on in the grants management process. Training can also help subrecipients expand or increase their services and improve their performance. Evaluations by third parties (such as consultants) are also valuable moni-

> **METHODS FOR MONITORING SUBRECIPIENT ACTIVITIES**
>
> - Review single audits
> - Arrange for limited-scope audits
> - Schedule site visits
> - Review subrecipient reports
> - Require prior approval for certain activities
> - Require third-party evaluations
> - Provide technical assistance and training
> - Make telephone calls and use other means of communication such as e-mail
> - Follow subrecipient coverage in the news

toring tools because they can provide cost-effective yet targeted reviews of subrecipient activities.

One of the most important facets of the grant/subgrant process is to stay informed. Pass-through entities and subrecipients alike can use such communication tools as telephone interviews and e-mail to stay abreast of activities and changes to programs and policies relevant to a particular award. Critical to a good pass-through subrecipient relationship and solid grant performance is effective communication (discussed further in Chapter 5). Open communication can help ensure that the subaward runs smoothly. Moreover, pass-through entities can stay informed by monitoring local and national media (newspapers, magazines, radio and television) for news about their subrecipients. Frequently, news stories and features will shed light on the successes or problems of a nonprofit or governmental subrecipient.

Which tools should a pass-through entity use to monitor its subrecipients? Should it use several of them, all of them, or none of them? Which practices are best for a particular type of subrecipient (community organization, local government agency, school district, etc.)?

Before selecting the best monitoring tool for a particular subrecipient, there are several factors a pass-through entity should consider. First, the pass-through entity should determine the purpose of the monitoring activity. Then it should consider the risk of noncompliance associated with the subrecipient. Additionally, the pass-through entity should assess its available monitoring resources.

By identifying the purpose and objectives of the monitoring effort, a pass-through entity can select the best monitoring techniques. Most pass-through entities monitor their subrecipients to ensure compliance with program requirements and identify any problems with the administration and performance of the award. But there are other reasons for monitoring such as identifying whether subrecipients need technical assistance. Monitoring also can be used to follow up on findings identified in an earlier monitoring visit, document review or audit to ensure that corrective action has been taken.

Thus, a pass-through entity that wants to monitor a subrecipient's general compliance with the subgrant agreement may require a more comprehensive monitoring plan that involves the review of financial and progress reports, site visits and, in the case of subrecipients spending $500,000 or more in federal money, a review of the single audit report. In contrast, monitoring a subrecipient for corrective action of an earlier finding may require more limited monitoring such as reviewing a revised report from the subrecipient.

Pass-through entities also may want to monitor the quality of a subrecipient's performance. For instance, monitoring could focus not only on the number of children receiving breakfast under the U.S. Department of Agriculture's School Breakfast program but on the quality and kinds of food provided. Similarly, a pass-through entity might look beyond the number of individuals trained and employed through WIA programs to the kind of training being provided and the quality of the instructors. These are issues pass-through entities may address when monitoring subrecipients that have single audits conducted because an audit generally does not address quality-of-service issues.

SPECIAL GRANT CONDITIONS FOR HIGH-RISK SUBGRANTEES

Both the grants management common rule and Circular A-110 discuss special treatment for sub-grantees that have had one or more of the following problems and are considered "high-risk":

- a history of unsatisfactory performance;

- financial instability;

- an inadequate management system that does not meet the standards mandated in OMB's grants management circulars;

- failure to comply with the terms and conditions of previous subawards; or

- is not otherwise responsible.

A pass-through entity that subawards funds to a high-risk subgrantee can incorporate any of the following special conditions or restrictions into the agreement:

- requiring that subrecipients be paid on a reimbursement basis;

- withholding the authority to proceed to the next phase of the project until the pass-through entity receives evidence of acceptable performance;

- requiring additional or more detailed financial reports;

- requiring the subgrantee to obtain technical or management assistance; or

- establishing additional prior approvals.

If a pass-through entity decides to impose additional restrictions on a high-risk subgrantee, it should notify the subgrantee of the following:

- the nature of the additional restrictions;

- the reasons for imposing them;

- the corrective action that the subgrantee must take before the pass-through entity will remove the restrictions; and

- the method by which the subrecipient can request reconsideration of the restrictions.

Pass-through entities may want to cite the applicable grant administration circular as authority for imposing additional restrictions.

Pass-through entities may be looking for success stories that they can share with other subrecipients in the same program. They also can use monitoring tools to determine if they are doing their job as a pass-through entity. Are there problems or gaps in communication that need to be addressed? Or do they have a good working relationship with the subrecipient?

Once a pass-through entity has identified the purpose of its monitoring efforts, it should also consider the risk that a particular subrecipient will not comply with the applicable requirements in the subaward.

When determining risk, the pass-through entity should consider factors such as the size of the subawards administered by subrecipients and the percentage of the pass-through entity's total federal funds awarded to subrecipients. The greater risk generally will be with those subrecipients that receive larger subawards.

For example, if a pass-through entity subawards a large portion (e.g., 75 percent) of its federal awards to 10 subrecipients that each spend less than $500,000 in federal funds annually, then the pass-through should determine the most effective method for monitoring these funds. To do so, it would balance the cost of monitoring the subrecipients against the size of the subawards and the percentage of the pass-through entity's total federal awards that are passed through. If, for example, the pass-through entity provides the majority of these funds to two subrecipients, it might perform more extensive site visits to the two largest subrecipients and review the documentation supporting the requests for reimbursement from the other eight subrecipients. On the other hand, if a pass-through entity subawards only a small percentage of its federal awards to subrecipients, the risk to the pass-through entity will most likely be low. Therefore, the pass-through entity's monitoring procedures could be more limited.

A pass-through entity also should consider the complexity of the compliance requirements. A more complex program usually will require more monitoring because there is a greater chance of noncompliance with at least some of the program requirements. Also, complex programs often involve larger amounts of federal funds, which invite more attention from pass-through entities. For example, state educational agencies (SEAs) subaward Eisenhower Professional Development funds to LEAs to help improve teacher skills. Each LEA can use the money for a variety of activities such as individual training or group training. States, however, must develop methods for tracking the funds and ensuring all of an LEA's activities support the program's goals. This may require detailed reports and site visits.

Another important factor to consider is an organization's experience with administering a federal subaward. A subrecipient that has administered the same program for several years often will require less monitoring than a subrecipient that is administering an award for the first time.

A first-time subrecipient may have to submit more financial and progress reports and receive more visits from the pass-through entity than a more experienced subrecipient. How much monitoring is conducted will depend on whether the pass-through entity is familiar with the subrecipient, perhaps from another subaward agreement, or has reviewed the subrecipient's prior single audits, if they are available.

If an experienced subrecipient has made changes in program staff, a pass-through entity may monitor their activities more closely because the new staff members may not be as familiar with the subaward requirements.

The subgrantee's prior monitoring results will have a great influence on future monitoring efforts by the pass-through entity. Thus, if a subrecipient has such problems as submitting incomplete or late reports or not having records available for review during an onsite visit, the pass-through entity most likely will slate that subrecipient for additional monitoring.

The type of award will affect the frequency and type of monitoring that a pass-through entity performs. When a pass-through entity awards a single-year subaward, it has to perform all of the monitoring during the year-long award period. In the case of a multi-year subgrant, a pass-through entity can spread its monitoring effort over the life of the agreement, perhaps concentrating its efforts at the beginning when a subrecipient is new to the program and at the end when the subaward is winding up.

Another important factor a pass-through entity must consider in selecting the best techniques for monitoring its subrecipients is the amount of resources a pass-through entity can devote to subrecipient monitoring, including the cost of the monitoring and the staff and time required.

No grantee has unlimited resources, even for subrecipient monitoring. Therefore, it must determine the most efficient and effective method to allocate its resources

> **FACTORS TO CONSIDER WHEN ASSESSING A SUBRECIPIENT'S RISK**
>
> - Size of the subaward administered by a subrecipient
> - Percentage of a pass-through entity's total federal funds awarded to subrecipients
> - Complexity of the subaward requirements
> - Subrecipient's experience with administering a federal subaward
> - Subrecipient's prior monitoring and audit results
> - Type of subaward (single year v. multiyear)

while obtaining assurance that its subrecipients are properly administering their subawards and accounting for program funds.

A pass-through entity most likely will devote more resources to monitor the subrecipients that receive the most funds. For example, an SEA may pass through funds from the School Breakfast, National School Lunch and Special Milk programs to local schools. However, if 60 percent of the funds passed through go to five LEAs while the remaining 40 percent of funds are distributed to 15 other LEAs, the state agency may be willing to pay more to monitor the five LEAs than the remaining 15 LEAs. The state agency may make more onsite visits or provide more training and technical assistance to the subrecipients receiving the larger amount of money.

Similarly, a pass-through entity that has limited staff but many subrecipients may choose to rely primarily on desk reviews of progress reports, reimbursement requests and other records. When onsite visits are necessary to adequately monitor subrecipients, the pass-through entity may send staff to subrecipients on a rotating basis rather than trying to visit every subrecipient each year. By visiting each subrecipient once every two or three years, the pass-through entity can monitor one-half or one-third of its subrecipient's each year.

Single Audits

For subrecipients that expend at least $500,000 a year in federal funds, primary recipients have a valuable monitoring tool at their disposal – the subrecipients' Circular A-133 audit. All state and local governments, colleges and universities, and nonprofit organizations that expend $500,000 or more of federal awards in a fiscal year must have a single audit. Primary recipients must ensure that such subrecipients have their audits performed.

However, audits of subrecipients spending less than $500,000 are not required by Circular A-133 and the cost of these and other audits (e.g., financial statement audits) are unallowable. Pass-through entities, therefore, must rely on other methods to monitor these subrecipients or pay for the cost of the audit with nonfederal funds.

The single audit provides the auditor's opinion on the subrecipient's financial statements. Because many federal assistance programs do not require recipients or subrecipients to have a financial statement audit, a subrecipient's single audit report may provide the pass-through entity with information on the subrecipient's financial statements and any related compliance problems that it might not have otherwise. The single audit also includes a report on the subrecipient's internal controls. While the auditor does not give an opinion on internal controls, his or her report should identify significant deficiencies and material weaknesses that relate to the subrecipient's administration of federal programs and that the pass-through entity should ensure are corrected. The single audit report provides information on a subrecipient's compliance with program-specific and cross-cutting (e.g., cost principles) regulations, including a list of findings and questioned costs.

The single audit report also includes the subrecipient's corrective action plan, which identifies how the subrecipient will remedy any problems identified by the auditor and prevent them from recurring. Primary recipients should review the plan to make sure the planned corrective action is allowable and will be made in a timely fashion. They also should determine if the subrecipient needs any technical assistance. In addition, they may want to plan additional monitoring to ensure the corrective action is taken.

Once the single audit is complete, it is the subrecipient's responsibility to submit the final single audit report to the pass-through entity if there are findings affecting the pass-through entity. The pass-through entity can review the audit results for any audit findings and the subrecipient's planned corrective action to determine whether the subrecipient is complying with the subaward requirements.

The single audit has limitations. Auditors only test a subrecipient's compliance with program requirements for "major programs." Major programs include the subrecipient's larger programs and programs which the auditor determines have a higher risk of noncompliance. Smaller programs and low-risk programs are excluded from the audit and may be audited as infrequently as once every three years.

REVIEWING A SINGLE AUDIT REPORT

A single audit report contains information about a subrecipient's use of federal money and compliance with program objectives. Primary recipients should review the following components of a subrecipient's single audit report as part of its monitoring efforts:

- the auditor's opinion on the financial statements;

- the auditor's report on internal control;

- the auditor's report and opinion on compliance with laws and regulations that could have an effect on major programs;

- the schedule of findings and questioned costs; and

- the subrecipient's corrective action plan.

Additionally, the auditor's testing is required to cover only 50 percent of the subrecipient's programs although, in many cases, auditors test closer to 90 percent of the programs. Therefore, there is the potential for many programs to go unaudited. Moreover, subrecipient single audit reports usually are not available until nine months after the end of the subrecipient's fiscal year. If there are problems, the pass-through entity may not be able to correct them before they are repeated.

In most instances, pass-through entities that review single audit reports from their subrecipients still perform additional monitoring such as site visits or document reviews. In fact, if a pass-through entity's only method of monitoring a subrecipient is reviewing its single audit report, it risks a finding in its own single audit report for failure to adequately monitor its subrecipients.

Some pass-through entities choose not to rely on the single audit as a monitoring tool at all, preferring instead to rely on their own additional desk reviews and onsite visits. These pass-through entities can monitor areas of a program that an auditor would not test, such as quality-of-service issues (e.g., appropriateness of the service provided). Additionally, they can look at programs administered by a subrecipient that are not tested as part of the single audit either because they are too small or they are not high-risk. Early identification of problems is another incentive for pass-through entities to do additional monitoring. Rather than waiting nine months to learn that one or more subrecipients have been charging certain costs incorrectly because of poorly written program guidance, the pass-through entity can identify and remedy the problem before it leads to larger unallowable costs that must be recovered from the subrecipient or possibly the pass-through entity.

Other pass-through entities rely on the single audit report to monitor their subrecipients' activities, but also perform supplementary monitoring. If a subrecipient's single audits regularly report no findings affecting its subawards, then the pass-through entity may feel comfortable relying more heavily on the single audit results and less so on its supplementary monitoring activities to ensure compliance. In contrast, if a subrecipient's single audits report findings that affect the pass-through entity's awards, the pass-through entity may increase its monitoring activities – performing additional visits and reviewing additional reports. Pass-through entities can plan their monitoring activities accordingly.

Still other primary grantees scale back their monitoring of subrecipients that must have single audits (organizations spending at least $500,000 annually). Instead, they concentrate their resources on those small subrecipients that are exempt from Circular A-133's audit requirements. Therefore, it is important that subrecipients let their pass-through entities know what their total federal expenditures will be and thus whether they will have a single audit performed.

Limited-Scope Audits

Pass-through entities that award funds to subrecipients that are exempt from single audit requirements should consider arranging for limited-scope audits to monitor those subrecipients. The cost of a limited-scope audit is allowable only if the subrecipient has not had a single audit. Primary grantees would have to pay for (using nonfederal funds) limited-scope audits of subrecipients that have single audits performed.

A pass-through entity would hire an auditor to perform the limited-scope audit because such audits only include agreed-upon procedures engagements performed in accordance with either generally accepted auditing standards (GAAS) or attestation standards. They must be paid for and arranged by the pass-through entity and not the subrecipient. Pass-through entities should note that audits are limited to the following types of compliance requirements:

- activities allowed or unallowed;

- allowable costs/cost principles;

- eligibility;

- matching, level of effort and earmarking; and

- reporting.

When a primary grantee hires an auditor to perform a limited-scope audit, the primary grantee must determine the procedures to be used and compliance areas to be reviewed. The pass-through entity will need to base these determinations on its needs, as well as the needs of other audit report users such as federal awarding agencies.

For example, if an auditor performs a limited-scope audit of reports the subrecipient submitted, the pass-through entity would have to specify that the auditor test whether the subrecipient's records support the information included in the reports.

A limited-scope audit may be a cost-effective technique to monitor a specific area of compliance for a group of subrecipients that are exempt from single audit rules. For instance, a pass-through entity that subawards program funds for which eligibility determinations are very important (e.g., the TANF program) must ensure that subrecipients are complying with the eligibility regulations. A pass-through entity can hire an auditor to perform

---

ARRANGING FOR AN AGREED-UPON PROCEDURES ENGAGEMENT

GAAS defines an agreed-upon procedures engagement as one in which an accountant is engaged by a client to issue a report of findings based on specific procedures performed on the specific subject matter of specified elements, accounts or items of a financial statement. The client engages the accountant to assist users in evaluating specified elements, accounts or items of a financial statement as a result of the needs of the users of the report. Because users require that findings be independently derived, the services of an accountant are obtained to perform procedures and report his or her findings. The users and the accountant agree upon the procedures to be performed by the accountant that the users believe are appropriate.

Because users' needs may vary widely, the nature, timing and extent of the agreed-upon procedures may vary as well; consequently, the users assume responsibility for the sufficiency of the procedures since they best understand their own needs. In an agreed-upon procedures engagement performed in accordance with GAAS, the accountant does not perform an audit and does not provide an opinion or negative assurance relating to the fair presentation of the specified elements, accounts or items of a financial statement. Instead, the accountant's report on agreed-upon procedures should be in the form of procedures and findings.

Similarly, AICPA's attestation standards state that an agreed-upon procedures engagement is one in which an accountant is engaged by a client to issue a report of findings based on specified procedures performed on the subject matter of an assertion, which is any declaration or set of declarations taken as a whole by a party responsible for it. Under the attestation standards, the client engages the accountant to assist users in evaluating an assertion as a result of the needs of the users of the report.

---

an agreed-upon procedures engagement of its subrecipients' compliance with eligibility requirements, rather than having to train their own personnel. Using the criteria defined by the pass-through entity, the auditor would perform a targeted evaluation and provide a report for each subrecipient that describes the procedures performed and any findings.

If there are a large number of subrecipients to be monitored, the pass-through entity can enter into one auditing contract (or maybe a few to spread the work) to perform agreed-upon procedures for all subrecipients administering the program in question. The auditing firm can perform the engagements on a cyclical basis. For example, if a pass-through entity hires the firm to perform procedures on 60 subrecipients spending less than $300,000, the firm and pass-through entity could agree to a three-year monitoring cycle. The firm would perform procedures on one-third of the subrecipients each year, which would provide the pass-through entity with some assurance about compliance with eligibility determination rules. In addition, the pass-through entity could direct the firm to perform procedures on higher-risk subrecipients (e.g., more incidents of noncompliance) more frequently.

> ### FOR-PROFIT SUBRECIPIENTS
>
> Pass-through entities that subaward funds to for-profit organizations can arrange for these subrecipients to have an agreed-upon procedures engagement. Because for-profit subrecipients are not subject to Circular A-133, the engagement could cover compliance areas other than the five specified in the circular (e.g., eligibility, reporting).

Onsite Visits

Onsite visits can be a useful tool for pass-through entities to ensure that subrecipients are complying with program requirements. During an onsite visit, a pass-through entity can:

- inspect a subrecipient's facilities and operations to ensure they comply with governmentwide and program requirements (e.g., eligibility determinations, Section 504 of the Rehabilitation Act of 1973);

- interview staff to ensure they are informed of and carry out program policy and regulations;

- review documentation and records such as invoices and payrolls that support subrecipient reports;

- view delivery of program services such as training;

- become familiar with subrecipient operations and staff; and

- learn about the subrecipient's progress and problems.

Many subaward agreements include provisions for onsite visits. Based on the type of subaward, a pass-through entity should be able to foresee if site visits will be necessary. The agreement should specify the number of visits that the pass-through will make to enable both the pass-through and the subrecipient to plan for those visits (see Fig. C-3 in Part C of this manual). The subaward agreement, however, does not have to specify the time or nature of the onsite reviews. Primary grantees and their subrecipients must negotiate the details of when the visits occur once the agreement is signed. Subrecipients should be aware that pass-through entities may make additional visits if they feel it is necessary such as to check on whether the subrecipient corrected a previously identified problem. For example, a monitoring visit may reveal a subrecipient receiving CDBG funds is building a facility that does not comply with the Americans With Disabilities Act. The pass-through entity would most likely schedule a follow-up visit to ensure that the facility has been modified to accommodate disabled individuals.

> ### WHEN ARE ONSITE VISITS APPROPRIATE?
>
> Onsite visits are more costly than some other types of monitoring because they require staff to prepare for the visit, travel to the subrecipient and review its operations. Many pass-through entities opt for onsite visits for subawards that require closer supervision:
>
> - programs with complex compliance requirements;
> - high dollar programs;
> - a program newly authorized by Congress;
> - programs with prior audit or monitoring findings;
> - high profile programs in which the federal awarding agency, Congress or the public have an interest;
> - programs administered by inexperienced subrecipients or subrecipients that have inexperienced staff;
> - programs where the subrecipient has requested an onsite visit; and
> - subrecipient sites that have not been visited recently.

Planning Onsite Visits

There are several steps to planning an onsite visit. A pass-through entity and subrecipient need to plan when the visit will take place. They also need to schedule the actual visit and develop an agenda for the meeting. Both parties need to review pertinent documents and files that are relevant to the subaward.

Pass-through entities and their subrecipients need to plan when the pass-through entity will make its monitoring visit. The timing of the visit will depend on several factors such as the availability of pass-through entity staff and resources and the areas that the pass-through entity plans to review during its visit (e.g., financial transactions, environmental records).

Exactly when the onsite visit will occur also will depend on the type of subaward. If a subrecipient administers an award that is renewed every year (for example, a school district that receives school breakfast and lunch program funds), the pass-through entity may schedule a regular visit for each recipient. In the case of a school district, the pass-through entity probably would schedule the visit during the school year, so it could review the school's records, conduct interviews with school staff and ensure that only eligible students are receiving the subsidized meals.

In contrast, if a subrecipient has a grant for a one-time project such as building low-income housing a pass-through entity may schedule monitoring visits at different intervals of the subaward period, as time and resources permit. For example, when a subrecipient buys a parcel of land on which it will build low-income housing, the primary grantee may visit to inspect the location. As the building progresses, the pass-through entity might make visits to ensure the construction actually is proceeding, the builder is following the subrecipient's plans, construction is completed and the facility complies with program requirements.

Lastly, pass-through entities may want to consider making unscheduled visits to high-risk subrecipients to ensure they comply with program requirements throughout the term of the subaward.

A pass-through entity and subrecipient may want to establish a schedule that will enable both organizations to prepare for onsite visits. The schedule could list specific dates, particularly if the subaward involves regular activities (e.g., job training) that the pass-through entity can monitor any time. Or the schedule could be linked to specific events such as the benchmarks in a building's construction. If a pass-through entity does establish a schedule for its visits, it should allow for a few changes to accommodate unplanned

---

GEORGIA GETS A BLUE RIBBON FOR ITS CDBG MONITORING PROGRAM

In the early 1980s, the state of Georgia Department of Community Affairs initiated a monitoring process that involved ongoing reviews of local CDBG recipients through one- or two-day local visits. During these visits, staff reviewed activities such as procurement and financial management practices and inspected construction in progress. Making timely visits and providing advice before the local government proceeds on a particular project has proved to be effective in ensuring compliance with program requirements and also in keeping paperwork to a minimum.

Over the years, Georgia has continued to use this approach, making minor adjustments to make the system more efficient. The key to its success is an experienced staff of program representatives who are continually visiting subrecipients. The staff report findings and help ensure that they are promptly resolved. By doing so, Georgia has kept major instances of noncompliance to a minimum.

Georgia deploys its program representatives in the field and emphasizes frequent one-on-one contacts with representatives of local governments. Written correspondence is kept to a minimum, and the strategy of making several short visits to each local government rather than one comprehensive monitoring visit to review program compliance has proven to be effective. Program representatives are in a position to counsel local government officials at critical stages of the development process. They monitor all activities in all applicable compliance areas and make an immediate verbal report to the locality. Letters are written only to notify the local government of a finding.

The program representatives have worked with the same local governments over several years and have become familiar with each community's needs. They can also advise local government officials about which CDBG activities have the most potential to meet their needs. In some instances, the program representatives have dissolved barriers between state and local governments and have become trusted advisers on community development matters.

As a result of these monitoring practices, Georgia has corrected most of the instances of noncompliance quickly – before they became serious.

Source: U.S. Department of Housing and Urban Development, Blue Ribbon Practices in Community Development, http://www.hud.gov:80/ptw/docs/ga14.html.

---

events. Some pass-through entities and subrecipients, however, may prefer to negotiate the details of each visit as the need arises.

When the time for the monitoring visit draws near, a pass-through entity should schedule the exact time first with a telephone call, followed by a letter of confirmation (see Fig. 4-1). The letter should contain the following information to help a subrecipient prepare for the visit:

- date of the visit;

- purpose;

- agenda;

- individuals to be interviewed; and

- documents and operations to be reviewed.

FIG. 4-1
ONSITE MONITORING CONFIRMATION LETTER

To: [insert subrecipient contact name]

From: [insert pass-through entity contact name]

Date: [insert date]

Subject: [Onsite Monitoring Visit for Community Development Block Grant (CDBG) program]

This memorandum is to confirm the CDBG program onsite monitoring visit of the CDBG subaward agreements, [insert agreement numbers], to be conducted [insert date and time of site visit].

I will review, at a minimum, the files indicated below, although I may choose to review any and all CDBG-related documents, if appropriate:

- application and contract;
- financial management;
- procurement and contracting;
- Americans With Disabilities Act/Section 504 of the Rehabilitation Act of 1973;
- construction contracts;
- labor standards;
- environmental review records; and
- civil rights.

Please ensure that all files are available for review during this onsite visit and that all personnel responsible for this contract can meet with me to respond to questions or concerns. Such personnel includes the finance director, the program administrator and any other personnel that deals with the documents identified above.

If possible, I would prefer a room where I can review files before or after the visit to the program site. Prior to the conclusion of the visit, I will discuss any questions and concerns with you and attempt to resolve as many issues as possible.

Should you have any questions please contact me at [insert telephone number].

To better plan their monitoring visits, pass-through entities may want to develop program-specific monitoring policies and checklists for use by their staffs. By using the checklists, the staff can perform more efficient visits, reviewing only relevant administrative and compliance areas, and apply uniform monitoring procedures to its subrecipients. When preparing the checklist, the pass-through entity should include all of the areas it needs to review to get an assurance that the subrecipient is meeting its obligations under the subaward agreement. (Pass-through entities that monitor small awards to only a few subrecipients may not need to develop policies to ensure uniformity.) However, pass-through entities should build some flexibility into their policies to allow for the unexpected. Areas that a pass-through entity should consider covering in their checklist include:

- accounting and financial management policies and procedures, including internal control systems;

- personnel policies and procedures;

- procurement policies and procedures;

- property records and inventory;

- environmental review record;

- labor policies and procedures;

- Americans With Disabilities Act and Section 504 of the Rehabilitation Act of 1973 compliance;

- eligibility determinations;

- program income records and reports; and

- other program-related compliance areas that are material to the subaward.

By reviewing some or all of these areas, a pass-through entity can verify during an onsite visit that a subrecipient's records support the periodic status reports provided to the pass-through entity and confirm the subrecipient's compliance with program requirements.

To help subrecipients prepare for their onsite visit, pass-through entities may find it more efficient to give the subrecipients a copy of the checklists so they know what the pass-through entity will be reviewing and can adequately prepare for the visit. It also may be less costly to provide the subrecipients with this guidance at the beginning of the subaward process rather than at the end of the process as follow-up advice in a management decision on a finding. Additionally, if there are any forms that the subrecipient may have to complete during the visit, the pass-through entity may want to provide those to the subrecipient in advance. The subrecipient can complete the forms and have them ready at the time of the visit.

Conducting the Onsite Visit

When the visit begins, a pass-through entity and subrecipient should discuss the purpose of the visit, the documents to be reviewed and the people to be interviewed. While all of this information is set out in the monitoring visit letter, the pass-through entity or subrecipient may want to make changes to the agenda. For example, the subrecipient may have identified a problematic area that requires the pass-through entity's technical advice.

During an onsite visit, a primary grantee has an opportunity to review a subrecipient's provision of program services (e.g., providing job training, building housing) on a first-hand basis. The pass-through entity can confirm that the subrecipient is providing the services in compliance with program regulations (e.g., the subrecipient is providing job training only to individuals that meet certain age or income requirements). To do this, the pass-through can interview both beneficiaries and staff. It can also review the documents and records related to the program areas it wants to monitor (e.g., financial and accounting systems, program-specific requirements) using the checklists it developed (see Fig. 4-2).

At the completion of the site visit, the pass-through entity should conduct an exit conference to clarify any questions and share its initial findings and recommendations.

Follow-Up

The pass-through entity should prepare a written report of its findings and recommendations following the site visit. The report should address each area that the pass-through entity reviewed as part of the monitoring visit (e.g., financial management, environmental policies and procedures, program compliance). The report should be added to the subrecipient's file. In the final monitoring report, the pass-through entity should list all of the monitoring checklists it used during the visit, so when staff prepare for future monitoring efforts (e.g., desk reviews, audits, onsite visits), they can find all of the records pertaining to the subrecipient.

The pass-through entity also should prepare a follow-up letter to the subrecipient that discloses any monitoring findings, makes recommendations to correct those findings, offers technical assistance if necessary and requests a corrective action plan (see Chapter 6). To ensure the subrecipient corrects the problem, the pass-through entity might schedule additional monitoring visits or request certain reports. For example, if a subrecipient built a facility using federal funds, and the facility did not meet federal accessibility standards, the primary recipient's management may need to make a return visit to verify that the subrecipient made changes to the facility.

Document Reviews

Pass-through entities can perform desk reviews of documentation and reports as a method for monitoring subrecipient activities. Desk reviews generally are less expensive than other monitoring methods (e.g., limited-scope audits) because pass-through entity staff do not have to travel or gather data, and they can target specific areas of compliance. By performing document reviews, a pass-through entity can determine whether

---

FIG. 4-2
COMMUNITY DEVELOPMENT BLOCK GRANT PROGRAM

Financial Management System

Recipient: _____

Agreement Number: _____

A. Pre-Visit File Check

1. Number of requests for payment: _____

3. Total disbursed to date: _____

5. Follow-up needed from prior visits or audits:

Onsite Monitoring Form

Monitoring Date: _____

Reviewer: _____

2. Amount requested to date: _____

4. Balance: _____

_____

_____

B. Onsite Visit

Ask for a copy of the revenue and expense ledger for this contract. Expense ledger should be itemized to show each expenditure. Note that this will likely cover two to three fiscal years, and we need ledgers for the entire length of the contract. Ledgers can be requested in the appointment memorandum, so they will be available at the onsite visit. Ledgers should be reviewed before sending the follow-up letter.

	Yes	No	N/A	Comments

1. Internal Controls

a. Title of person(s) who approves expenditures: _____

_____

b. Title of person(s) who signs checks: _____

_____

c. Title of person(s) responsible for general ledger transactions: _____

_____

2. Disbursements (random sample of two requests for payment)

a. Request No.   Amount: _____

Date received: _____

Date deposited: _____

All funds disbursed within 10 days:

b. Request No.   Amount: _____

Date received: _____

Date deposited: _____

All funds disbursed within 10 days:

c. No improper costs incurred prior to release of funds date

FIG. 4-2 (CONTINUED)

	Yes	No	N/A	Comments

3. Source Documentation

Files should contain original records, invoices, vouchers and documents – select two items and trace through the system.

<u>Request for Payment No.</u>　　Amount　　<u>Item</u>

a. _____　　　　　　_____

b. _____　　　　　　_____

c. approval to pay on each　　| | | |　_____

4. CDBG Funded Staff

a. Names/Title

_____　　　　　　_____

_____　　　　　　_____

_____　　　　　　_____

b. Engaged in activities as in application　| | | |　_____

c. Time records signed by employee and supervisor　| | | |　_____

5. Program Income

a. Records indicate source, date, amount and deposit account　| | | |　_____

b. Disbursements for eligible activities　| | | |　_____

c. Program income spent prior to additional requests for funds (unless revolving loan fund)　| | | |　_____

d. Payments timely　| | | |　_____

6. Property Management

a. Fixed assets ledger lists all assets acquired with CDBG funds and includes: description, serial identification number, acquisition date, invoice, unit, cost and total cost, location, use, condition, documentation of disposition　| | | |　_____

b. Inventory agrees with subrecipient's application　| | | |　_____

7. Other Items

a. Indirect cost documentation, if applicable　| | | |　_____

b. Audits: file contains and identifies location of all audits and related correspondence　| | | |　_____

c. Follow-up actions from prior visits or audits were implemented　| | | |　_____

a subrecipient is complying with financial, environmental, labor and other compliance requirements.

Subaward agreements generally authorize the pass-through entity to perform document reviews. For example, subrecipients must submit all requests for payment to the pass-through entity for approval and often have to include supporting invoices or receipts. Many pass-through entities also require periodic reports (e.g., quarterly or annually) from their subrecipients that include financial information or performance data with respect to the goals and objectives of the federal programs. Additionally, the subaward should contain provisions that give the pass-through entity access to all program-related materials for the purposes of reviews, site visits and audits.

Financial Monitoring

Most pass-through entities should develop some financial monitoring procedures to ensure that subrecipients:

- request the correct amount of federal funds;

- use the funds for program-related purposes;

- ensure only authorized personnel request funds;

- deposit funds in the proper account; and

- otherwise properly account for federal funds spent.

For example, pass-through entities monitoring subrecipient payments can require their subrecipients to identify in advance the official(s) authorized to request federal reimbursement (e.g., providing a signature card for the pass-through entity's files) and the bank or other institution where the pass-through entity will make any deposits. In addition, when any subrecipient makes a reimbursement request, the pass-through may want to require the subrecipient to provide not only a request for the money but an explanation (including supporting documentation such as payroll records) of how funds will be used (e.g., to pay subcontractors). Using this information, the pass-through entity would be able to verify not only that the proper parties requested the funds but also that the funds were being used for allowable program purposes. For example, if a subrecipient requests money to pay a subcontractor, the pass-through entity could verify against the documentation that the subcontractor is not debarred or suspended and that it actually performed the required work.

Monitoring Compliance With Other Requirements

Pass-through entities can perform document reviews to monitor subrecipient compliance with program-specific requirements throughout the subaward period, identifying problems and correcting them early on. Some pass-through entities begin performing desk reviews when a subrecipient submits a grant application, checking whether the subrecipient has included all of the necessary information. When an organization receives a subaward, the pass-through can monitor all facets of the subaward using desk reviews. For example, if a subrecipient receives a Community Development Block Grant (CDBG) subaward for a public housing facility, the pass-through entity can monitor every phase of the construction and completion of the facility. When the subrecipient purchases the land for the facility, the pass-through entity should ensure the subrecipient is complying with environmental regulations and notice requirements. For example, the pass-through entity may review and approve the necessary public notices to ensure they contain the language required by the program regulations and are published within the required time period. When the subrecipient hires construction contractors, the pass-through should consider reviewing the subrecipient's internal procurement procedures, the request for proposal that was issued and the construction agreement. In addition, the pass-through entity may want to review the subcontractor's payroll records to ensure compliance with Davis-Bacon Act requirements. Once the facility is completed and running, the pass-through entity may want regular reports on the facility's maintenance.

Planning Document Reviews

Both pass-through entities and subrecipients can plan for upcoming document reviews to make them more efficient and mitigate problems. Those pass-through entities that administer several federal programs may want to develop a monitoring cycle, performing document reviews of different programs at different times of the year. For example, a pass-through entity that administers the U.S. Department of Agriculture's Summer Food Service Program for Children, which provides meals for low-income children during the summer, might begin desk reviews in the spring when subrecipients are in their planning stages, increase the reviews over the summer as the program is performed and conduct any follow-up during the fall and winter months. At the same time, the pass-through entity may gear up desk review monitoring for other programs such as the School Breakfast Program, which provides breakfast to low-income children during the school year, when it is finishing up work on the Summer Food Service program subrecipients. By establishing a monitoring cycle, pass-through entities and subrecipients should go through the monitoring process more efficiently. Pass-through entities can allot the necessary resources and staff to perform the desk reviews and any necessary follow-up, and subrecipients can prepare and provide the proper reports and documents to the pass-through entities within established time frames.

Financial and Progress Reports

Beyond looking at a subrecipient's specific transactions (e.g., a request for reimbursement or a request for proposal), many pass-through entities require subrecipients to prepare periodic financial or progress reports.

The financial reports usually provide an overview of the subrecipient's financial status and include information concerning the subrecipient's total expenditures and program income. Some federal agencies require subrecipients to complete certain financial reporting forms such as standard form SF-269, *Financial Status Report* (see Fig. 4-3), or an agency-specific form. However, most federal agencies allow the pass-through entity to develop its own financial reporting form. In many instances, pass-through entities require more detailed information than is called for by SF-269 such as a line item comparison of budgeted and actual expenditures. When developing a financial reporting form, a pass-

FIG. 4-3

FINANCIAL STATUS REPORT
(Long Form)
(Follow instructions on the back)

1. Federal Agency and Organizational Element to Which Report is Submitted	2. Federal Grant or Other Identifying Number Assigned By Federal Agency		OMB Approval No. **0348-0039**	Page of pages

3. Recipient Organization (Name and complete address, including ZIP code)

4. Employer Identification Number	5. Recipient Account Number or Identifying Number	6. Final Report ☐ Yes ☐ No	7. Basis ☐ Cash ☐ Accrual

8. Funding/Grant Period *(See instructions)* From: (Month, Day, Year)	To: (Month, Day, Year)	9. Period Covered by this Report From: (Month, Day, Year)	To: (Month, Day, Year)

10. Transactions:	I Previously Reported	II This Period	III Cumulative
a. Total outlays			0.00
b. Refunds, rebates, etc.			0.00
c. Program income used in accordance with the deduction alternative			0.00
d. Net outlays *(Line a, less the sum of lines b and c)*	0.00	0.00	0.00
Recipient's share of net outlays, consisting of:			
e. Third party (in-kind) contributions			0.00
f. Other Federal awards authorized to be used to match this award			0.00
g. Program income used in accordance with the matching or cost sharing alternative			0.00
h. All other recipient outlays not shown on lines e, f or g			0.00
i. Total recipient share of net outlays *(Sum of lines e, f, g and h)*	0.00	0.00	0.00
j. Federal share of net outlays *(line d less line i)*	0.00	0.00	0.00
k. Total unliquidated obligations			
l. Recipient's share of unliquidated obligations			
m. Federal share of unliquidated obligations			
n. Total Federal share *(sum of lines j and m)*			0.00
o. Total Federal funds authorized for this funding period			
p. Unobligated balance of Federal funds *(Line o minus line n)*			0.00
Program income, consisting of:			
q. Disbursed program income shown on lines c and/or g above			
r. Disbursed program income using the addition alternative			
s. Undisbursed program income			
t. Total program income realized *(Sum of lines q, r and s)*			0.00

11. Indirect Expense	a. Type of Rate *(Place "X" in appropriate box)* ☐ Provisional ☐ Predetermined ☐ Final ☐ Fixed			
	b. Rate	c. Base	d. Total Amount	e. Federal Share

12. Remarks: Attach any explanations deemed necessary or information required by Federal sponsoring agency in compliance with governing legislation.

13. Certification: **I certify to the best of my knowledge and belief that this report is correct and complete and that all outlays and unliquidated obligations are for the purposes set forth in the award documents.**

Typed or Printed Name and Title	Telephone (Area code, number and extension)
Signature of Authorized Certifying Official	Date Report Submitted August 1, 2007

Previous Edition Usable
NSN 7540-01-012-4285

269-104

200-498 P.O. 139 (Face)

Standard Form 269 (Rev. 7-97)
Prescribed by OMB Circulars A-102 and A-110

FIG. 4-3 (CONTINUED)

FINANCIAL STATUS REPORT
(Long Form)

Public reporting burden for this collection of information is estimated to average 30 minutes per response, including time for reviewing instructions, searching existing data sources, gathering and maintaining the data needed, and completing and reviewing the collection of information. Send comments regarding the burden estimate or any other aspect of this collection of information, including suggestions for reducing this burden, to the Office of Management and Budget, Paperwork Reduction Project (0348-0039), Washington, DC 20503.

PLEASE <u>DO NOT</u> RETURN YOUR COMPLETED FORM TO THE OFFICE OF MANAGEMENT AND BUDGET.

Please type or print legibly. The following general instructions explain how to use the form itself. You may need additional information to complete certain items correctly, or to decide whether a specific item is applicable to this award. Usually, such information will be found in the Federal agency's grant regulations or in the terms and conditions of the award (e.g., how to calculate the Federal share, the permissible uses of program income, the value of in-kind contributions, etc.). You may also contact the Federal agency directly.

Item	Entry
1, 2 and 3.	Self-explanatory.
4.	Enter the Employer Identification Number (EIN) assigned by the U.S. Internal Revenue Service.
5.	Space reserved for an account number or other identifying number assigned by the recipient.
6.	Check *yes* only if this is the last report for the period shown in item 8.
7.	Self-explanatory.
8.	Unless you have received other instructions from the awarding agency, enter the beginning and ending dates of the current funding period. If this is a multi-year program, the Federal agency might require cumulative reporting through consecutive funding periods. In that case, enter the beginning and ending dates of the grant period, and in the rest of these instructions, substitute the term "grant period" for "funding period."
9.	Self-explanatory.
10.	The purpose of columns, I, II, and III is to show the effect of this reporting period's transactions on cumulative financial status. The amounts entered in column I will normally be the same as those in column III of the previous report *in the same funding period*. If this is the first or only report of the funding period, leave columns I and II blank. If you need to adjust amounts entered on previous reports, footnote the column I entry on this report and attach an explanation.
10a.	Enter total gross program outlays. Include disbursements of cash realized as program income if that income will also be shown on lines 10c or 10g. Do not include program income that will be shown on lines 10r or 10s.

For reports prepared on a cash basis, outlays are the sum of actual cash disbursements for direct costs for goods and services, the amount of indirect expense charged, the value of in-kind contributions applied, and the amount of cash advances and payments made to subrecipients. For reports prepared on an accrual basis, outlays are the sum of actual cash disbursements for direct charges for goods and services, the amount of indirect expense incurred, the value of in-kind contributions applied, and the net increase or decrease in the amounts owed by the recipient for goods and other property received, for services performed by employees, contractors, subgrantees and other payees, and other amounts becoming owed under programs for which no current services or performances are required, such as annuities, insurance claims, and other benefit payments.

Item	Entry
10b.	Enter any receipts related to outlays reported on the form that are being treated as a reduction of expenditure rather than income, and were not already netted out of the amount shown as outlays on line 10a.
10c.	Enter the amount of program income that was used in accordance with the deduction alternative.
Note:	Program income used in accordance with other alternatives is entered on lines q, r, and s. Recipients reporting on a cash basis should enter the amount of cash income received; on an accrual basis, enter the program income earned. Program income may or may not have been included in an application budget and/or a budget on the award document. If actual income is from a different source or is significantly different in amount, attach an explanation or use the remarks section.
10d,	e, f, g, h, i and j. Self-explanatory.
10k.	Enter the total amount of unliquidated obligations, including unliquidated obligations to subgrantees and contractors.

Unliquidated obligations on a cash basis are obligations incurred, but not yet paid. On an accrual basis, they are obligations incurred, but for which an outlay has not yet been recorded.

Do not include any amounts on line 10k that have been included on lines 10a and 10j.

On the final report, line 10k must be zero.

Item	Entry
10l.	Self-explanatory.
10m.	On the final report, line 10m must also be zero.
10n,	o, p, q, r, s and t. Self-explanatory.
11a.	Self-explanatory.
11b.	Enter the indirect cost rate in effect during the reporting period.
11c.	Enter the amount of the base against which the rate was applied.
11d.	Enter the total amount of indirect costs charged during the report period.
11e.	Enter the Federal share of the amount in 11d.
Note:	If more than one rate was in effect during the period shown in item 8, attach a schedule showing the bases against which the different rates were applied, the respective rates, the calendar periods they were in effect, amounts of indirect expense charged to the project, and the Federal share of indirect expense charged to the project to date.

SF-269 Back (Rev. 7-97)

through entity should consider what information it needs and how it will use the information to evaluate a subrecipient's progress.

A subrecipient's progress report explains the subrecipient's progress toward achieving subaward goals and objectives (see Fig. 4-4). (The goals and objectives often are described either in the subaward agreement, reference regulations or the subrecipient's original application, which usually is incorporated into the subaward.) While a few federal agencies have developed program reporting formats for use by subrecipients, most pass-through entities must develop their own. Circular A-110 and the grants management common rule both state that performance reports should include the following information:

- a comparison of actual accomplishments with the goals and objectives established for the period;

- reasons why goals were not met; and

- other pertinent information, including analysis of cost overruns or high unit costs.

When reviewing subrecipient financial reports, the pass-through entity should make sure that the information is accurate and complete. Has the subrecipient provided all of the requested information? Do all of the figures add up? For example, if a subrecipient is paid in advance, the pass-through entity should verify that the amounts drawn down by

---

FIG. 4-4
SAMPLE PROGRESS REPORT

Date_____

Subrecipient Contact Person _____

Subrecipient Name _____

Subaward Number_____

Pass-Through Entity Contact Person _____

Report Number and Period _____

Progress Achieved Toward Project Goals and Objectives _____

_____

_____

Goals	Target	Actual	Unit Costs	*Problems/Resolution
Goal No. 1 (e.g., provide medical care to children under age 5)				
Goal No. 2				
Goal No. 3				
Goal No. 4				

*The subrecipient should indicate the problems encountered, why goals were not met and how it plans to resolve the problems.

---

the subrecipient match with the actual expenditures it reported. The pass-through entity also should compare the subrecipient's actual expenditures to those budgeted. Discrepancies may indicate problems that should be followed up on if the subrecipient is spending money either too quickly or too slowly.

As with the financial reports, the pass-through entity should review subrecipient progress reports to determine if adequate progress is being made toward the subgrant goals and objectives. If there are problems, determine whether any follow-up action is needed.

When required reports are overdue, the pass-through entity should contact the subrecipient to remind them of the requirement. An informal telephone reminder may be all that is necessary. But if the report fails to appear, the pass-through entity may want to send a formal letter specifying the report that is required, the date it was due and the provisions of the subgrant agreement or program regulations that require the report.

Pass-through entities should try to establish standard monitoring procedures and checklists for performing desk reviews of subrecipient reports. Because most subrecipients perform similar activities and provide similar reports, pass-through entities can re-use these checklists to save time and apply uniform monitoring procedures to subrecipients. Pass-through entities should make part or all of the checklists available to their subrecipients (and if they do not, subrecipients may want to ask for them), so the subrecipients can make sure they are properly carrying out the subaward and preparing the correct reports and documentation. Pass-through entities may find it more efficient and less costly to provide guidance at the beginning of the subaward process rather than at the end of the process as follow-up advice in a management decision on a finding.

Pass-through entities may need to supplement document reviews with onsite monitoring. By visiting the subrecipient, the pass-through entity can review the underlying documentation (e.g., payroll, applications or receipts) that support subrecipient reports, conduct staff interviews and view the actual site and services being delivered.

If a desk review discloses problems, the pass-through entity is responsible for informing the subrecipient and prescribing corrective action (e.g., repaying funds). In response to the finding, the pass-through may schedule follow-up desk reviews (and onsite visits, if necessary) and require additional reports to ensure the subrecipient has corrected the problem.

Prior Approvals

Circular A-110 and the grants management common rule require most subrecipients to get prior written approval from the pass-through entity for most major changes to the budget or the scope of work once the subaward is finalized. Examples of changes that require prior approval are:

- revisions that would result in the need for additional funding;

- transfer of funds allotted for training;

- revisions in the scope or objectives of the subaward;

- the need to extend the period of availability of funds; and

- changes in key personnel (e.g., the principle investigator of a research project).

In addition, the cost principles require subgrantees to obtain prior written approval from pass-through entities to charge certain costs to their subaward such as travel and special facilities rearrangement and alterations.

By requiring a subrecipient to get prior approval for such expenditures or changes, the pass-through entity can monitor the activities of the subrecipient. If certain costs or changes are not chargeable to the subaward, the pass-through entity can inform the subrecipient before the subrecipient incurs unallowable costs. Similarly, if the subrecipient needs to change a key staff member, this may signal problems with subaward administration. The pass-through entity may need to perform additional monitoring until a new staff person is hired and becomes familiar with the subaward requirements.

Both Circular A-110 and the grants management common rule state that requiring prior approvals is an effective method to monitoring "high-risk" subgrantees. By requiring certain prior approvals, the pass-through entity and subrecipient work closely throughout the subaward period and the pass-through entity stays informed of subrecipient activities.

By the same token, primary grantees have the discretion to waive prior approval requirements for reliable subrecipients to ease their administrative burden.

Third-Party Evaluations

A pass-through entity may require as part of the subaward agreement that subrecipients have an outside consultant specializing in grants administration review their operations.

CITY USES CITIZENS ADVISORY COMMITTEE TO EVALUATE ITS CDBG PROGRAM

The city of Santa Maria, Calif., sought to manage CDBG programs according to program and statutory requirements. While delivering quality services to beneficiaries, the city must ensure that program funds are expended in a timely manner; that performance reports are complete, timely and accurate; that CDBG-funded programs are eligible activities that benefit low- and moderate-income residents; and that the new consolidated planning requirements are met.

The city's staff works closely with a citizens advisory committee to ensure that programs and activities reflect community needs. In terms of day-to-day administration, performance reports are prepared carefully and completely, and program activities are classified properly. Corrections, when they are required, are submitted in a timely fashion, and responses are prompt to requests for supplemental information.

This practice provides an example of a city combining a strong commitment to citizen participation with an unusual attention to detail in administering its housing and community development programs. City staff have developed particular expertise in administering affordable housing programs. Contractors and subrecipients are informed of their responsibilities under the CDBG program, and they are monitored on a yearly basis. The city has avoided audit or monitoring findings, achieving a high level of performance with program funds.

Source: U.S. Department of Housing and Urban Development, Blue Ribbon Practices in Community Development, http://www.hud.gov:80/ptw/docs/ca30.html.

The consultant generally would review the subrecipient's various systems (e.g., financial management, property management, procurement) and prepare a report that identifies any problems and makes recommendations for improvements. Before hiring a consultant, both pass-through entities and subrecipients need to consider who will pay for the evaluation and whether the costs are chargeable to the federal award – are they reasonable, allowable and allocable?

There are other types of independent evaluations that pass-through entities should consider reviewing as part of their efforts to monitor subrecipients. Besides paid consultants, pass-through entities and subrecipients should consider having other interested groups evaluate their program such as beneficiaries of the subrecipient's services or community organizations operating in the same community where the subrecipient provides its services. These groups may provide valuable insights about problems with the services or benefits provided or areas where the subrecipient could increase its services.

Technical Assistance and Training

Training is an effective means of ensuring that subrecipients, especially new ones, are familiar with the governmentwide and program-specific requirements that apply to their subaward. By providing training, the pass-through entity can answer questions, recommend techniques for carrying out the subaward that have been successful with previous subrecipients and develop a partnership with its subrecipients. Similarly, pass-through entities may want to provide subrecipients with training when there is a major change in program policy and the pass-through entity wants to ensure that all subrecipients understand and correctly implement the change.

Pass-through entities can provide more targeted technical assistance to individual subrecipients. During a desk review or monitoring visit, the pass-through entity may identify a problem that will require technical assistance. For example, a primary grantee may discover that a subrecipient does not have effective internal controls over its financial accounting and cash management systems. This may require the primary grantee's staff to work with the subrecipient to develop a new internal control system. This kind of targeted assistance can be costly because it requires substantial staff time. However, the long-term benefits of setting up successful internal controls may include fewer overpayments by the pass-through entity, fewer findings and possibly an internal control system that can be shared with other subrecipients.

Informal Monitoring

Telephone calls and e-mail communication are probably the least costly and time-consuming methods of monitoring available. Such tools provide pass-through entities with the opportunity to ask a subrecipient questions about financial and progress reports and other documents submitted for review. Informal communication enables the pass-through entity to interview subrecipient staff about various subaward issues without having to make an onsite visit. Also, because telephone calls can be made and e-mail can be sent frequently and with less planning (e.g., when to make monitoring visit, what record to review) than other forms of monitoring, these types of procedures can help a pass-through entity develop a closer partnership with its subrecipients.

NJ CITY USES TECHNICAL ASSISTANCE PARTNERSHIPS TO MONITOR CDBG SUBRECIPIENTS

The city of Elizabeth, N.J., wanted to develop a more comprehensive system for ensuring subrecipients' compliance with program requirements and for simultaneously assisting subrecipients to improve performance.

The city's strategy for monitoring and managing subrecipients includes a detailed risk analysis of all the subrecipients, onsite and remote monitoring, and continuous technical assistance and staff interviews.

The city provides each agency with program-specific technical assistance that helps establish effective partnerships with its subrecipients. The city gives personal attention to each agency by providing ongoing technical assistance – both onsite and at its offices. City staff review each subrecipient's past operational and fiscal performance. In addition to examining relevant records and reports, the city meets with subrecipients to discuss problems and issues in order to get an overall sense of how the agency is doing. City staff emphasize a broad perspective in their technical assistance approach: assistance is provided in regulatory compliance, as well as in project delivery, outreach and performance. Finally, the city has designed and is implementing workshops to better acquaint subrecipient agencies with the entire grant process.

As a result of technical assistance provided to a group counseling and therapy provider for survivors of domestic abuse, the subrecipient was able to expand services from approximately 100 clients served per year to 140 clients. More generally, the city's approach to subrecipient monitoring focuses on improving the subrecipients' capacity to serve its clients.

Source: U.S. Department of Housing and Urban Development, Blue Ribbon Practices in Community Development, http://www.hud.gov:80/ptw/docs/nj10.html.

Like any other monitoring techniques, pass-through entities and subrecipients need to prepare for the telephone interview. The pass-through entity should schedule a time for the interview with the subrecipient, if it is going to involve complex questions, cover several areas or require a large amount of time. Routine questions and advice should be reserved for separate telephone calls.

When scheduling a telephone interview, a pass-through entity should inform a subrecipient of the purpose of the interview, issues that will be addressed during the call, who should be present for the call, how long it will take and any other information necessary (e.g., documents that the subrecipient should have on hand).

To prepare for the call, the pass-through entity and subrecipient both should review the relevant subaward provisions and administrative and programmatic regulations. The pass-through entity also should review the subrecipient's file.

The pass-through entity should make the call at the appointed time and identify the parties to the call from both the pass-through entity and the subrecipient. It should review the purpose of the call and follow the agenda, making sure the scheduled issues are covered. At the close of the call, the pass-through entity should summarize the results of the telephone interview, including any findings. The pass-through entity should indicate whether any follow-up will be necessary.

Both the pass-through entity and the subrecipient should take notes during the interview (or get permission to record it on tape). Once the call is complete, both sides should review their notes and make final copies for their files. If either side has any questions about what was said, a follow-up call may be necessary.

The pass-through entity also should prepare a final report to the subrecipient that summarizes the telephone call, identifying the issues addressed, any findings and recommendations for corrective action or improvement. The report should be added to the subrecipient's file. If the subrecipient disagrees with any aspect of the final report, it should contact the pass-through entity immediately. Otherwise, the subrecipient is responsible for taking any required corrective action and informing the pass-through entity when it is completed.

While there are a variety of tools available for subrecipient monitoring, a pass-through entity must choose those that will work best for its subrecipients. In making this choice, it should always keep in mind that its monitoring efforts should ensure that a subrecipient is meeting performance goals and objectives and administering its federal funds in compliance with the subaward requirements.

Regardless of the type of monitoring tool chosen, a pass-through entity should keep a detailed record of monitoring activities and other vital information related to all subawards. Thus, for each monitoring effort, a pass-through entity should prepare for its files a report that lists the monitoring date, the type of monitoring that was performed and the purpose of the monitoring activity. It should also identify any subrecipient staff or beneficiaries who were interviewed. The pass-through entity also should describe the monitoring results and any follow-up that is needed. This will enable the pass-through entity to better assess the subrecipient's compliance, plan future monitoring activities and prepare its own reports and records.

Costs of Monitoring

A pass-through entity may charge to its federal awards the cost of the following monitoring tools:

- reviewing reports submitted by subrecipients;

- performing site visits to the subrecipient to review financial and programmatic records and observe operations;

- arranging for limited-scope audits (i.e., agreed-upon procedures engagements) of certain areas, such as eligibility (when the subrecipient does not have a single audit performed); and

- reviewing single audits (for subrecipients spending less than $500,000, single audit costs are not reimbursable).

CHECKLIST FOR SUBRECIPIENT MONITORING RESULTS

A pass-through entity should keep a record of monitoring activities and other vital information related to all subawards.

✔ Subrecipient name and address

✔ Program name

✔ Subrecipient contact person

✔ Subaward agreement number

✔ Date of monitoring

✔ Type of monitoring procedure

   ❑ telephone call

   ❑ financial/progress report review

   ❑ onsite visit

   ❑ limited-scope audit (or other agreed-upon procedures engagement)

   ❑ audit review

✔ Purpose of the monitoring

   ❑ Review program progress and compliance with subaward requirements

   ❑ Perform follow-up review

   ❑ Other

✔ Subrecipient staff contacted/interviewed as part of monitoring

✔ Beneficiaries contacted/interviewed as part of monitoring

✔ Related reports (e.g., financial status reports)

✔ Monitoring results

   ❑ findings

   ❑ recommendations

   ❑ required corrective action (e.g., report, site visit)

   ❑ necessary technical assistance

✔ Subrecipient contact person responsible for follow-up

✔ Pass-through entity contact person responsible for follow-up

✔ Deadline for corrective action

Communication Between Pass-Through Entities and Subrecipients

Effective communication between pass-through entities and subrecipients during the subaward agreement period is essential to ensuring that the subrecipient performs the activities or services required by the agreement in compliance with the applicable program laws and regulations.

The pass-through entity needs to convey to the subrecipient the kinds of activities that the subrecipient must perform and any applicable laws and regulations with which the subrecipient must comply. Similarly, in many instances (e.g., performing a research grant), the subrecipient must inform the pass-through entity, usually through its application or proposal to perform the subaward, how it intends to perform the activities or services required in the subaward. For instance, a subrecipient that is performing a research subgrant for a university generally must provide a budget for its work, a list of the personnel that will be working on the subgrant and a list of the equipment needed to do the research. Beyond the terms of the agreement, pass-through entities and subrecipients will need to convey additional information to each other. Pass-through entities may have to inform their subrecipients about changes in program regulations and subrecipients, in turn, may have questions about subaward terms or changes in personnel. Therefore, pass-through entities and subrecipients should maximize the various tools of communication available to them.

> ### INFORMATION FOR SUBRECIPIENTS
>
> To help ensure that subrecipients understand all of the relevant laws, regulations and guidelines that apply to the subaward, pass-through entities should consider preparing a package of information that provides the following, as appropriate:
>
> - program authorizing legislation;
> - excerpts of program regulations;
> - relevant public policy laws (e.g., the Davis-Bacon Act);
> - the *Catalog of Federal Domestic Assistance program listing;*
> - OMB Circulars (e.g., Circular A-110);
> - excerpts of the *Federal Acquisition Regulation;*
> - relevant state laws; and
> - guidelines developed by the pass-through entity.

Importance of the Subaward Agreement and Other Guidance

Perhaps the most important form of communication between the parties is the subaward agreement. It describes both the pass-through entity's and subrecipient's roles and responsibilities, the activities or services to be performed, and the applicable laws and regulations (see Chapter 3). It is the first document that either party should review when questions arise regarding the subaward.

Many pass-through entities prepare handbooks and other guidance for subrecipients that explain further the program's requirements and include important information such as program laws and regulations and OMB circulars. Such guidance also may describe additional requirements imposed by the pass-through entity. By providing such documents, pass-through entities help ensure that subrecipients, particularly new subrecipients, understand all of the relevant regulations and guidelines. And subrecipients get a more complete picture of what is required of them.

Whether a pass-through entity prepares such guidance depends on several factors, including the number of subrecipients the pass-through has to oversee, the size of the subawards it makes, the need for such guidance and whether the benefits outweigh any related costs. For example, some state agencies have developed labor or environmental guidelines that subrecipients must follow when performing housing rehabilitation or other construction activities under the CDBG program. State agencies have developed such guidelines because they subaward a large portion of their CDBG funds to county and city governments and other entities. In many cases, the state making the subaward may include the guidelines by reference in the subaward agreement (see Fig. C-1 in Part C of this manual). If so, the subrecipient must follow them to comply with the agreement's requirements.

Even if guidelines prepared by the pass-through entity are not referenced in the subaward agreement, subrecipients should read the guidelines because they can provide additional information for carrying out the award such as describing the reports that the subrecipient must prepare. For example, the Library of Michigan, which awards subgrants to certain public, private, research, and elementary and secondary libraries under the Library Services and Technology Act (LSTA), has developed the *LSTA Subgrant Program Guidelines.* The guidelines address several areas such as reimbursement policies and procedures, the procurement of property and services, and copyrights. Under the section on reports, it states that "during the grant year, the Library of Michigan will send forms to subgrantees for reporting project progress. These reports request information pertinent to project expenditures, as well as progress on project objectives. This information is required for federal and state reporting and must be submitted in a timely fashion." It also notes that site visits may be conducted on a random basis.

Need for Dialogue Between Pass-Through Entities and Subrecipients

In most cases, the information in the agreement and any additional policy documents is just the beginning of an ongoing dialog between a pass-through entity and its subrecipients. Subrecipients frequently need to ask their pass-through entities questions about the subgrant agreement and its compliance requirements that are not answered in the subaward agreement or other guidance. In fact, many pass-through entities provide question and answer sessions for subrecipients during the application process. At these sessions, the pass-through entity answers questions about various aspects of the subawards such as modifying the scope of work, the applicable compliance requirements and the payment process. The pass-through entity also can explain the policies and procedures (e.g., the accounting or procurement systems) that the subrecipient is expected to have in place.

Subrecipients, especially those that are administering an award for the first time, may have questions for the pass-through entity during the course of the subaward. For example, a subrecipient may have a question about whether a certain cost is allowable. Additionally, a subrecipient may want to ask the pass-through entity if a change in the subaward such as adding personnel or purchasing new equipment needs prior approval from the pass-through entity. Pass-through entities should encourage subrecipients to ask questions and try to provide the answers quickly and clearly. If both parties deal with questions as they arise, they can prevent potential problems such as noncompliance or unallowable expenditures, which if not caught can lead to findings during an audit or review and possibly a reduction or complete loss of federal funding.

Most pass-through entities try to keep these type of communications informal, but depending on the nature of the subrecipient's question, a pass-through entity may want to document the answer in writing. Also, if a subrecipient identifies a problem such as a breakdown of its internal control, it may want to inform the pass-through entity in advance rather than having the pass-through entity discover it through an audit or monitoring visit. A pass-through entity or auditor probably would be more assured if the subrecipient has found a problem, informed the pass-through entity and is working to correct it.

Pass-through entities may need to contact subrecipients about changes in grant requirements. Federal agencies update program regulations frequently, and while subrecipients are responsible for following the most current compliance requirements, pass-through entities also should inform their subrecipients of applicable federal regulations and related changes to ensure that the program is successful. Circular A-133 states that pass-through entities should "advise subrecipients of requirements imposed on them by federal laws, regulations and the provisions of contracts or grant agreements as well as any supplemental requirements imposed by the pass-through entity." For instance, pass-through entities that are aware of changes to income guidelines that affect the eligibility of certain beneficiaries of program services should communicate this information to any affected subgrantees. Also, subrecipients should be made of aware of other changes such as a new address or contact person for the pass-through entity.

How pass-through entities choose to communicate this information may vary depending on the number of subrecipients they have, the importance of the regulatory changes and the pass-through entity's resources. Some pass-through entities with a large number of subrecipients may send an official letter that explains the changes, while others may telephone if they have only a few subrecipients. Pass-through entities that rely on the telephone may want to keep a record of calls with subrecipients as part of the subgrant file.

Pass-through entities also may want informal updates on the progress from subrecipients without waiting for formal reports or audits. Some pass-through entities schedule regular meetings with subrecipients. The frequency of the meetings depends on the nature of the subaward, how near the subrecipients are to the pass-through entity and how much oversight the pass-through entity wants to exercise. In one case, the program director for a Midwestern medical school that subawards U.S. Department of Education funds for health education training to nonprofit organizations attends the subrecipients' board meetings because of their proximity. In this way, the medical school is able to ascertain on a regular basis that the subrecipients are performing the activities set forth in the subaward.

During these informal meetings, subrecipients should discuss any problems they may be having rather than waiting for a formal monitoring visit or progress report and get advice from the pass-through entity on potential remedies. Subrecipients also can use the informal meetings to report program successes such as achieving program goals or reducing administrative costs.

Many pass-through entities, including those that contact their subrecipients on a more informal basis, specify in the subaward agreement that the subrecipient must submit financial or progress reports during the course of the subaward. These reports may be in addition to or in lieu of a Circular A-133 audit, depending on whether the subrecipient's federal expenditures exceed the circular's audit threshold. However, the subaward agreements quite frequently do not fully explain the reporting that subrecipients must provide to the pass-through entities. Pass-through entities may have to further explain to the subrecipients the type of reporting required.

For example, a disaster funding agreement between the state of Florida and its subgrantees requires the subgrantees to provide quarterly progress reports. The pertinent language in the agreement states:

> The first report is due three months after the date of execution of this agreement and quarterly thereafter until the work has been completed and approved through final inspection. All reports shall be provided using the attached quarterly report form. ... The grantee may require additional reports as needed. The subgrantee shall, as soon as possible, provide any additional reports requested by the grantee.

If the pass-through entity needs any additional reports, it should contact the subrecipient as soon as possible to explain what information the report should contain and where and when it should be submitted. Providing the subrecipient with the most information possible about the required report will help ensure the subrecipient submits information the pass-through entity needs to oversee the subaward.

Similarly, pass-through entities should contact their subrecipients to schedule monitoring visits. While most subaward agreements specify that the pass-through entity has the right to visit the subrecipient, they generally don't specify when the visits take place or what the pass-through entity will inspect. An example of subaward monitoring language is as follows: "The subgrantor will schedule two monitoring visits with the provider on the following basis to evaluate the progress and performance of the program and provide technical assistance."

Pass-through entities, therefore, usually must contact subrecipients to schedule their visits. When contacting the subrecipient, pass-through entities may want to let the subrecipients know the areas of the program they want to focus on and the records they want to review during their visit. This should help the

---

PREPARING FOR A SITE VISIT

When scheduling a visit to a subrecipient's program site, a pass-through entity should consider providing the subrecipient with the following information, so it can prepare for the visit:

- the visit's purpose;
- the pass-through entity contact person;
- records to be reviewed;
- areas of the program site to be visited or observed;
- employees to be interviewed; and
- beneficiaries to be interviewed.

---

visit go smoothly and efficiently. And if the pass-through entity does not volunteer this information, subrecipients should go ahead and ask for it.

There may be instances when a pass-through entity does not inform a subrecipient of an inspection, preferring instead to "surprise" the subrecipient. While these types of visits are not common, they give subrecipients greater incentive to keep their books and records in order. However, a pass-through entity may want to consider the effect a surprise approach to monitoring might have on its relationship with its subrecipient.

During the monitoring visit, the pass-through entity and subrecipient should maintain an open discussion rather than waiting for the pass-through entity to issue its report on the visit. By talking during the visit, the pass-through entity can alert the subrecipient to problems such as noncompliance with program regulations or accounting errors that it discovers. This gives the subrecipient an opportunity to explain why it is not a problem or possibly correct it before the pass-through entity leaves.

Once the monitoring visit is over, the pass-through entity should prepare a report of the results that includes any findings and send it to the subrecipient. The report also should contain the pass-through entity's recommendations and technical advice for improvement and how the subrecipient should follow up. The subrecipient should take the opportunity to comment on the report, indicating where it disagrees with the pass-through entity, and providing a corrective action plan to address any findings and implement the pass-through entity's recommendations. The pass-through entity should indicate in the report whether it will require additional reports or inspections as a result of the monitoring visit. If so, the pass-through entity and subrecipient will have to work together to schedule subsequent visits and reports.

Communication About Subrecipient Single Audits

The amount of monitoring, both document reviews and onsite visits, that a pass-through entity performs depends on whether a subrecipient has a single audit performed in accordance with Circular A-133 (see Chapter 4). When a pass-through entity knows that a subrecipient will have a Circular A-133 audit performed, it may reduce the amount of monitoring it performs because it can rely on the single audit to identify problems with or provide assurance about a subrecipient's compliance with program requirements.

Under Circular A-133, a subrecipient must provide any pass-through entity with a copy of its single audit report when the pass-through entity is affected by findings reported in the schedule of findings and questioned costs or disclosed in the summary schedule of prior audit findings. Otherwise, a subrecipient must send its pass-through entity a letter stating that the subrecipient had a single audit performed and there were no audit findings affecting the pass-through entity's subawards.

Pass-through entities, however, should not wait to receive a subrecipient's single audit report to determine what level of additional monitoring is required. They must determine a subrecipient's federal expenditures early enough in the subaward period to conduct effective monitoring. While a pass-through entity can identify those subrecipients to which it awarded $500,000 or more in federal funds or that had single audits conducted in previous years, it cannot identify all of its subrecipients that will have a single audit. Therefore, to identify how much monitoring it will have to do, a pass-through entity should require as part of the subaward agreement that subrecipient inform the pass-through entity what their federal expenditures are and whether they are going to have single audit done. Many pass-through entities require their subrecipients to complete a certification letter that provides this information (see Fig. 5-1).

Using this information, the pass-through entity can set up a monitoring plan for each subrecipient. To monitor a subrecipient that does not have a single audit, pass-through entities will have to develop a more comprehensive review plan that focuses on such areas as the subrecipient's financial records and program compliance. In contrast, pass-through entities can focus monitoring efforts on areas that are not covered in a single audit such as performance objectives (e.g., qualitative issues that auditors do not test), or they can focus on certain subrecipients that are deemed high-risk because of prior findings, the amount of money they receive, the complexity of the program or other reasons.

Contacting the Federal Awarding Agency

Federal agencies generally are not involved in the management or monitoring of subrecipients. This is because the subrecipients receive their federal funds through agreements with pass-through entities. Therefore, because subrecipients and federal agencies do not have a contractual relationship, they are not directly linked. When preparing any financial or progress reports or having an audit performed, the subrecipient should submit any results to the pass-through entity. Similarly, questions about the subaward also should be directed to the pass-through entity. This is not to say that subrecipients are prohibited from contacting federal agencies.

In fact, a subrecipient may need to contact the federal awarding agency directly when the pass-through entity cannot answer its questions about the subaward. For example, a subrecipient may need to contact the federal awarding agency for the CFDA name and number of a program it administers to complete the *Data Collection Form for Reporting on Audits of States, Local Governments and Nonprofit Organizations* (SF-SAC). The pass-

---

Fig. 5-1
Single Audit Certification Letter

Date
Subrecipient Contact Person
Subrecipient Organization Name
Street Address
City, State, Zip

RE: Subrecipient Audit Requirements of OMB Circular A-133
        Contract between [insert pass-through entity's name] and [insert subrecipient's name]
        for the period of [insert date] through [insert date] under [identify subaward by name/
        CFDA number/amount of award]

Dear [insert subrecipient contact person]:

[Insert the pass-through entity's name] is subject to the requirements of Office of Management and Budget (OMB) Circular A-133, *Audits of States, Local Governments and Nonprofit Organizations*. As such, Circular A-133 requires [insert pass-through entity's name] to monitor our subrecipients of federal awards and determine whether they have met the audit requirements of the circular and whether they are in compliance with federal laws and regulations.

Accordingly, we are requesting that you check one of the following, provide all appropriate documentation regarding your organization's compliance with the audit requirements, sign and date the letter and return this letter to me at your earliest convenience.

1.____   We have completed our Circular A-133 audit for fiscal year ended [enter date]. A copy of the audit report and a schedule of federal programs by major program are enclosed. (If material exceptions were noted, please enclose a copy of the responses and corrective actions taken.)

2.____   We expect our Circular A-133 audit for fiscal year ended [insert date] to be completed by [insert expected completion date]. A copy of our audit report will be forwarded to [insert pass-through entity's name] within 30 days of receipt of the report. A schedule of federal programs is enclosed.

3.____   We are not subject to a Circular A-133 audit because:
           ____ We are a for-profit organization.
           ____ We expend less than $500,000 in federal awards annually.
           ____ Other (please explain) _____

_____   _____
Type or Print Name   Title

_____   _____
Date   Signature

Please address all correspondence to:
            Pass-Through Entity Contact Person
            Pass-Through Entity Name
            Street Address
            City, State, Zip

Your prompt attention to this matter is greatly appreciated. If you have any questions please contact me at [insert telephone number for pass-through entity contact person].

Sincerely,

Pass-Through Entity Contact Person

---

through entity often does not have the CFDA information because it is a subrecipient itself and did not receive the CFDA information from its pass-through entity.

Additionally, under most subaward agreements, subrecipients must make their records available for inspection by not only the pass-through entity but also the federal awarding agency.

While the federal agency is not directly involved in subrecipient management, they want to ensure that subrecipients are spending federal awards in accordance with program requirements and that the pass-through entities are monitoring their subrecipients' activities. Therefore, pass-through entities' monitoring procedures are audited during their single audit. The results of the audit, including any findings regarding subrecipient monitoring, are sent to the federal awarding agency.

Beyond reporting the results of their single audits to their federal awarding agencies, pass-through entities may want to contact program officials or auditors at the federal agency. They may have questions about program regulations or subaward provisions that affect how their subrecipients perform the program activities or about monitoring procedures. For example, a subrecipient may want to purchase a piece of equipment not listed in the approved budget. Before the pass-through entity approves the purchase, it may contact the grantor agency to ensure the piece of equipment is an allowable expense under the federal award. By contacting the federal awarding agency for answers to subrecipient questions, the pass-through entity can help ensure its subrecipient complies with program requirements and properly manages their federal funds. It also is a method for monitoring subrecipient activities.

Monitoring Follow-Up

6

Regardless of whether primary grantees make onsite visits or review documents and audits, the results of these monitoring efforts must be conveyed to the subrecipients. When doing so, problem areas that need to be corrected, as well as examples of successful program administration, should be identified. Recommendations and corrective actions needed should also be noted. For example, a university that finds a nonprofit subrecipient performing biomedical research has inadequate time sheets can provide samples of how time sheets should be prepared when it informs the subrecipient of the finding. In addition to offering subrecipients recommendations for corrective action, the pass-through entity also can provide more specific technical advice and training directed toward the subrecipient's problem.

Once a subrecipient receives its pass-through entity's recommendations, it must take steps to correct any problems found and prevent recurrence of similar problems. If necessary, the subrecipient may need to consult the pass-through entity for additional advice or to make sure that its plan of action is allowable under the federal program. The subrecipient also should keep the pass-through entity informed of its follow-up progress and let the pass-through entity know when the problems have been remedied.

A pass-through entity must ensure that the subrecipient has taken the necessary steps to correct the problems identified. To do so, the pass-through entity may request additional follow-up reports and documentation from the subrecipient, and in some cases, it may make a follow-up visit to the subrecipient. For example, a state housing agency that discovers a contractor is building public housing facilities that do not satisfy Section 504 of the Rehabilitation Act of 1973, which prohibits discrimination against disabled individuals by federal programs, may make a follow-up visit to verify that the facilities now accommodate persons with disabilities.

Pass-Through Entity Responsibilities

When a pass-through entity completes an onsite visit or a document review or receives a copy of an auditor's limited-scope audit report, it must inform the subrecipient of the findings. Even if the pass-through entity has communicated the results of the review to the subrecipient informally (e.g., at the onsite visit or over the phone after a desk review), it should send an official letter confirming those results (see Fig. 6-1). The letter should identify:

- specific problems (e.g., misspent funds, problems with internal control, noncompliance with program requirements);

- the type of corrective action required (e.g., repaying federal funds, establishing new policies or procedures);

- whether a corrective action plan is necessary;

- the time frame for the subrecipient to take the corrective action;

- technical assistance that is available from the pass-through entity, if appropriate;

- any additional reports that the subrecipient may have to provide to the pass-through entity; and

- any additional monitoring the pass-through entity will perform to verify that the corrective action has taken place (e.g., site visit to view renovated facilities, document review of new policy or revised account ledgers).

Similarly, if the monitoring did not disclose any problems, the pass-through entity should confirm the results in writing to the subrecipient. It may congratulate the subrecipient and encourage it to continue any successful practices.

Subrecipients should ask their primary grantees when they plan to issue a monitoring follow-up letter. Often, a pass-through entity may include such information in its program guidance. The sooner a pass-through entity issues a letter, the sooner a subrecipient can make any needed corrections.

While monitoring follow-up often takes place after the pass-through entity completes its monitoring activity, pass-through entities and their subrecipients can take the opportunity to begin follow-up and corrective action while the monitoring activity is still going on. Pass-through entities performing site visits can inform subrecipients immediately when they discover problems such as misspent funds, internal control deficiencies or inadequate compliance with eligibility, matching or other program requirements. Then pass-through entities and subrecipients can work together to determine what corrective action will be necessary while the pass-through entity is onsite. In some instances, it may be possible for a subrecipient to begin corrective measures during the onsite review. For example, a pass-through entity may determine that certain ineligible beneficiaries have been receiving program services. Before the pass-through entity's staff leaves, the subrecipient may have drafted new policies to properly identify only eligible beneficiaries.

Reviewing a Subrecipient's Single Audit Report

When the pass-through entity receives a copy of a subrecipient's single audit report, it must issue a management decision within six months of receiving the report if that

---

FIG. 6-1
MONITORING FOLLOW-UP LETTER

August 2, 2006

Subrecipient Contact Name _____

Subrecipient Name _____

Subrecipient Address _____

Response Due Date _____

Agreement Number _____

Dear [Insert Subrecipient Contact Name]

This letter is a follow-up of my monitoring visit on [insert date] of Community Development Block Grant (CDBG) agreement [insert agreement number]. I appreciate the time you took to show me the CDBG files and the completed Waste Water Expansion project. I also enjoyed meeting and talking to [insert names and titles of individuals interviewed].

I reviewed files dealing with financial management and labor standards, and I performed a general overview of all CDBG files. I wish to acknowledge that the files provided were all readily available and well organized.

Following are items of recommendation for future CDBG grants and items that require a response. Please respond to those items in **bold** by the due date indicated above.

1. The [insert the subrecipient organization name] provided notification to unsuccessful bidders for the Waste Water Expansion project but it did not include the [subrecipient organization name's] protest procedure in either the bid package or the notification. **Please provide a copy of the [insert subrecipient organization's name] protest procedure for bidders wishing to protest an award and ensure that future notifications include such.**

2. I noted that you do not have a complete set of CDBG handbooks and information bulletins. They are a useful tool for CDBG grant administration and may also answer questions that arise during the application process. Please ensure that the [insert the subrecipient organization name] obtains a set of handbooks and bulletins if it plans to apply for future CDBG grants.

3. I was unable to review the [insert the subrecipient organization name] procurement policy and procedures. **Please submit a copy.**

4. A special survey was conducted for the Waste Water Expansion project but the backup documentation was not available for review. **Please provide documentation of that survey, including: tabulation sheets, all completed surveys and how the survey was publicized.**

5. The leverage ledger was incomplete as it documented only $76,000 rather than the $82,000 as stated in the application. **Please complete the ledger and send a copy to me.**

Should you have any questions about this or other CDBG related subjects, please feel free to contact me at [insert telephone number].

Sincerely,

[insert pass-through entity's contact name]

CDBG Program

---

report discloses any findings. In the management decision, the pass-through entity must state whether it sustains the audit findings identified in the auditor's report, the reasons for its decision and the corrective action that the subrecipient must take. If the subrecipient has not completed the necessary corrective action, the pass-through entity should include a timetable for completion. The management decision should also specify any appeals procedures that are available to the subrecipient.

Subrecipients should note that a pass-through entity may request additional information or documentation before it issues a management decision. Also, they should initiate corrective action within six months of receiving their audit report and proceed as quickly as possible.

Pass-through entities should remember that if a subrecipient's single audit disclosed no findings that related to awards provided by the pass-through entity, the subrecipient does not have to send the pass-through entity a copy of its single audit report. Instead, the subrecipient must send a letter to the pass-through stating that the subrecipient had a Circular A-133 audit and that no findings affecting awards provided by the pass-through entity were reported.

After reviewing a subrecipient's single audit report, the pass-through entity should consider whether it is necessary to adjust its own records. As part of the finding-resolution process, the pass-through entity should estimate the total unallowable costs for each subrecipient finding and consider the need to adjust its financial records and federal expenditure reports. Failure to do so should be considered by the auditor in forming his or her opinion on the primary recipient's major program compliance.

Subrecipient Responsibilities

Once a pass-through entity informs a subrecipient of the monitoring results, the subrecipient should take any corrective action prescribed by the pass-through entity such as repaying the misspent funds or changing its policies or practices to prevent further noncompliance with the subaward requirements. If the pass-through entity provides the monitoring results through a follow-up letter, the subrecipient may want to respond to the pass-through entity with its own letter, explaining how it has already corrected or plans to correct any findings (see Fig. 6-2).

A subrecipient must correct the problem in the time period specified by the pass-through entity. To demonstrate its corrective action to the pass-through entity, a subrecipient may have to:

*   provide revised documentation or a report for the pass-through entity to review (e.g., revised accounting ledger entry); or

*   undergo a follow-up visit by the pass-through entity (e.g., to review a change in operations).

If a subrecipient disagrees with a finding disclosed during monitoring, it should negotiate with the pass-through whether it must take corrective action. In some instances, pass-through entities have established appeal procedures.

FIG. 6-2
SUBRECIPIENT MONITORING VISIT LETTER RESPONSE

August 28, 2006

Pass-Through Entity Contact Name
CDBG Program
Pass-Through Entity Address

      Re: [Insert Contract Number]

Dear [Insert Pass-Through Entity Contact Name]:

This letter is in response to your monitoring visit letter of [insert date]. I will respond to your concerns in the order presented in your letter.

1. Enclosed is a copy of the [insert the subrecipient organization name] protest procedure as addressed in our purchasing policies. We will ensure that future bid documents related to CDBG contracts include the protest procedure.

2. Enclosed is a check for $60.00. Please send me a copy of all CDBG handbooks and information bulletins that are currently available.

3. Enclosed is a copy of the [insert the subrecipient organization name] procurement policy and procedures.

4. Enclosed are the tabulation sheets and marketing information for our special survey of 2005 pertaining to the Waste Water Expansion project. Because the survey area was very large and we had a high response rate, I did not include all 234 survey responses. I spoke with you on [insert date] regarding this and was instructed to send a sampling of 15 completed responses. Those are enclosed.

5. Enclosed is a copy of the completed ledger documenting the full amount of $82,000.

Please call me if you have any other questions or concerns.

Sincerely,

[Insert the Subrecipient Contact Name and Title]

encl: Procurement Policies (includes protest procedure)
            Check for $60.00
            Special Survey documents

To ensure the subrecipient corrects the problem, the pass-through entity might schedule additional monitoring visits or request certain reports. For example, if a nonprofit performing job training has been charging the same costs inconsistently, as both direct and indirect costs, the state agency that subawarded the money should require the nonprofit to submit revised reimbursement requests that treat the costs consistently.

Importance of Follow-Up

Failure by either the pass-through entity or the subrecipient to carry out their follow-up responsibilities could have serious consequences. If monitoring is performed and problems are identified, but neither party ensures corrective action is taken, the problems could be compounded, leading to more serious findings. For example, a monitoring visit may reveal that a subrecipient is determining program or benefit eligibility incorrectly. However, if the subrecipient does not correct its eligibility determination process and the pass-through entity just lets it go, the subrecipient's unallowable costs for providing benefits to ineligible persons will continue to grow, potentially costing the federal government hundreds of thousands of dollars. Remember, both the subrecipient and the pass-through entity are liable for misspent federal funds.

MONITORING FOLLOW-UP: LOOKING AT THE BIG PICTURE

Pass-through entities should look at the overall results of their monitoring to identify:

* recurring problems unique to one program of which the federal awarding agency should be informed;

* opportunities to better monitor funds they subaward; and

* recurring problems with individual subrecipients.

Like the pass-through entity, the subrecipient should look at the overall monitoring results to identify:

* recurring problems that affect several programs (e.g., an inadequate financial accounting system) and need to be corrected;

* effective methods to administer subawards and comply with program requirements that can be applied to other subawards; and

* program-specific problems that may require a change in the way the pass-through or federal agency administers the program.

Furthermore, an auditor performing a pass-through entity's single audit may determine that the pass-through entity does not have an adequate subrecipient monitoring system because of the pass-through entity's failure to follow up on identified findings. The auditor most likely would identify a significant deficiency and possibly a compliance finding in the pass-through entity's single audit report. If the lack of adequate subrecipient monitoring was material to a major program, it also could affect the auditor's opinion on whether the pass-through entity complied with laws, regulations and the provisions of its grant agreement that could have a direct and material affect on major programs. For example, an auditor could modify its opinion if a pass-through entity that subawarded 90 percent of its federal funds did not perform adequate subrecipient monitoring follow-up and, therefore, did not have an adequate subrecipient monitoring system.

As discussed above, a subrecipient that fails to correct monitoring findings risks incurring additional unallowable costs. It also could suffer additional sanctions, such as the pass-through entity withholding program funds or suspending the subaward until the necessary corrective action is taken. More stringent sanctions might include termination of the subaward, denial of refunding and debarment and suspension.

In many instances, the subaward may specifically address the need for parties to follow up on monitoring and the potential sanctions that could result if they do not. An example of such a provision is as follows:

> The grantor will monitor the performance of the subrecipient against goals and performance standards required herein. Substandard performance as determined by the grantor will constitute noncompliance with this agreement. If action to correct such substandard performance is not taken by the subrecipient within a reasonable period of time after being notified by the grantor, subaward suspension or termination procedures will be initiated.

Auditor Review of Monitoring Activities

7

Organizations that pass through funds to subgrantees need to provide assurance to their federal awarding agencies that they are properly monitoring their subrecipients' use of federal funds and following up on any problems that are identified as a result of the monitoring. Therefore, OMB included guidance in its *Circular A-133 Compliance Supplement* for auditors on reviewing grantees' procedures for monitoring subrecipients as part of performing a single audit. Auditors will review the pass-through entities policies and records to verify that pass-through entities have internal controls in place to ensure monitoring is carried out and that they actually monitor their subrecipients. Additionally, auditors will look at whether the procedures ensure that federal funds are used by subrecipients for authorized purposes in compliance with applicable laws and regulations and that program performance goals are achieved.

How Auditors Test Subrecipient Monitoring

When selecting and performing activities to monitor subrecipients, primary grantees should keep in mind that OMB's guidance requires an auditor to test only a pass-through entity's programs that are large or otherwise at-risk for noncompliance with program requirements – "major programs." Once the auditor has selected the pass-through entity's major programs, he or she should inquire whether the entity provided program funds to subrecipients. Thus, if the pass-through entity made no awards to subrecipients from a major program, the auditor would not perform any tests for monitoring.

In contrast, when awards were made to subrecipients, the auditor must determine whether the amount of subawarded funds was material to the major program involved. The auditor uses his or her judgment to determine if it is material. Pass-through entities should note that certain federal programs contain requirements that generally will make their subawards material to a major program. For example, a state must subaward at least 90 percent of its CDBG funds. When such a large percentage of funds is passed through to subrecipients, the auditor would test a state's procedures for monitoring subrecipients administering CDBG subawards.

When the amount of subawarded federal funds is material in relation to a major program, the auditor reviews the pass-through entity's subrecipient monitoring activities. The auditor would develop audit procedures for testing the pass-through entity's subrecipient monitoring procedures by reviewing the number, size, and complexity of subawards provided.

Pass-through entities should note that auditors will look at both subrecipient and vendor relationships. An auditor may determine that a pass-through entity's relationship with a vendor is, in substance, a subaward to a subrecipient and, therefore, is subject to monitoring. If the pass-through entity has not monitored these entities sufficiently, the auditor most likely will issue a finding. Pass-through entities must look closely at the substance of the relationship when determining whether they should issue a contract to a vendor or a subaward to a subgrantee (see Chapter 2).

As part of the single audit, an auditor must review the subrecipient monitoring controls a pass-through entity has in place. A pass-through entity's controls should provide reasonable assurance that federal award information and compliance requirements are clearly conveyed to subrecipients, subrecipient activities are monitored and the impact of any subrecipient noncompliance on the pass-through entity is evaluated. Also, grantees must ensure that subrecipients have required audits, and must take appropriate follow-up action on audit findings.

If an auditor determines that a primary grantee does not have effective internal controls in place, the auditor would include a significant deficiency in the grantee's single audit report. (A significant deficiency indicates there are sufficient deficiencies in the internal controls over compliance requirements, including subrecipient monitoring, that could affect a pass-through entity's ability to administer the federal program in accordance with applicable program requirements.) Then the auditor would do additional testing to determine the overall extent of the pass-through entity's noncompliance with subrecipient monitoring requirements. In contrast, if the entity's controls appear to be effective in detecting material noncompliance in subrecipient monitoring, then the auditor would identify those key controls the entity had in place and test that the controls were operating as designed.

Therefore, in anticipation of its single audit, a pass-through entity should assess whether it has adequate subrecipient monitoring controls in place. Questions that a primary grantee should ask include whether the primary recipient's management supports subrecipient monitoring objectives, whether there are written policies that explain its subrecipient monitoring policies and whether there are sufficient records of its monitoring efforts.

As part of the audit, pass-through entities can expect an auditor to test award documents to ascertain if they made subrecipients aware of award information, specifically CFDA information, award name and federal awarding agency, and requirements imposed by laws, regulations, and the provisions of contract or grant agreements pertaining to the program. The auditor also would review the subaward agreement to verify that the activities approved in it were allowable. The auditor would review the grantee's documentation supporting its monitoring activities aimed at ensuring federal funds were used for authorized purposes.

This review would also include procedures to verify that the pass-through entity monitors activities of subrecipients exempt from Circular A-133, using such techniques as a limited-scope audit or document review. Additionally, an auditor would verify that a pass-through entity required its subrecipients subject to Circular A-133 to have the required audits.

When subrecipients are required to have an audit in accordance with Circular A-133, an auditor would verify that a pass-through entity received a copy of the audit reports, as necessary. (Circular A-133 does not require a subrecipient to provide a pass-through entity with a copy of the audit report when there are no findings that affect that pass-through entity.) Pass-through entities should be aware that review of a subrecipient's single audit report generally should be only one element of an adequate monitoring system. Document reviews and other procedures should also be performed.

Additionally, an auditor would verify that a pass-through entity issues management decisions on a timely basis for any audit or monitoring findings disclosed and require subrecipients to take timely corrective action on deficiencies identified. If there were disallowances for subrecipient questioned costs, the auditor would determine whether credits were properly reflected in the pass-through entity's records.

Auditors also will look at whether a pass-through entity identified the total amount of federal awards provided to subrecipients from each program in its schedule of expenditures of federal awards for the single audit. Circular A-133 requires pass-through entities to prepare the schedule, which lists all of its federal expenditures for the year by federal agency and program, and include the amount of subawards made, if practical. A pass-through entity that cannot identify the federal money it gave to subrecipients should raise a red flag for auditors. This would indicate that the pass-through entity is not tracking its subawards adequately.

The primary recipient may have to adjust its financial records and its federal expenditure reports to reflect certain costs incurred by the subrecipient that were identified as unallowable during an audit or review. Failure by the primary recipient to make the necessary adjustments to its records and reports would be considered by the auditor when preparing its final single audit report.

Potential Audit Findings and Their Effect

Primary recipients should be aware of the kinds of findings they may receive from an auditor if they do not have an adequate subrecipient monitoring system. If a primary recipient's monitoring system is not sufficient to ensure a subrecipient's compliance with the subaward and applicable laws and regulations, an auditor would note a significant deficiency. The auditor also might report a material weakness if the primary recipient's internal controls over subrecipient monitoring for a program do not reduce the risk that noncompliance with applicable federal and program requirements may occur without detection. In addition, the auditor would consider whether the insufficient monitoring system should be reported as a finding of noncompliance. Should a primary recipient receive any such findings, it would have to correct them and take steps to prevent their recurrence.

A pass-through entity also could receive a qualified opinion as part of its single audit report, depending on the nature of the findings reported by the auditor. The auditor would draw an overall conclusion on whether the pass-through entity is in material compliance with subrecipient monitoring requirements. That conclusion would help the auditor to determine whether he or she can give an opinion on compliance for major programs. (Circular A-133 requires an auditor to give an opinion on whether an auditee complied with laws and regulations that could have a direct and material effect on major programs.) An auditor generally would modify his or her opinion on compliance if a primary recipient's lack of subrecipient monitoring was pervasive, and compliance with subrecipient monitoring requirements was material to the program. For example, if the pass-through entity did not perform adequate monitoring procedures and 90 percent of the program was subawarded, the auditor most likely would modify its opinion on compliance.

An auditor also would consider the effect of inadequate subrecipient monitoring on his or her opinion on the auditee's financial statements. If amounts passed through to subrecipients are considered material to the pass-through entity's financial statements, the auditor may need to alter his or her opinion on the financial statements. In making this determination the auditor should review evidence of whether its subrecipients administered the subawards in compliance with laws and regulations. The auditor can accomplish this by, for example, reviewing the results of limited-scope audits.

When reviewing a pass-through entity's subrecipient monitoring system, auditors want to see if the organization has a monitoring system in place. Many primary recipients that rely on single audits to monitor their subrecipients have no other form of monitoring in place. With the increased audit threshold, many of these subrecipients no longer have single audits. As a result, primary grantees need to use new methods for reviewing subrecipient activities. They must set up procedures to ensure that they provide their subrecipients with the required compliance information. They need to identify the areas they want to monitor, the reports and other documentation that subrecipient must provide and the staff that will oversee the monitoring effort.

Auditors also will look for monitoring activities that ensure subrecipient compliance with certain program-related requirements. Auditors generally will test the areas of allowable costs and activities, matching requirements, eligibility requirements and reporting. Are subrecipients performing allowable activities under the subaward? Are they only charging allowable costs to the federal program? Have they complied with any requirement to obtain matching funds from nonfederal sources? Are they providing benefits and services to eligible individuals only? Have they complied with all applicable financial and performance reporting requirements?

Pass-through entities may want to monitor subrecipient compliance with certain requirements that are unique to the award or the program. Auditors will look for and review the procedures used to monitor those areas. For example, a state that passes through job training funds to a nonprofit organization may request performance reports that describe number of individuals trained and other services provided by the subrecipient. It also may request financial reports, as well as invoices and other documentation to monitor allowability of the nonprofit entity's expenses. In another example, a medical school awarded federal funds to a nonprofit to provide training services. All of the nonprofit entity's grant-related bills are paid by the medical school, so it can review the subrecipent's activities and expenses to ensure they are allowable.

A common problem among pass-through entities is a lack of documentation of monitoring activities. Therefore, entities should maintain files for each subrecipient that contain any financial and progress reports that the subrecipient submits, the single audit report, and other documentation provided by the subrecipient. A pass-through entity should keep any completed checklists its staff may have used to perform onsite or desk reviews of subrecipient activities. Other documents to file include copies of any notes or follow-up letters sent in response to onsite visits or telephone interviews. Finally, a pass-through entity may want to maintain a record of each monitoring activity performed for a subrecipient. The record would include information such as the name of the subrecipient and subaward agreement number. It would identify the type and amount of federal program funds passed through. It would describe briefly the type of monitoring activity performed (e.g., document review, telephone monitoring), the date of the activity, the persons contacted, the activities and records reviewed and the results of the review.

Internal Control Assessment Checklist

A pass-through entity must ensure it has internal controls in place to support its subrecipient monitoring objectives. Therefore, it may want to ask itself the following questions:

Control Environment

- Does the "tone at the top" demonstrate management's commitment to monitoring subrecipients?

- Is management intolerant of overriding established procedures to monitor subrecipients?

- Is the entity's organizational structure and its ability to provide the necessary information flow to monitor subrecipients adequate?

- Are sufficient resources dedicated to subrecipient monitoring?

- Are the knowledge, skills and abilities needed to accomplish subrecipient monitoring tasks defined?

- Do individuals performing these tasks possess the knowledge, skills and abilities required?

- Do subrecipients demonstrate that:

  - they are willing and able to comply with the requirements of the award; and

  - they have accounting systems, including the use of applicable cost principles, and internal control systems adequate to administer the award?

- Are appropriate sanctions taken for subrecipient noncompliance?

Risk Assessment

- Do key managers understand the subrecipient's environment, systems and controls sufficiently to identify the level and methods of monitoring required?

- Do mechanisms exist to identify risks arising from external sources affecting subrecipients such as risks related to:

  - economic conditions;

  - political conditions;

  - regulatory changes; and

  - unreliable information?

- Do mechanisms exist to identify and react to changes in subrecipients such as:

  - financial problems that could lead to diversion of grant funds;

  - loss of license or accreditation to operate the program;

  - rapid growth;

  - new activities, products or services; and

  - organizational restructuring?

Control Activities

- Does an official written policy exist establishing:

  - communication of federal award requirements to subrecipients;

  - responsibilities for monitoring subrecipients;

  - process and procedures for monitoring;

  - methodology for resolving findings of subrecipients' noncompliance or weakness in internal control; and

  - requirements for and processing of subrecipient audits, including appropriate adjustment of pass-through entity's accounts?

- Describe how subrecipients' compliance with audit requirements is monitored. The techniques that may be used include the following:

  - determining by inquiry and discussion whether the subrecipient met thresholds requiring an audit under Circular A-133;

  - if an audit is required, assuring that the subrecipient submits the report, reporting package or the documents required by the latest circular or recipient's requirements;

  - following up on reported deficiencies related to programs funded by the recipient; and

  - if a subrecipient was required to obtain an audit in accordance with Circular A-133 but did not do so, following up with the subrecipient until the audit is completed and taking appropriate actions such as withholding further funding until the subrecipient meets the audit requirements.

- Describe the follow-up system used to track reported subrecipient deficiencies and resolution actions.

- Describe how subrecipients' compliance with federal program requirements is monitored. The following techniques may be used:

  - issue timely management decisions for audit and monitoring findings to inform the subrecipient whether the corrective action planned is acceptable;

  - maintain a system to track and follow-up on reported deficiencies related to programs funded by the recipient and ensure that timely corrective action is taken;

  - contact subrecipients regularly and make appropriate inquiries concerning the federal program;

  - review subrecipient reports and follow-up on areas of concern;

  - monitor subrecipient budgets;

  - perform site visits to subrecipients to review financial and programmatic records and observe operations; and

  - offer subrecipients technical assistance where needed.

- Are the federal award information (e.g., CFDA title and number, award name, name of federal agency, amount of award) and applicable compliance requirements identified to subrecipients?

- Do agreements with subrecipients specify the compliance requirements applicable to the federal program, including the audit requirements of Circular A-133?

Information and Communication

  - Do standard award documents used by the nonfederal entity contain:

    - a listing of federal requirements that the subrecipient must follow (items can be specifically listed in the award document, attached as an exhibit to the document or incorporated by reference to specific criteria);

    - the description and program number for each program as stated in the CFDA (if the program funds include pass-through funds from another recipient, the pass-through program information should also be identified); and

    - a statement signed by an official of the subrecipient, stating that the subrecipient was informed of, understands and agrees to comply with the applicable compliance requirements?

- Is there a record-keeping system in place to ensure that documentation is retained for the time period required by the recipient (applies to subrecipients only)?

- Are procedures in place to provide channels for subrecipients to communicate concerns to the pass-through entity?

Monitoring

- Has a tracking system been established to ensure timely submission of required reporting such as:

- financial reports;
- performance reports;
- audit reports;
- on-site monitoring reviews of subrecipients; and
- timely resolution of audit findings?

- Are supervisory reviews performed to determine the adequacy of subrecipient monitoring?

A Sample Audit Process

As part of a broader effort to review the management of grant programs within the Department of Health and Human Services, in 2004 the Office of Inspector General conducted a series of audits examining states' subrecipient monitoring activities under the Foster Care program. To do this, the OIG developed a set of "measurable criteria" based on federal grants management requirements. Auditors and pass-through entities may find this tool useful as an example or template for creating their own subrecipient monitoring checklist.

As the OIG explained, pass-through entities are required to "monitor the activities of subrecipients as necessary. ... However, HHS has issued no further guidance or delineation on what kind or level of monitoring is considered necessary." So the OIG auditors crafted a set of specific measurements that were applied during their evaluations of states' Foster Care program administration.

In its subrecipient monitoring assessment model, the OIG said states must have at least one fiscal monitoring mechanism and one program monitoring mechanism in place, and must provide subgrantees with specific information about the award and accompanying responsibilities.

The OIG used two primary tools to carry out its evaluations: interviews with staff; and a review of states' subgrantee files. Interviews included discussions with fiscal, program and licensing staff, and were based on a set of standard questions. The OIG asked staff to describe each of their monitoring mechanisms. Their descriptions included how frequently those mechanisms were used to collect information, how the information was reviewed, and how the state followed up on problems that were identified during this process.

The results of these interviews then were used as a basis for reviewing subgrantee files. For example, if staff indicated that the state requires monthly fiscal reports, the OIG expected each subgrantee file to have 12 fiscal reports, along with evidence that those reports included the type of review and follow up described by the state staff.

Finally, the OIG wanted to determine whether states had provided the required award and regulatory information to their subgrantees during the initial communication process (i.e., in the written subgrant agreement). The OIG looked at whether the state:

- delineated the federal requirements in any way, (e.g., in a single audit manual);

- cited the federal requirements (e.g., 45 C.F.R. Part 74); or

- implied the requirements (e.g., "subgrantee is responsible for all applicable state and federal requirements"). This latter language was the minimum level of information that the OIG considered acceptable.

Any state that did not have the proper documentation on file was given an opportunity to provide that information to the OIG, but those that failed to do so were considered not to be in compliance with program and governmentwide regulations.

OIG officials said they found it "straightforward" to assess states' communication of required information to subgrantees. However, to assess program and fiscal monitoring mechanisms, more specific criteria were needed.

They broke down fiscal and program monitoring into three basic components: collecting information; reviewing the information collected; and following up on identified problems.

Two examples of acceptable follow-up activities were an approval or a corrective action letter from the state to each subgrantee after an annual site visit; or a letter or phone call that was made only when a subgrantee's progress report indicated a problem. For subrecipients that were required to have a single audit, the OIG looked to ensure that states followed up on all audit findings within six months.

Program and fiscal monitoring mechanisms had to meet two standards. First, the mechanism had to be appropriate. It had to include all three basic components mentioned above (collecting information, reviewing information and following up on problems). Further, the mechanism had to be designed to monitor all subgrantees.

The monitoring mechanism also had to be "functioning," the OIG concluded. For the HHS OIG, this meant that at least 75 percent of the subgrantee monitoring files had to include sufficient documentation indicating that the mechanism had been carried out. "While we would expect the monitoring to be documented in all files, we wanted to allow for a small amount of error in states' documentation of their monitoring," the OIG explained.

Fig. 7-1 contains relevant checklists and discussions from the HHS OIG assessment protocol. The entire document can be downloaded from the Web at http://oig.hhs.gov/oei/reports/oei-05-03-00062.pdf.

FIG. 7-1

► **C R I T E R I A**

CRITERIA DEVELOPMENT

Grants management requirements for States monitoring of subgrantees are general. States are required to "monitor the activities of subrecipients as necessary to ensure that Federal awards are used for authorized purposes in compliance with laws, regulations, and the provisions of contracts or grant agreements and that performance goals are achieved." HHS has issued no further guidance or delineation on what kind or level of monitoring is considered "necessary." Thus, to assess whether States are monitoring their subgrantees "as necessary," it is essential to define measurable criteria.

To develop criteria based on the general grants management requirements, we consulted various grants management sources. Specifically, we reviewed:

o   Federal requirements, including 45 C.F.R. Part 74, 45 C.F.R. Part 92, and OMB Circular A-133;

o   OMB Circular A-133 compliance supplements;

o   applicable HHS grants management guidance;

o   subgrantee monitoring guidance produced for other HHS programs;

o   guidance for other Federal departments;

o   industry guidance from Management Concepts and Thompson Publishing Group;

o   grants management reports from the Government Accountability Office (GAO), OIG, ASAM, and Assistant Secretary for Planning and Evaluation; and

o   Single Audit reports containing subrecipient monitoring findings for States' foster care programs.

We presented our criteria to staff from ASAM in its draft form. The ASAM staff found our criteria to be reasonable and consistent with Federal requirements.

Fig. 7-1 (continued)

CRITERIA

We developed these criteria as a set of minimum standards based on Federal grants management requirements. Our goal was to develop criteria specific enough to be measurable, yet general enough to allow for variation in how States execute their monitoring of subgrantees.

Our criteria set forth the following framework for assessing whether or not States were monitoring "as necessary": States must have at least one fiscal monitoring mechanism and one program monitoring mechanism in place. In addition to assessing States' program and fiscal monitoring systems, we also examined their adherence to requirements related to communicating required grants management information.

FEDERAL REQUIREMENTS	CRITERIA
Program and Fiscal Monitoring	
States must: --"monitor the activities of subrecipients as necessary to ensure that Federal awards are used for authorized purposes in compliance with laws, regulations, and the provisions of contracts or grant agreements and that performance goals are achieved." [OMB Circular A-133, §__.400(d)(3)] --"manage and monitor each project, program, subaward, function or activity supported by the award." [45 C.F.R. § 74.51(a)] --"monitor grant and subgrant supported activities to assure compliance with applicable Federal requirements and that performance goals are being achieved." [45 C.F.R. § 92.40(a)]	States must have at least: --**one fiscal monitoring mechanism, and** --**one program monitoring mechanism**
Communication of Required Information	
States must provide subgrantees with the "best information available to describe the Federal award." [OMB Circular A-133, §__.400(d)(1)]	States must at least inform subgrantees that the grant includes Federal funds.
States must advise subgrantees of requirements imposed on them by Federal laws and regulations. [OMB Circular A-133, §__.400(d)(2)]	States must inform subgrantees of Federal grants management requirements.

FIG. 7-1 (CONTINUED)

USING CRITERIA TO ASSESS STATES' MONITORING OF SUBGRANTEES: DATA COLLECTION AND ANALYSIS

This section demonstrates how we applied our criteria to assess States' monitoring of subgrantees in the foster care program. First, we present our methodology for collecting data from States, including three key data collection instruments from our inspection. Each instrument is presented in a half-page format and is followed by brief definitions and instructions for use. Then, we turn to our analysis, which consisted of comparing the data we collected with our criteria.

Data Collection

We examined States' subgrantee monitoring through interviews with staff and a review of States' subgrantee files.

Interviews with monitoring staff. To understand the complexities of State monitoring systems, we began by interviewing staff members responsible for monitoring subgrantees. Typically, this included interviews with fiscal, program, and licensing staff. We also reviewed policies, protocols, and guidance related to subgrantee monitoring.

We used structured interviews aimed at gaining a full understanding of the complex design of States' systems for monitoring subgrantees. We asked staff to describe each of their monitoring mechanisms, including how frequently mechanisms were used to collect information, how the information was reviewed, and how the State followed up on problems that were identified during this process.

The following Monitoring System Summary table summarizes the design of a State's monitoring system, based on information gathered in interviews and by reviewing monitoring protocols. After completing the Monitoring System Summary, we used it as a guide when conducting subgrantee file reviews. The summary provides information about which monitoring mechanisms each subgrantee should have received and indicates what documentation to expect in the file. The summary is also useful at the analysis stage, when assessing whether the design of a State's monitoring system meets our criteria.

Fig. 7-1 (continued)

Monitoring System Summary					
State:					
Monitoring Mechanism	**Frequency**	**Review**		**Follow-up**	
FISCAL MONITORING					
PROGRAM MONITORING					

Monitoring Mechanism:
> List the name of the monitoring mechanism. This could include progress reports, site visits, financial reports, independent audits, State-performed audits, or other such approaches. Single Audits should be included under fiscal monitoring. If the mechanism does not apply to all subgrantees, indicate the subset for which the mechanism applies. Example: Monthly Progress Reports for group homes.

Frequency:
> The number of times the mechanism should be used in your sample timeframe (we used 1 year). Example: for Monthly Progress Reports, Frequency = 12.

Review:
> Enter **Y** if State staff indicate that they review submitted information, or enter **N** if they indicate that they do not review. For monitoring that the State conducts directly, such as site visits, review should be coded **N/A**. *Check the shaded box* within the column if staff indicate that their review is documented.

Follow up:
> Enter **Y** if State staff indicate that they follow up with subgrantees, or enter **N** if they indicate that they do not follow up. *Check the shaded box* within the column if staff indicate that their follow up is documented.

FIG. 7-1 (CONTINUED)

Review of States' subgrantee monitoring files: After gaining an understanding of how States intended to monitor their subgrantees, we used structured data collection instruments in our review of subgrantee files. To verify whether States' monitoring systems were functioning as the State described, we reviewed documentation of monitoring in a sample of subgrantee case files. For example, if a State requires monthly fiscal reports, we reviewed each file for evidence of 12 fiscal reports. Next, we reviewed the file for evidence that the 12 reports had the type of review and follow-up described by the State.

We also assessed whether States met Single Audit requirements in those States that required their subgrantees to have a Single Audit. Namely, we assessed whether States followed up on all subrecipient audit findings within the six-month time period.

In cases where States were unable to provide us with documentation of their monitoring activities onsite, we allowed them additional time to locate and send us the documentation. In cases where documents were unavailable, States were not given credit for carrying out monitoring for these particular subgrantees.

We used the following Subgrantee Monitoring File Review worksheet to record information from an individual subgrantee file. First, the analyst enters the monitoring mechanisms and documentation expected, using information in the Monitoring System Summary table and from interviews. Then the analyst reviews the subgrantee monitoring file and records what documentation is actually found in the file. After completing a file review for each selected subgrantee, these worksheets can be aggregated and used when analyzing whether States' monitoring mechanisms are functioning as States described.

FIG. 7-1 (CONTINUED)

Subgrantee Monitoring File Review						
Subgrantee ID# _____			State _____			
Monitoring Mechanism	**Frequency**		**Review**		**Follow-up**	
	Expect	Actual	Expect	Actual	Expect	Actual
FISCAL MONITORING						
PROGRAM MONITORING						

Monitoring Mechanism: List the name of the monitoring mechanism. Example: Monthly Progress Reports.

Frequency (expect): The number of times the mechanism should be used annually. Example: for Monthly Progress Reports, Frequency (expect) = 12.

Frequency (actual): The number of times the mechanism was actually used for the sample year according to documentation in the monitoring file. Example: for a file that reflects 10 Monthly Progress Reports for the year, Frequency (actual) = 10.

Review (expect): The number of times evidence of review is expected annually. If State staff indicate that they do not document their review, this number should be zero.

Review (actual): The number of times review was documented (e.g., check marks or other notations indicating review) for the sample year.

Follow up (expect): The number of times evidence of follow-up is expected annually, or 'U' for unknown (e.g., if the State only follows up in cases where a problem is identified).

Follow up (actual): The number of times evidence of follow-up was found. Example: for a file that includes documented follow-up for 8 of 12 Monthly Progress Reports, Follow-up (actual) = 8, even if the file contains evidence of multiple follow-up actions for individual reports.

FIG. 7-1 (CONTINUED)

Review of States' subgrantee contracts and other communication: To assess whether States had communicated required grants management information to subgrantees, we reviewed State contracts, and other forms of up-front communication to subgrantees. Specifically, we reviewed documents for language informing subgrantees that they were receiving Federal foster care funds and language informing subgrantees of Federal grants management requirements.

The Contract, Policy Manual, Other Communication checklist is used to review contracts and other forms of up-front communication between the State and its subgrantees. The analyst can use the checklist to record which requirements the State has communicated to its subgrantees. After completing a checklist for each selected subgrantee, these checklists can be aggregated and used when analyzing whether States communicated information as required.

Fig. 7-1 (continued)

Contract, Policy Manual, Other Communication Checklist

Subgrantee ID# _____   State _____

I. Identify Federal awards UPFRONT by informing each subgrantee of the best information available to describe the Federal award. [OMB Circular A-133, §__.400(d)(1)]

> 1. Identify that the subgrantee's award includes Federal funds, at least implying that funds are Title IV-E foster care funds.
> ____ Yes   ____ No

II. Advise subgrantees of requirements imposed on them by Federal laws or regulations. [OMB Circular A-133, §__.400(d)(2)]

> 1. 45 CFR Part 74 or OMB Circular A-110, grants management requirements are:
> ____ Explained   ____ Cited   ____ Implied   ____ Not included

> 2. OMB Circular A-133 Single Audit requirement (if applicable) are:
> ____ Explained   ____ Cited   ____ Implied   ____ Not included

> 3. Subgrantees are required to pass through these requirements to any subcontractors.
> ____ Yes   ____ No

> 4. Subgrantees are required to permit appropriate officials of the Federal agency and pass-through entity to have access to records and financial statements.
> [OMB Circular A-133, §__.400(d)(7) and §__.200(d)]
> ____ Yes   ____ No

I. Identify Federal Awards:

Check <u>Yes</u> if funds are identified to subgrantee as Federal.

II. Advise subgrantees of:

45 CFR Part 74 and OMB Circular A-133 requirements:

Check: <u>Explained</u> if Federal requirements are delineated in any way, (e.g., in a Single Audit manual).
  <u>Cited</u> if Federal requirements are cited but not explained, (e.g., "45 C.F.R. Part 74").
  <u>Implied</u> if Federal requirements are implied, but not cited or explained, (e.g., "Subgrantee is responsible for all applicable State and Federal requirements"). This is the minimum States had to communicate to meet our criteria.

Pass through requirements:

Check <u>Yes</u> if the subgrantee is specifically informed that it must pass through requirements to any subcontractors that the subgrantee hires.

Access to records and financial statements:

Check <u>Yes</u> if subgrantee is specifically informed that it must allow oversight entities this access.

FIG. 7-1 (CONTINUED)

Analysis of States' Monitoring of Subgrantees

In analyzing the data we collected from States, we found it straight-forward to assess States' communication of required information to subgrantees using our criteria. However, to assess States' program and fiscal monitoring mechanisms, we needed to further define our criteria.

We broke down fiscal and program monitoring into three basic components: collecting information, reviewing the information collected, and following up on identified problems. We defined follow-up to include communication back to the subgrantee regarding the results of the State's monitoring. Here are two acceptable examples: (1) the State sends a letter of approval or corrective action to each subgrantee after the annual site visit; (2) the State follows up by letter or phone call only when a subgrantee's progress report indicates a problem.

In States where subgrantees are required to have a Single Audit, we defined follow-up to include the specific Single Audit requirement that States follow up on all audit findings within six months.

We operationalized our criteria to include standards for mechanisms' design and functioning. Specifically, program and fiscal monitoring mechanisms must meet the following standards:

o   Mechanism design is appropriate: The mechanism must be designed to include all three basic components: collecting information, reviewing the information collected, and following up on identified problems. Further, the mechanism must be designed to monitor all subgrantees.

o   Mechanism is functioning: The mechanism must be functioning for all three basic components: collecting information, reviewing the information collected, and following up on identified problems. Use of the mechanism must be documented for 75 percent of the subgrantee monitoring files reviewed. While we would expect the monitoring to be documented in all files, we wanted to allow for a small amount of error in States' documentation of their monitoring.

Part B: Selected Management Issues

How to Write Subgrant Agreements

Introduction

This chapter will discuss how to write subgrant agreements. The chapter will review the applicable federal policies on the subject, and then discuss issues related to format and style as well as substance. Readers should take a broad perspective here and hold any existing agreements they might be using up against the approach and model discussed. Figures 8-1 through 8-5 provide a review of the information presented.

Challenges to Writing Subgrant Agreements

Writing subgrant agreements is a major challenge that pass-through entities face in grants administration. First, no single form has the U.S. government seal of approval or, for that matter, anybody else's seal of approval. Second, pass-through entities have to have the authority to subgrant. In some cases, the program design that is involved with the federal program assumes that the pass-through entity has the authority to subgrant to somebody else. (Most state government grantees have been doing subgrants for years and have been expected to do it in terms of passing a significant amount of the federal funds on to lower organizations.) But absent program design approaches, Office of Management and Budget (OMB) Circulars A-102 and A-110 both make it clear that to transfer substantive activity to a third party, pass-through entities must have federal agency permission. In A-102 authority is contained in the common rule implementing the Circular in Section __. 30, and in OMB Circular A-110, which applies to educational institutions, hospitals and nonprofit organizations, authority is contained in Section __.25. Authority must arrive either from federal regulation or from the program legislation.

Subgrants vs. Contracts

Keep in mind that subgrant agreements are not contracts. While a subgrant has some of the features of a contract, in the sense that it's a legal document – it provides for an offer and acceptance; consideration; and rights and remedies for both parties – a grant agreement or a subgrant agreement is a unique document. It is not a generic legal contract.

Also, it is important to differentiate subgrants from purchase contracts in federal practice. The conceptual framework for making this distinction comes out of the Federal Grant and Cooperative Agreement Act. This act is not applicable but is relevant. What the Federal Grant and Cooperative Agreement Act did was to differentiate at the federal level between situations where the federal government was buying goods or services, and situations where the federal government was trying to assist somebody who was a nonfederal party. In fact what the law said was, if the principal purpose behind the federal activity was to buy, acquire, purchase or procure something for the federal government's use or benefit (remember its principaled purpose not exclusive purpose), then that would be treated as a purchase contract administered under the Federal Acquisition Regulation. On the other hand if the principal purpose of the federal transaction was to assist, stimulate or support a nonfederal party in the conduct of a public program authorized by law, then that would be treated as an assistance transaction. The instruments used to carry it out would be either grants or cooperative agreements. (See Fig. 8-1.)

The difference between a grant and a cooperative agreement is not an administrative one; it is a programmatic one. In cooperative agreements, federal agency involvement during performance on a substantial basis is anticipated, whereas in a grant it is not. But from an administrative standpoint, the instruments are the same. Now why is that relevant to writing subgrant agreements? Because the federal rules in OMB Circulars A-102 and A-110 differentiate lower tier relationships on roughly the same basis. While the Federal Grant and Cooperative Agreement Act doesn't apply to those lower tier relationships, Circulars A-102 and A-110 both have procurement standards that relate to purchase transactions – §__.36 in A-102 and §__.40-48 in A-110. These explain to grantees how to buy goods or services using federal funds. The flip side is that both of those circulars contain instructions for dealing with subgrants or subawards. In Circular A-102's common rule §__.37, the term "subgrant" is used. In A-110, §__.5, the term "subaward" is used. However, the definitions in the two circulars are essentially the same. Subgrants or subawards are an award of federal financial assistance between an entity that has already received a grant and a lower tier organization. This definition is embellished further by requirements contained in OMB Circular A-133. Circular A-133 sought to differentiate between

---

FIG. 8-1
DIFFERENTIATING SUBGRANTS FROM PURCHASE CONTRACTS – THE POLICIES

- Conceptual Framework
  - The Federal Grant and Cooperative Agreement Act *(not applicable but relevant)*
- Purchase Transactions
  - OMB Circular A-102 Common Rule, Section _.36
  - OMB Circular A-110 Sections _.40-.48
- Subgrants
  - OMB Circular A-102 Common Rule, Section _.37
  - OMB Circular A-110 Section _.5
- Audit-Related
  - OMB Circular A-133, Sections _.210 and _.400(d)

situations where a subrecipient relationship existed versus situations where a vendor relationship existed. (The terms "subrecipient" and "subgrantee" are synonymous. The terms "vendor" and "contractor" also are synonymous.) Basically a purchase transaction is a transaction conducted with a vendor, and a subgrant transaction is a transaction conducted with a subgrantee or subrecipient.

Terminology

Fig. 8-2 presents terminology for parties to a subgrant. A term that was introduced in Circular A-133 is the term "pass-through entity." A pass-through entity is an organization that receives federal assistance from an entity above it – whether it is directly from the federal government or from another grantee – and then in turn subgrants the funds to somebody else. In many cases, that pass-through entity is in fact the primary grantee. For example, a lot of state agencies are the prime grantee subgranting to a lower tier organization. But it's entirely possible that the "other organization" a state agency is subgranting to is turning around and subgranting themselves. OMB in trying to fully dispose of all the possible relationships introduced the term "pass-through entity." Another term, or another set of terms to keep in mind, are the terms "competition" and "application." Under the purchase rules contained in Circulars A-102 and A-110, the requirement is that a grantee must enter into purchases to the maximum extent practicable using free and open competition. This doesn't mean that a grantee can't sole source a purchase, but the burden is on the grantee to justify the sole source as an exception to the normal practice. No governmentwide policy requires competition for subgrants. There may be individual federal programs where the program legislation or the program regulations require

competition and there may be lots of grantees who as a matter of good administrative practice and the desire to create a defendable system for awarding funds have pursued competition. That segues into another other pertinent term, "application." "Application" is a term of federal assistance as distinct from the term "proposal," which is normally a term of procurement or purchasing. When a grantee or subgrantee is submitting a document to an awarding agency, they are submitting an application. Using the correct terminology can be helpful in the discussion of how these instruments ought to be put in place and what ought to be contained in them.

FIG. 8-2
USING THE CORRECT TERMINOLOGY

- Subgrant
- Subgrantee
- Subrecipient

- Pass-through Entity
- Primary Grantee
- Grantee

- Competition
- Application

States Making Subgrants to Other Governmental Units

Fig. 8-3 delves into the details of writing subgrants. Unfortunately the federal government hasn't made this as easy as might be desirable. And, making the process easy may not be possible given the variety of organizations that are involved in this sort of exercise. Different requirements manifest themselves in the process depending on who the awarding agency is and who the pass-through entity is. This discussion will start with subgrants by states made to other governmental units, which are covered in Section __.37(a) of Circular A-102's common rule. OMB instructs that the state government follow state law and procedure for awarding subgrants. However, in many states there isn't any state law or procedure because they have relied heavily on federal policies with respect to how these subgrants are done. Other states might have to consider what their state law and procedures say about how to carry out a subgrant instrument. But as far as the federal government is concerned the following items are required:

- Include clauses required by federal statutes and executive orders.

- Ensure that subgrantees are aware of those requirements, which is accomplished via the subgrant agreement.

- Ensure a provision for recordkeeping compliance is included in all cost reimbursable subgrants. (This introduces the possibility that some subgrants may be fixed obligation grants. Many organizations don't use these, but the point is that if the subgrant involves settlement based upon the incurrence of allowable cost, then state governments have to tell the subgrantee to keep records in accordance with Section __.42 of Circular A-102's common rule.)

- Conform advances to subgrantees substantially to the same standards as federal advances to the grantee.

State governments are covered by the Cash Management Improvement Act. Each state government has a separately negotiated agreement with the U.S. Treasury Department on how the advances to them will be handled. Basically what OMB was saying is, based on the way the state gets paid (i.e., advanced payment based on a checks paid arrangement or check clearance arrangement), the state needs to advance funds to subgrantees substantially to the same standards. OMB's point is that if a state is getting advanced payment, then that state should be advance paying their subgrantees. The state shouldn't be paying its subgrantees after the fact.

This discussion introduces another point that needs to be made clear. Having a cost reimbursable agreement has nothing to do with when the cash shows up. It has to do with how settlement occurs at the end. That is why the recordkeeping issue and the cash payment issue are separated in Circular A-102.

States Making Subgrants to Nongovernments

A different set of rules applies to states making grants to nongovernments. OMB Circular A-110 §__.5 requires state governments to flow through to nongovernmental organizations the requirements of Circular A-110. The objective of this procedure is to assure that those nongovernments are following the same rules with respect to subgrants that they would be following if they got the money directly from a federal agency. This requirement also reinforces the notion that OMB likes to assure that uniform administrative requirements are imposed on grantees regardless of how many hands touched the funds in the interim. This introduces another wrinkle here with respect to states, and that is subgrants by states using block grant funds which were authorized by the Omnibus Budget

---

FIG. 8-3
DELVING INTO THE DETAILS

- Subgrants by States to Governments
  - Follow State Law and Procedure
  - Include Clauses Required by Federal Statutes and Executive Orders
  - Ensure Subgrantees are Aware of Requirements
  - Ensure Provision for Recordingkeeping Compliance in Cost Reimbursable Subgrants
  - Conform Advances of Funds to Subgrantees Substantially to the Same Standards as Federal Advances to the Grantee
- Subgrants by States to Non-governments
- Subgrants by States using Block Grant Funds (OBRA of 1981)
  - Impose Requirements Included in Circular A-110
- Subgrants by Other Types of Governments to Governments
  - Include Clauses Required by Federal Statutes and Executive Order
  - Ensure Subgrantees are Aware of the Requirements
  - Include a Provision for Compliance with Federal Agency Implementation of the A-102 Common Rule
- Subgrants by Other Types of Governments to Non-governmental Organizations
  - Impose Requirements Included in Circular A-110
- Subgrants by Non-governmental Organizations to Governments
  - Impose Requirements Included in the Circular A-102 Common Rule
- Subgrants by Non-governmental Organizations to Other Non-governmental Organizations
  - "Flow-through" Applicable Provisions of Circular A-110

Reconciliation Act of 1981 and by subsequent statute. With respect to nonprofit organizations, imposing requirements included in Circular A-110 §__.5 would also be expected under those circumstances.

Other Types of Subgrants

Another type of subgrant agreement might be subgrants made by other types of governments to governments, government to government but not a state. (See Fig. 8-3.) For example, this could be a county government subgranting to a municipal government or a municipal government subgranting to a township. Requirements for these are contained in Section __.37(b) of Circular A-102's common rule. The bullets under that listed item on Fig. 8-3 are the requirements. Grantees must include clauses required by federal statutes and executive orders and ensure that subrecipients are aware of those requirements. Communicating this information in the subgrant agreement is important, but there's absolutely nothing to preclude a prime grantee from also providing instruction or training about what those requirements really entail. Finally, grantees should include a provision for compliance with the federal agency's implementation of the OMB Circular A-102 common rule. The federal agency involved in this particular discussion is the federal agency whose funds are being subgranted by the governmental unit.

The last types of subgrant agreements to discuss are subgrants made by other types of governments to nongovernmental organizations and nongovernmental organizations to one another. In the case of subgrants by other governments to nongovernmental entities the imposition of requirements comes out of Circular A-110 §__.5. A county government subgranting to a local community-based nonprofit organization would be expected to flow through Circular A-110's requirements, not Circular A-102's. Fig. 8-3 shows the requirements for nongovernmental entities subgranting to other parties. This includes colleges and universities, hospitals and other nonprofits. If they are subgranting to a governmental unit, they are expected to impose the requirements contained in Circular A-102's common rule. Subgrants by nongovernmental organizations to other similar entities would flow through the applicable provisions of Circular A-110.

This discussion goes through a fairly complex list, but the bottom line is the expectation that the subrecipient follow requirements that would have applied to it had the federal funds arrived on its doorstep directly from the government. This is the principle that any type of pass-through entity needs to keep in mind when writing subgrant agreements.

Practicalities and Substance of Subgrant Agreements

Get History

Fig. 8-4 shows some of the practicalities as well as the substance of what goes into subgrant agreements. Most pass-through entities work off existing agreements. The problem with relying on existing documents is that in many cases the documents have not changed in years. The challenge is to improve the document and make sure it is in full compliance with the federal requirements. If your organization has some existing history on the agreement, this information might be useful when updating it. When was it drafted? By whom? How often has it been amended? What policies were in effect at the time it was drafted? All of this information may be helpful.

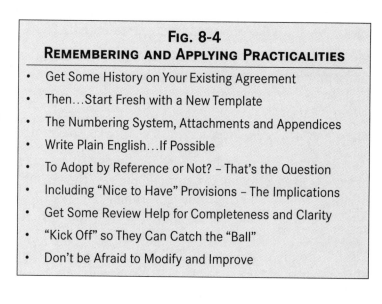

Fig. 8-4
Remembering and Applying Practicalities

- Get Some History on Your Existing Agreement
- Then...Start Fresh with a New Template
- The Numbering System, Attachments and Appendices
- Write Plain English...If Possible
- To Adopt by Reference or Not? – That's the Question
- Including "Nice to Have" Provisions – The Implications
- Get Some Review Help for Completeness and Clarity
- "Kick Off" so They Can Catch the "Ball"
- Don't be Afraid to Modify and Improve

Start with New Template

When your organization starts the updating process, it is a good idea to start with a new template. A good template to use is a structure that goes according to the life events in the life of a grant. What goes on during pre-award in terms of application and certifications, and then what goes on in post-award. Items such as payment and expenditure and requirements for documentation and reporting all fall into place in the post-award period.

Simplify Numbering

Another issue to address in restructuring the document is to simplify the numbering system. The numbering system and approach toward attachments and appendices can be a real impediment to a clear subgrant agreement. It is strongly recommended not to use the outline format; Roman Numeral 1, Capital A, Arabic 1, lower case a, etc. Readers can get lost easily while trying to read and follow along in an outline format. It makes a lot more sense to be simple, to present the numbering system in consecutive Arabic numbers 1 through whatever. With respect to items that are detailed or ancillary, put those in attachments or appendices that are referenced in the numbered provisions of the document. Of course, this simplified numbering system may not be appropriate in every circumstance.

Write in Plain English

Writing the subgrant agreement in plain English is important for several reasons. First, it makes the language more approachable and understandable to a wider audience. Second, it helps eliminate confusion from overly technical jargon or overly wordy sentences. The federal government itself has done a lot of work done on this particular subject. The office of the Federal Register, which is part of the National Archives, has done a fair amount of work trying to get federal employees who write regulations to write in plain English. A guidebook dealing with plain English regulations writing is available on the National Archives Web site, which is http://www.nara.gov (standing for National Archives Records Administration). The guidebook contains some good hints. An example of a federal product written in plain English is the governmentwide suspension and debarment rules, contained in Title 2 C.F.R. Part 180.

Adopt Federal Policy by Number

One of the issues that frequently comes up with subgrant agreements is whether to adopt a particular federal policy by reference. An example might be the imposition of the applicable cost principles. There's no expectation that a subgrant agreement will include the whole text of Circular A-87 for state and local governments or Circular A-122 for nonprofits in the text of the agreement. But if the agreement references anything and adopts it by reference to that subgrant agreement, then grantees should provide a copy of that to the subgrantee, or provide them with information about how to access it on the Internet or elsewhere.

Limit 'Nice-to-Have' Provisions

Another issue is including "nice-to-have" provisions. Many organizations tend to add provisions that they think will improve internal controls over the funds or that would indicate that the entity they're subgranting to is acting as a responsible party. But often these are not required provisions. For example, imposing requirements on a subgrantee to comply with tax law or with employment law. Obviously a grantee doesn't want to do business with an entity that isn't complying with those laws, but are these issues that should be included in the subgrant agreement? It might be better for the subgrant agreement to impose a responsibility to comply with all applicable laws and regulations having to do with organizational status, status as an employer, etc. without specifically referencing it. There are several reasons for handling "nice-to-have" provisions in this fashion. When an agreement has a provision that is not required, it creates a number of dynamics with respect to that agreement. First, the agreement needs to communicate the requirement, which hopefully it would do, but probably isn't necessary. Second, grantees are expected to then monitor the subgrantee to determine whether they complied with that requirement. Third, grantees are supposed to enforce that provision if it's not being complied with and, last, the grantee is imposing additional incremental costs on the subgrantee particularly if compliance was not routinely part of their normal organizational responsibility.

Review for Completeness and Clarity

A good business practice is to have the agreement reviewed for completeness and clarity. Once the document is in a final form, have a lay person read it to determine if he or she understands it and can grasp the details. Obviously, grantees should have a legal review as well. Having both a lay person review and a legal review helps grantees create a document that's not overly intimidating and ensures that the document will be a good road map for how the subgrant will be implemented. Once the subgrant agreement is drafted and ready to go, create a means to go through it with the subgrantee or the whole class of subgrantees involved. For example, hold a kick-off meeting at which the provisions are explained and clarifications can be given. ("Kick off so they can catch the ball.")

Improve the Agreement

Grantees should not be afraid to modify or improve the document. Many organizations tend to treat the final document as inviolate, but this language doesn't have to live on forever. Improvements or clarifications should be welcomed and can even be implemented in the form of an amendment if the agreement is already in place.

Fashioning the Subgrant Agreement

This section explains the substantive information that needs to be present in the agreement. Fig. 8-5 presents an outline of the topics discussed.

Intent

First, and foremost, state the intent. For example, "This is a subgrant of federal financial assistance from organization A here and after referred to as grantor to organization B here and after referred to as subgrantee or subrecipient." That terminology will let all those involved – from staff at the pass-through entity to the subgrantee and, equally importantly, to the independent auditors who will be auditing the subgrantee – that this is intended to be financial assistance and it is included within the scope of the Circular A-133 audit. This is not a purchase of service. It is not a vendor agreement.

FIG. 8-5
FASHIONING THE AGREEMENT

- State the Intent
  - e.g. "This is a subgrant of federal financial assistance from _____ (hereinafter referred to as "grantor") to _____ (hereinafter referred to as "subgrantee" or "subrecipient".
- Provide:
  - the CFDA Number
  - the award name and number
  - whether the award is for research and development
  - the name of the federal awarding agency
- Organize the Document Based on the Sequence of Events in the Life of the Award
- Punctuate Each Provision with:
  1. The Applicable Legal Citation
  2. The Date that the Provision was Introduced into the Agreement
- General Provisions
  - Evidence of Offer/Commitment of Funds
  - Acceptance
  - Notices
  - Responsible Parties
  - Venue
  - Severability
- Scope of Work
- Programmatic Requirements
- Performance Indicators and Measures
- Documentation of Pre-Award Understandings
  - e.g. Certifications and Representations
- Post-Award Actions
  - Payment
  - Expenditure Restrictions and Limitations
  - Cost Principles
  - Documentation Expectations
  - Reporting
- End of the Award Activities
  - Closeout
  - Continuation/Carryover
  - Audit
  - Continuing Responsibilities

FIG. 8-5 (CONTINUED)
FASHIONING THE AGREEMENT (CONTINUED)

- **Required** Public Policies Applicable to Federal Assistance
  - SF 424B
  - Suspension and Debarment, Terrorism
  - Drug-Free Workplace
  - Byrd Amendment (PL 101-121)
  - Stevens Amendment (PL 100-463)
- Other **Required** Public Policies
  - e.g. Applicable State Laws
- Public Policies That Do Not Apply (**By Their Terms**)

Required Information

The document must provide certain required information to the subgrantee. This requirement comes from Section 400(d)(1) of Circular A-133. The primary recipient or pass-through entity must tell the subrecipient the Catalog of Federal Domestic Assistance number of the program funds that it is providing. The award name and number should be provided from the standpoint of the prime grantee as well as any nomenclature that's being used in subgranting. Also, the document must indicate whether the award is for research and development, which is important for universities and hospitals, and the name of the awarding agency.

Many grantees and subgrantees have been through some rigor on this particular problem, because at the end of their fiscal year or during the field work of their independent audit, they're trying to get Catalog of Federal Domestic Assistance numbers, contacting awarding agencies and trying to backtrack to get this information. Pass-through entities should make sure this information is included in the agreement. Subgrantees should make sure this information is included before they sign the agreement, so that they are able to track it down when it's necessary at year end.

Organize the Document

Pass-through entities should organize the document based on the sequence of events in the life of the award – the life events that go on in pre-award, in post-award and after the grant. This section will outline a structure for organizing an agreement in this fashion.

Provisions Relating to Pre-Award

During pre-award, four events occur:

- Solicitation, the announcement of the availability of the funds

- Application

- Awarding agency review

- Actual issuance of the award document

Some readers may be thinking, if we're talking about issuing the award document what kinds of things would we need to include in the award that would relate to pre-award? An example would be adoption of the grant application and narrative as part of the agreement, adoption of any certifications or representations that were made by the applicant before the award was made. Those kinds of issues would be pre-award matters that ought to be incorporated right up front in the subgrant agreement.

Provisions Relating to Post-Award

Once the parties move into post-award, what are the administrative events that are going to occur? Arguably they are payment; expenditure, which would include limitations on the awards such as the applicable cost principles; requirements related to matching and cost sharing; treatment of program income; requirements related to necessary awarding agency approvals that might have to be granted during the life of the project (or prior approvals); and the period of performance of the award. All of those would be limitations in post-award.

Other issues during post-award that should be addressed in the agreement are reports and records – what information is going to have to be transmitted back to the awarding agency in the form of performance or financial reports – and what kind of record retention is going to be expected. For many of these provisions, pass-through entities can go to the applicable OMB administrative circular as implemented by the federal awarding agency and pick up those requirements and plug them into the agreement as being the applicable provisions that must be followed.

Provisions for Once the Award is Over

After the award is over, there are still issues of continuing accountability for property or records, and the rights of the awarding agency to audit and disallow costs. Both Circulars A-102 and A-110 provide a nice template for applicable language. It is a good idea to use these as the terms and conditions in the agreement.

Legal Citations

Punctuate each provision with the applicable legal citation. The legal citation may come out of federal statute, but more likely it's going to come out of programmatic regulations or administrative regulations issued by the awarding federal agency. It is important to be sure that agreements are clear in their legal or regulatory references. In many cases in agreements that are unclear, problematic or internally inconsistent, someone has taken some language from someplace, but it's not abundantly clear from where. Unless legal or regulatory citations are clear, users of the agreements can be confused about whether a provision is actually a firm legal requirement or something the pass-through entity just threw into the agreement. Put in the citations and put in the date the provision was introduced into the agreement so it will be clear that if something has changed from a policy standpoint at the federal level or even at the grantee or pass-through entity level those provisions can be updated in an appropriate manner.

General Provisions

This section discusses some of the general provisions pass-through entities should include in the subgrant agreement. (See Fig. 8-5.)

Evidence of an offer or a commitment of funds and acceptance. These provisions deal with the identification of how much the pass-through award is, what the expectations are with respect to nonfederal funds and evidence of acceptance on the part of the subgrantee.

Notices and responsible parties. A provision related to notices, notices to the parties, should be included to clarify that if something needs to be changed or if enforcement action is going to be taken, who the responsible legal parties are for each entity – the pass-through entity and the recipient.

Venue. The agreement should address which law will govern if a dispute arises. Will it be the law of the state in which the pass-through entity is located? That may be where the subgrantee is located as well, but there are numerous situations, particularly in the nongovernmental sector, where the two parties are not located in the same political jurisdiction.

Severability. A provision should be included that says if any provision of the agreement is declared null and void that doesn't preclude the rest of the agreement from being fully enforceable.

Scope of Work

Earlier this chapter asserted that the scope of work needs to be part of the agreement. Where does that come from? Presumably from the application, the project narrative or plan that was submitted by the subgrantee. In a sense, the subgrantee has control over the scope of work, but presumably the awarding agency has looked at that document as well and may have made modifications. So the scope of work should be an agreed-upon provision.

Programmatic Requirements

This refers to the program statute authorizing the federal grant program from whom funds come as well as the program regulation. This information can be included in the prime grant agreement that the pass-through entity received. But if that's not the case, pass-through entities should go back to the Catalog of Federal Domestic Assistance (CFDA), which is also online at http://www.usa.gov, and look up the program statute and program regulation within the five digit CFDA number that's presented.

Performance Indicators and Measures

The Government Performance and Results Act has been in place at the federal level for a number of years now. This legislation has forced federal agencies to develop performance indicators and measures to determine where their programs are effective. It has had a ripple effect down into the grantee community for those programs that are implemented through federal assistance. It may very well be that because of imposition of those requirements from the federal government to the first tier or through a pass-through entity, those requirements have to flow down as well to the lower tier organization, to show benchmarks or evidence of success.

Documentation of Pre-Award Understandings

Pre-award understandings come about through certifications and representations. Standard Form 424B is the statement of assurances for nonconstruction programs, and has citations to the general laws and presidential executive orders that apply across the board to all federal assistance activities. Examples include certifications and assurances relating to certain civil rights laws, such as Title 6 of the Civil Rights Act of 1964, and references to certain environmental laws, such as the National Environmental Policy Act and the Endangered Species Act. The applicant has said in the pre-award phase it will comply with these if the assistance is awarded. The subgrant agreement needs to remind subgrantees either by full-text replication or by reference that certifications and representations are in place. Another pre-award understanding that may be relevant has to do with particular types of costs. Each of the OMB cost principles (A-21 for colleges and universities, A-87 for state and locals and A-122 for nonprofit organizations) has in its introduction a discussion of advanced understandings. These identify unique or particularly problematic types of costs that may not have been specifically mentioned in the cost principles, but for which it may be wise to obtain an advanced understanding with the awarding agency on or before performance begins. The absence of having an advanced understanding doesn't mean the cost is unallowable. It just means that in post-award it may be more difficult to establish allowability.

Post-Award Actions

As mentioned earlier, Circulars A-102 and A-110 provide a template for applicable language for post-award issues. Types of provisions that may need to be included in the subgrant agreement regarding post-award actions include:

- Payment requirements, which have to do with advanced payment as well as cash management expectations.

- Expenditure restrictions and limitations such as the period for availability of funds requirements related to matching and cost sharing of program income.

- Applicable cost principles. Actions that will require the prior approval of the awarding agency before they're taken; the flow-through of applicable cost principles. (Keep in mind that if different types of organizations are involved in a subgrant agreement, the agreement needs to differentiate the cost principles. For example if a state government is subgranting to a nonprofit organization, the state government should not be imposing A-87, which applies to it, but rather should be imposing A-122, which applies to the lower tier nonprofit.)

- Documentation expectations. This describes the types of documentation that will be required to be generated and held by the recipient and subrecipient and be available for review either by auditors or others trying to determine that actions were taken properly.

- Reporting. This includes financial and performance expectations. Circular A-102 is explicit on this, A-110 is less so, but one of the concerns that OMB had in A-102 is the idea that prime grantees not impose more stringent or detailed reporting requirements on their subgrantees than the primes were facing from the federal government. In a sense, OMB was trying to protect subgrantees from overzealous pass-through entities. This is good advice even if a pass-through entity can't find specific instructions not to do it. Pass-through entities need to recognize that when they are imposing reporting requirements they are imposing burden as well as cost down to a lower level. Pass-through entities should ask themselves "are those going to be reports that we actually rely on and we need to have in that kind of frequency?"

End of Award Activites

The last lifecycle phase to address in a subgrant agreement is end of the award activities. These include closeout, continuation/carryover, audit, and continuing responsibilities.

Closeout. For closeout, issues to address in the subgrant agreement are the actions that the subgrantee will need to take to close out the project and what will be done by the primary recipient in response to it.

Continuation and carry over. Under what circumstances is continuation and carry over allowed? Many pass-through entities have experienced situations where the amount of time that was given for performance was circumscribed by the fact that the award wasn't in place until things like congressional appropriations were made and other sorts of problems were resolved, which may have meant grantees and subgrantees didn't have a full program year to implement. At the end of the program year there's an unobligated balance. Is that unobligated balance something that can be carried forward automatically? Is it something that has to be subject to approval? Under what circumstance is a no-cost extension appropriate? Those are the kinds of issues that need to be addressed regarding continuation and carryover.

Audit requirement. Organizations acting as subrecipients must include the funds received as a subrecipient within the scope of their annual Circular A-133 audit. (Payments received for goods and services provided as a contractor or vendor are not considered to be federal awards and subject to A-133.) Putting in an A-133 provision is totally appropriate unless the subgrantee is a commercial entity, which is possible, or a non-U.S. based entity. Neither of those types of organizations are subject to A-133 requirements.

Continuing responsibilities. These include the issue of continued retention of records, handling of property that was purchased with grant funds and may be staying with the subgrantee or may be sought to be returned, and then finally the right to audit and adjust claims if warranted.

Required Public Policies Applicable to Federal Assistance

Fig. 8-5 identifies the broad public policy requirements, such as civil rights laws and environmental laws, that subgrants should address. Standard Form 424B, which is a document that OMB issued as a certification on the front-end, is a good template for use on the back-end to establish expectations. 2 C.F.R. Part 180 contains the common rule for suspension and debarment in nonprocurement or assistance activities. Subgrantees are required to represent that they are not suspended or debarred. But the rules that were revised in 2003 actually put the onus on the prime grantee to determine whether a potential subgrantee is suspended or debarred by checking the EPLS list, the Excluded Parties List System. If the pass-through entity wants to put this in as a term and condition of the award, it should do so with a provision that says the subgrantee agrees that it is not suspended or debarred, that it won't do business with anybody who is, and if any conditions related to that agreement change, it will notify the grantee.

The drug-free workplace requirement imposes certain procedural responsibilities on a grantee or subgrantee to maintain a drug-free workplace by posting certain notices, adopting specific policies, and conducting enforcement activity. Those procedural steps are also contained in a governmentwide common rule that is contained in 2 C.F.R. Part 180.

The Bird Amendment, named for the senator from West Virginia, establishes the expectation that federal funds will not be used for "award-specific lobbying." Award-specific lobbying involves attempting to get favored treatment from the legislative branch of government in terms of an award or favored treatment from an executive branch agency of government. This is not general lobbying having to do with trying to take a position on legislation or on regulations; it is a very narrowly focused set of requirements. Making reference to the Bird Amendment and Public Law 101-121 would be an appropriate provision to include.

Finally, the Steven's Amendment, which is named for the senator from Alaska, has to do with the disclosure of the fact that federal funds are being used. To a large extent the Steven's Amendment requirement is being met by the requirement in Circular A-133, which says the prime grantee needs to let the subgrantee know that the funds that it is receiving had federal identity and what federal program they came from.

Other Required Public Policies

Section .__ 400(d)(2) of Circular A-133 discusses the fact that the pass-through entity is expected to inform subrecipients of applicable laws, regulations, and terms and conditions, as well as any supplemental requirements imposed by the pass-through entity. The supplemental requirements that OMB had in mind here were truly legal requirements; things that because of state law or regulation an organization might be forced to include that the federal government might not necessarily know about. It is difficult to generalize about what those sorts of requirements might be. In certain states they may be fairly prolific whereas in other places they may be non-existent. It is important to ask the question whether any of those requirements are present and whether they are truly required.

Public Policies That Do Not Apply

This leads to the issue of public policies that do not apply by their terms, such as tax laws, employee classification laws, or the requirements of the Fair Labor Standards Act. For example, some subgrant agreements have included provisions requiring subrecipients to follow the Fair Labor Standards Act. But, organizations have to follow the Fair Labor Standards Act regardless of whether they have received a dime of federal money. Making it a term and condition of the federal award or subaward may not make a whole lot of sense. Another example, which is an isolated case, is a subgrant agreement that included within the agreement the expectation that the subgrantee would follow the United States Constitution.

A lot of extra provisions often get loaded in subgrants which by their terms don't apply. And don't forget that when extraneous provisions get included, pass-through entities create an expectation of information, of monitoring, of enforcement, and of paying the cost of all of that. Adding extra provisions probably doesn't make sense. There's plenty enough to include in subgrant agreements just based on what has been discussed in this chapter.

Troubleshooting
Subrecipient Monitoring

Introduction

There are few topics in the world of federal assistance that have generated as much angst as subrecipient monitoring. Because as much as 75 percent of federal funds awarded each year are passed through to lower tier organizations, primary grantees are feeling a lot of pressure to monitor and account for these subgrants. Independent auditors who perform single audits and similar reviews determine whether primary grantees have sufficiently monitored their subrecipients to ensure compliance with applicable terms and conditions and determine whether performance goals were achieved. But it is long before the auditors arrive that primary grantees need to have efficient and sound practices in place to ensure they are monitoring subgrants effectively. Guidance on monitoring subrecipients is sparse and scattered. But there are many logical and sensible practices grantees can adopt to implement a sound subrecipient monitoring program.

Monitoring subrecipients of federal grant funds is a topic that usually does not arise until independent auditors arrive to conduct single audits. Auditors are expected to test, among other requirements, a grantee's system for monitoring federal subawards. But the grantee's system or methods of monitoring must be in place and honed long before the subaward agreement is signed. Moreover, the primary grantee's system (including internal controls) for administering federal funds can be used as a starting point for developing monitoring procedures. Just how soundly subrecipient monitoring is carried out will depend on how well the controls over monitoring are designed and operated. But each subaward and each subrecipient is different, so monitoring procedures for each agreement need to be tailored – there is no one-size-fits-all approach.

Primary grantees have long had to oversee and monitor subawards they made with lower tier organizations (subgrantees). The OMB Circular A-102 common rule (for state and local government grantees) and OMB Circular A-110 (for university, hospital and nonprofit

> Monitoring is the continuous collection of relevant information about a subrecipient and its performance.

SUBRECIPIENT OR VENDOR?

The following is a quick checklist that can help determine whether an entity is a subrecipient or a vendor. These are only general attributes. An entity could have characteristics of both a vendor and a subrecipient. Similarly, not all entities will meet all of the listed characteristics. It is important to use your judgment and look at the nature of the arrangement to determine whether the entity is a subrecipient or vendor.

Subrecipient

- Determines who is eligible
- Has performance measured against program objectives
- Makes program decisions
- Is responsible for ensuring that federal requirements are met
- Uses federal funds to carry out a program, not to provide goods or services

Vendor

- Provides goods or services within normal business operations
- Provides similar goods or services to many different purchasers
- Operates in a competitive environment
- Provides goods or services that are ancillary to the program
- Is not subject to compliance requirements.

---

grantees) both state that it is the responsibility of the primary grantee to monitor sub-awards, but neither policy elaborates on how that should be done. The focus on monitoring magnified with 1996 amendments to the single audit statute. Language was added to the law stipulating that primary grantees would be responsible for monitoring the activities of subrecipients "through site visits, limited scope audits or other means."

OMB's *Circular A-133 Compliance Supplement*, which is essentially an audit guide, cites the various sections of the OMB grants management and audit rules that address subrecipient monitoring and subawards. The compliance supplement identifies for auditors requirements that, if violated, would have a direct and material affect on federal grant programs. One of 14 key compliance areas listed in the compliance supplement that auditors test in an audit is subrecipient monitoring.

In discussing the OMB Circular A-102 common rule, Circular A-110 and Circular A-133, it is evident that nowhere in any of these policy documents are concrete checklists or guidelines to follow in monitoring subrecipients. There is no one-size-fits-all or cookie cutter approach to monitoring. Each subaward is different. So where does a grantee start when designing and implementing an effective monitoring program?

'Step Back' Phase

Grantees should begin to develop a monitoring program long before they sign agreements with subgrantees. Step back, start fresh and organize the process.

Review the Agreement You Are Using

Review what you have been using to monitor subgrantees and focus on the major phases of the lifecycle of a subgrant. First, review the agreement you have been using to subgrant funds. The agreement you should review is the one you use for subgranting funds, not any contract you might use to obtain services from a vendor.

One of the biggest issues in the area of subrecipient monitoring is determining whether an organization is a subrecipient or a vendor. The term subrecipient is synonymous with subgrantee, whereas the term vendor is synonymous with the term contractor as those terms are used in the OMB Circular A-102 common rule and Circular A-110.

One key point to consider is that a grantee can have a subrecipient relationship or a vendor relationship with different kinds of organizations. Federal rules do not preclude having a vendor relationship with a nonprofit organization or a local government. What is important is the nature of the relationship, not the nature of the parties to the relationship. Similarly, it is entirely possible in some federal programs that a subgrantee may be a commercial entity.

An agreement that calls for advanced payment is most likely a grant or subgrant relationship. Conversely, if an agreement stipulates payment after the fact or pay for performance, it is likely a contract or vendor relationship. Regarding cost sharing, if a lower tier organization is cost sharing or matching, the agreement is most likely a subgrant. It is unlikely that a cost contract will include a cost sharing or matching type provision.

In subaward agreements, primary grantees are required to identify the federal funds they are awarding to the subrecipient. This is accomplished by listing all Catalog of Federal Domestic Assistance Program numbers. The federal awarding agency is required to provide primary grantees with this information, and those recipients must alert subrecipients to it as well. These numbers are key because independent auditors use CFDA information to determine compliance with a particular program's requirements. In addition, the primary grantee is required to identify the federal requirements that are being imposed or passed through to the subrecipient, as well as to differentiate those requirements from requirements that the primary grantee may add to the relationship. Such primary grantee requirements might include state laws that state grantees must follow when subgranting funds to lower tier organizations (such as a local government or nonprofit organization).

'STEP BACK' PHASE

Review agreements

- Determine whether it is a subrecipient or vendor relationship
- Identify federal funds
- Identify applicable federal requirements
- Shed excess weight – remove irrelevant provisions
- Organize the document
- Provide citations

Determine application requirements

- Create a useful file
- Ask relevant questions

Checklist review

- Build in flexibility for the awarding agency
- Identify other ways to gather information
- Connect to the subgrant agreement

Prior to entering agreements with subrecipients, primary grantees should carefully review provisions that do not apply to the particular program or circumstances. For example, Title IX of the Education Amendments of 1972 prohibits discrimination on the basis of sex in federally funded education programs. It is limited to that particular set of programs. Therefore, it should not be included in noneducation related agreements.

Agreements should be organized according to the sequence of events that will occur throughout the life of the award. Provisions relating to pre-award or to the actual negotiation of the award should be at the beginning of the agreement. Provisions that relate to post-award should be in the middle. Primary grantees should also review the cycle of financing

---

AGREEMENT REVIEW

To inform recipients and subrecipients of applicable requirements, awarding agencies and pass-through entities should regularly review the terms of the agreements. Prudent practice at the beginning of each award cycle should be to:

- Review any current standardized grant or subgrant agreement documents to determine if any provisions need to be superseded or rescinded because of statutory and regulatory change.

- Review current award terms and conditions to determine which provisions must stay intact. While this may involve some research or interviews to determine the basis for all current provisions, it is a one-time action taken to ensure only necessary requirements are included.

- Once award provisions have been firmly reviewed, assure that each provision includes the statutory or regulatory citation that serves as the basis for the requirement and its effective date. Some grantors label the entire agreement in this manner but it is then difficult to tell what, if anything, was changed from previous versions. This more detailed approach creates an institutional record that is much easier to update.

---

within the grant so that, for example, the discussion of payment precedes the discussion of expenditure, which precedes the discussion of documentation, which precedes the discussion of reporting. Grouping provisions into broad categories is a logical and efficient way of organizing the subaward agreement. Finally, it is important to include citations to laws and regulations and other policies that are the basis for particular requirements imposed in the subaward agreement.

Review Subgrantee Application Requirements

Primary grantees should create a file on each applicant as early in the process as possible. This eliminates the need to gather information, a time-consuming process, in the post-award monitoring phase of a grant. Such a file could include background on the organization, its policies and procedures, information about its licensure, etc. Applicant files can be added to when the need arises. Another aspect of the submission requirements ought to be to ask important and relevant questions, such as whether an applicant is required to have a Circular A-133 audit, and have actually had one prepared. Does the applicant expect to spend $500,000 of federal funds during its fiscal year, from all sources? If the answer is "yes," that organization would be expected to have a Circular A-133 audit. On the other hand, if the answer is "no," the primary grantee knows that monitoring tools other than audits must be used. Another good question to ask applicants/subrecipients is what is their fiscal year cycle? Different fiscal year cycles mean different audit cycles, and this valuable information in the subrecipient's file allows the primary grantee to identify which subrecipients will have and submit Circular A-133 audit results.

Develop Checklists

Many primary grantees develop checklists for post-award monitoring. These checklists are used for site visits, document review and other monitoring techniques. Regardless of the checklists that are developed, primary grantees should build in flexibility. There may be other ways to gather information for monitoring purposes, such as reviewing files and corresponding with a subrecipient's other funders. These checklists should correspond to the subgrant agreement, i.e., the sequence that the subgrant agreement follows would be the sequence that would be followed in addressing oversight issues.

Pre-Award Techniques

During the pre-award stage, the primary grantee develops a set of procedures for how the subgrant relationship will operate. At this stage, many actions taken will alleviate much confusion and can help fashion the post-award events that will make the entire grant cycle easier for both the primary grantee and the subrecipient.

Assess the Applicant

Assessing the applicant organization is part of this phase. Assessing the applicant's responsibility involves such steps as determining whether the applicant has been suspended or debarred by the federal government. Primary grantees can check what is known as the excluded parties list system (www.epls.gov) to obtain that information. Additionally, primary grantees can use employer identification numbers to assess credit worthiness and the like. A review of an applicant's financial statements can be a good tool for assessing financial stability.

Another pre-award monitoring technique is to assess an applicant's financial, procurement and property management systems. OMB's Circular A-102 common rule and Circular A-110 spell out the grantee standards for these systems (see Fig. 9-1). In reviewing these systems, grantees can assess whether a particular applicant has procedures in place for efficiently and effectively managing federal assistance in compliance with applicable laws and regulations. These reviews can uncover weaknesses that might lead the primary grantee to attach special terms and conditions to an award.

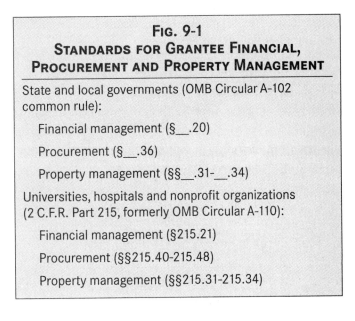

FIG. 9-1
STANDARDS FOR GRANTEE FINANCIAL, PROCUREMENT AND PROPERTY MANAGEMENT

State and local governments (OMB Circular A-102 common rule):

　　Financial management (§__.20)

　　Procurement (§__.36)

　　Property management (§§__.31-__.34)

Universities, hospitals and nonprofit organizations (2 C.F.R. Part 215, formerly OMB Circular A-110):

　　Financial management (§215.21)

　　Procurement (§§215.40-215.48)

　　Property management (§§215.31-215.34)

Finally, primary grantees should review prior award activity the applicant has had with the primary grantee as well as with other organizations. Contacting other sponsors, grantors and other pass-through agencies that have dealt with the applicant can provide good feedback about the applicant.

Review the Program or Project

Another pre-award technique is to assess the program or project. Primary grantees should review what can be monitored. What can the grantee assess during the life of the project from the standpoint of economy and efficiency and the use of funds and program results? Federal agencies have imposed performance indicators on primary grantees to assess their performance. These indicators can be incorporated into the subrecipient relationship as well.

PRE-AWARD TECHNIQUES

Assess the applicant
- Responsibility
- Financial stability
- Systems
- Prior award activity

Assess the program or project
- Determine what can be monitored
- Develop performance indicators

Tailor the agreement
- Determine any special "high-risk" conditions
- One size need not fit all

Organize your subgrant 'universe'
- Size of your award
- Size of the federal award portfolio
- Extent of your past experience

Tailor the Agreement

Many organizations use a single subgrant agreement for every subaward relationship they have. One size does not fit all. That is, primary grantees must tailor each agreement. One concept employed at the federal level is differential accountability. The notion behind differential accountability is that a grantor creates a relationship with a recipient based on the risk that exists within the relationship. Primary grantees can impose special conditions on recipients deemed high-risk. If an applicant has a history of poor performance, is not financially stable, has a management system that does not meet federal requirements, has not complied with terms and conditions of a previous award, or is not otherwise responsible, then special conditions can be imposed on that particular subrecipient. On the other end of the scale, subrecipients that have a history of good performance and sound financial management practices can be given greater flexibility in their subaward agreements.

Organize the Subgrant 'Universe'

One other pre-award tool is to organize the subgrant universe. Primary grantees should review all subrecipients and identify the size of their awards. The more funding that is awarded to a particular entity, the greater the differential accountability. Additionally, the size of a subrecipient's entire federal grant portfolio should be reviewed. If a subrecipient has a large grant portfolio, presumably there is greater oversight by other grantor agencies, and so it might not require a lot of additional oversight. However, contacting other funders of a subrecipient to determine how much oversight already exists can prove to be a useful step in determining the level of additional oversight needed.

Primary grantees should rely on their past experience. If a primary grantee has several new subrecipients that they have not done business with before, those subawards should have more attention than past subrecipients that have demonstrated good performance.

Post-Award Techniques

Once a subaward has been made to a subrecipient, there are numerous tools that can be used to monitor the subrecipient's progress and performance. "Kick-off" meetings are a good way to start the grant award cycle. These meetings are a good way to bring together primary grantee and subrecipient staff to discuss the grant program. As part of these meetings, a review of the subaward agreement and program can be conducted, and a detailed explanation of its provisions provided. Subaward provisions that might not be very clear can be discussed as well. While the best way to hold these kick-off meetings is in person, today's audio and Web conferencing technology allows these meetings to be held with no required travel.

Audits

Circular A-133 audits and limited-scope audits can be used to monitor subgrantees. Primary grantees can asks subrecipients for copies of audit reports and any management letters issued by the independent auditor, but there is no requirement that subrecipients automatically send audit reports to primary grantees. If a subrecipient has a single audit and there are no findings related to the funds awarded by the primary grantee and no issues related to prior findings from previous audits, the subgrantee should notify the primary grantee in writing that there were no findings. A subgrantee that does have audit findings related to a primary grantee's funds are required to send that awarding agency a copy of its audit report. The primary grantee is required to take affirmative action on those reports and to issue a management decisions related to the findings of that subrecipient within six months after receiving the audit report.

Limited-scope audits can be required of subgrantees, but the costs of those audits are not allowable as Circular A-133 audit costs because they do not meet Circular A-133's requirements or the audits were of organizations exempt from the circular. However, primary grantees are not precluded from charging federal funds for limited-scope audits as a tool for monitoring subrecipients, provided certain conditions are met. For example, a pass-through entity can hire an independent auditor or use its internal auditor to review a limited number of characteristics related to a subrecipient's compliance, allowable costs, cost principals, beneficiary eligibility, reporting, matching, level of effort, and earmarking. While limited-scope audits are not a cost-effective monitoring tool to use frequently, they can be useful for reviewing subrecipient performance in selected circumstances.

POST-AWARD TECHNIQUES

- Hold "kick-off" meetings so they can catch the ball
- Use A-133 audits (obtain, review, follow-up)
- Use limited-scope audits (A-133, §.230(b))
- Review financial and performance reports
- Document routine contacts
- Obtain and use third-party information
- Follow up on significant developments
- Conduct meaningful site visits
- Provide feedback and technical assistance
- Document, document, document

Review Financial and Performance Reports

Reviewing a subgrantee's financial and performance reports is a logical tool for monitoring interim performance. But reports are not always submitted in a timely fashion or they are sent to different staff of the primary grantee. For example, financial reports are usually sent to the finance office, while performance reports, narrative as they are, are sent to program staff. If there is no coordination between the two, these reports can be received but never actually reviewed. Primary grantees should ensure that financial and performance reports are submitted by subgrantees when expected and shared with all staff tasked with monitoring responsibilities.

Document Routine Contacts

Staff at subrecipient organizations should have regular contact with their primary grantees. Such communication can be via e-mail, telephone, and letters. Primary grantees should keep a file of all of this correspondence, so that if any issues arise at a later time, the files can be reviewed for resolution of any of these issues.

Using Third-Party Information

As suggested for pre-award preparation, primary grantees can contact other grantor agencies of a subrecipient to gain valuable information. Ask the grantor agencies whether they have done site visits or other kinds of oversight and determine whether those efforts can be relied on in lieu of conducting duplicative oversight.

Subgrantees are obligated to report significant developments, be they positive or negative, that may adversely affect performance under the award. Once a primary grantee has this information, it should follow up on the information (if action is needed) and document any action, such as providing assistance or taking corrective action. This documentation will serve as a tool for monitoring if issues arise later in the grant cycle.

Conduct Meaningful Site Visits

Conducting meaningful site visits is integral to an effective monitoring program. Primary grantees should focus on issues and obtain answers that cannot be obtained other than through face-to-face communication. Additionally, providing the subgrantee with feedback and technical assistance at site visits is essential. Using checklists when conducting site visits is helpful, but it is essential that such a checklist is tailored to the particular subaward and subgrantee.

Document, Document, Document

The mantra of grants management and subgrants management is document, document and document. Sound documentation of how a primary grantee monitored its subawards goes a long way in demonstrating federal program compliance and good grant stewardship.

Federal Cash Management – What Every Grantee and Subgrantee Should Know

10

Introduction

Federal cash management is a topic that keeps on giving. Unfortunately, what it often gives rise to are audit findings, as a number of well-publicized cases reveal. More broadly, the topic gives rise to many misconceptions among grantees as to what is actually expected of them. Not every cash management rule applies universally. State governments and their subgrantees are subject to distinctive rules because of federal statutory requirements under the Cash Management Improvement Act. Similarly, special rules apply to universities as they handle cash under student financial aid programs.

At the outset, it may be useful to explain why cash management is an important topic. First of all, how a grantee manages its funds is something that independent auditors can track readily. The OMB *Circular A-133 Compliance Supplement* sets out audit requirements that are applicable to all types of grantees, except commercial entities. Under that circular, auditors are expected to look at how a grantee manages its funds whenever a payment is made in advance. As a result, cash management problems crop up frequently in findings based on Circular A-133 audits. In fact, a search through the Federal Audit Clearinghouse database reveals cash management problems as the most prominent audit finding, outpacing allowable cost issues in recent years. Independent and federal auditors alike attend to this matter. A few years ago, the Department of Health and Human Services Office of Inspector General did a series of audits at universities across the country, from Harvard to Hawaii, looking for issues related to patterns and practices of cash management. As a result of those audits, some fairly significant findings arose with regard to several institutions. The U.S. Department of Education's Office of Inspector General has shown a similar interest in student financial aid cash management.

Indeed, federal agencies will take a hard look at the system that a prospective grantee already has in place, including financial management practices and policies, as part of their review before they make an award. The same review practice applies to primary grantees with respect to subgrantees. Does a prospective subrecipient have a financial system sufficiently well organized and controlled to warrant the type of payment that occurs in federal grants and subgrants? Were a grant awarded, could the recipient be trusted to handle what can, to some extent, amount to a risky proposition?

To avoid a negative public perception borne of negative media exposure is still another reason to manage federal funds properly. All too often, accusations or issues that arise during audits find their way into the front pages of local newspapers. Should that happen, would the grantee be able to successfully defend against the charges of irregularity? If the public comes away with the impression that the institution in question has been handling federal cash in a fast and loose manner, the damage may be long-term, even if the impression made actually is unwarranted.

CASH MANAGEMENT – SOME BASICS
• Methods of payment
• Timely disbursement of other grant-related revenue
• Fund control and accountability
• Cash depositories
• Prompt disbursement of federal drawdowns
• Crediting and reporting of interest earned

Applicable Federal Rates

The federal government imposes some rules regarding the methods that grantees and subgrantees may use to make payments. The timely disbursement of other grant-related revenue, such as program income and the like, figures into the discussion. Requirements also apply to funds control and accountability, which basically have to do with the custodial functions related to cash management. These rules identify eligible cash depositories, such as banks, where money can be held pending disbursement. How to provide prompt disbursement of federal drawdowns is another issue, one that attracts great interest in the audit community. Finally, the rules address how to credit and report interest earned.

Some special concerns that arise include the flow-through of cash to subrecipients. In organizations that operate programs where subgranting is built into the requirements, Congress intended that the means used to transfer money should be cash flow-through. Regarding awards in a discretionarily designed program that involves partnering with subrecipients, the concern is to keep the latter financed so that they can make expenditures in support of the overall program. Few federal rules apply to block grant programs, but among them are regulations of their cash management procedures. Finally, some concerns are exclusive. The Cash Management Improvement Act applies to states only, and it is institutions of higher education that need to concern themselves with how cash management is handled in the context of student financial aid.

The basic rules for cash management are in the OMB Circular A-102 common rule for state and local grant administration (see §§__.12, __.20, __.21, __.37 and __.41). OMB Circular A-110, which applies to colleges and universities, hospitals and nonprofit organizations, addresses the issue of interest refunds in its §§__.5, __.21, __.22 and __.52.

SPECIAL CONCERNS
• Flow-through to subrecipients
• Block grants
• States only – Cash Management Improvement Act
• Higher education only – student financial aid

RESOURCE DOCUMENTS

- OMB circulars and forms
  - OMB Circular A-102 common rule, §§__.12, __.20, __.21, __.37 and __.41
  - OMB Circular A-110, §§__.5, __.21, __.22 and __.52 (2 C.F.R. Part 215)
  - SF 272, 272a and instructions
- Treasury regulations
  - 31 C.F.R. Part 205
- Department of Education regulations
  - 34 C.F.R. §668.161
  - Audit guidance
  - OMB *Circular A-133 Compliance Supplement*– Part 3, cash management, and Part 6, internal controls

---

Standard forms 272 and 272a, with related instructions, are pertinent here. Similarly, the U.S. Department of Treasury has a set of regulations with cross-references to both OMB circulars A-102 and A-110. With regard to block grant requirements, 31 C.F.R. Part 205 applies. These regulations implement the Cash Management Improvement Act but, by definition, exclude certain types of payments from their coverage because they apply only to state governmental relationships with the federal government.

In addition, the Department of Education's student financial aid regulations (34 C.F.R. §668.161) deals with the cash management responsibilities that a higher education institution undertakes when it participates in such a program. Finally, it is important to note the audit guidance in the OMB *Circular A-133 Compliance Supplement*, especially Part 3, dealing with cash management, and Part 6, dealing with internal controls over cash management.

Cost Reimbursement and Methods of Payment

The question of how best to serve the grantee arises naturally, given that federal grants are, by their very nature, a form of assistance. Yet the payment of interest generally is an unallowable cost under OMB cost principles – Circular A-21 for colleges and universities, Circular A-87 for state, local and Indian tribal governments and Circular A-122 for non-profit organizations.

Does having a cost reimbursable agreement have any bearing on when the cash shows up? Why should the federal government, given its large projected budget deficit, borrow money so that grantees can draw it down and sit on it? What cash management does an auditor review, if there is no advance payment?

Payment in Advance

To begin to answer such questions, it may help first to address the methods of payment that are available. Section __.21 of the OMB Circular A-102 common rule and §__.22 of Circular A-110, are applicable to this discussion. Basically there are three methods to choose from, but the first one is preferred. In fact, both circulars state that

METHODS OF FEDERAL PAYMENT
• Advance (electronic funds transfer / Treasury check)
• Working capital advance
• Reimbursement
– Construction grants
– Special terms and conditions for high-risk grantees

grantees and subgrantees shall be paid in advance, provided they maintain a system that minimizes the time lapse between the transfer of funds from the government and their disbursement for grant purposes.

Working Capital Advance

A second payment option is what is known as a working capital advance. A federal agency may choose this option when a grantee needs financing for its project but does not have a system that meets the funds accountability requirements to minimize the time lapse between funds receipt and funds disbursement. Using this option, the awarding agency makes a one-time payment in advance of the award, up to a certain dollar amount. With every subsequent payment, the grantee must report its expenditures until they reach the same level as the initial first payment. In that way, the federal government is not at risk of a significant number of drawdowns by the grantee. This option often is exercised with organizations that do not have great financial management capacity and cannot finance their own operations any other way.

Payment by Reimbursement

A third option is payment by reimbursement. Payment reimbursement is not the same as cost reimbursement. The latter term refers to the final settlement that occurs at end of the award, based on assertions by the recipient or subrecipient of allowable costs. Payment by reimbursement, on the other hand, refers to instances where the grantee or subgrantee has itself disbursed cash out of its own resources and then requests payment after the fact.

Use of the payment by reimbursement option generally arises in two authorized circumstances. The first is construction grants. If the purpose of an award is exclusively to fund construction, the grantee will be paid by reimbursement and will submit a different financial report than will other grantees, namely, SF 271, "Outlay Report and Request for Reimbursement for Construction Programs."

Second, payment by reimbursement can be used as a punitive measure, in which case a grantee is paid after the fact, instead of in advance. Section 12 of the OMB Circular A-102 common rule identifies some of the possible remedies to cope with what is referred to as a high-risk grantee or subgrantee. If an organization has a history of poor performance, is not financially stable, does not have a management system that meets the requirements of the circular, or has not complied with the terms and conditions of a previous award, Circular A-102 instructs the awarding agency to impose special conditions. Among the conditions that can be imposed is payment by reimbursement. OMB Circular A-110, which sets out a similar provision in Section 14, does not spell out the special conditions that might be imposed. Nonetheless, it does authorize the imposition of such an arrangement on a nongovernmental entity, should the circumstances warrant.

Timely Disbursement

The issue of timely disbursement of other grant-related revenue may not involve large amounts of money, but it does pose the real possibility of audit vulnerability. Section 21(b) of the Circular A-102 common rule and 2 C.F.R. §215.22(g) (Circular A-110), together make it clear that any revenue received during the life of a project must be spent before additional federal cash is drawn down. Such revenue includes program income, rebates, refunds, recoveries from subgrantees, among other income.

TIMELY DISBURSEMENT OF OTHER GRANT-RELATED REVENUE

- OMB Circular A-102 Common Rule §__.21 (b)

- OMB Circular A-110, §__.22(g) (2 C.F.R. §215.22(g))

Such revenue can pose a vulnerability because the need for its timely disbursement is specifically set out in the cash management section of OMB *Circular A-133 Compliance Supplement.* This supplement is essentially a guide on how to test for compliance when performing a Circular A-133 audit. Invariably, the mention of such revenue alone is enough to prompt auditors to determine whether any money sits in an account while the recipient routinely draws down federal cash through the payment system.

Funds Control and Accountability

With regard to funds control and accountability requirements, the Circular A-102 common rule and Circular A-110 set out relevant standards, stating that grantees and subgrantees must develop and maintain internal controls over cash, property and other assets. The intent of such internal controls is to provide reasonable assurance that such assets will be safeguarded and used for proper purposes. If the internal control system for cash is a weak one, the possibility of problems with cash management is certainly present. Making it a practice to insure grants funds is but one indication that the internal control system is a strong one.

FUNDS CONTROL AND ACCOUNTABILITY

- Internal controls over cash

- Written cash management procedures

- Timing of drawdowns

- Routine disbursement schedules

- Special/emergency disbursements

- Reconciliations

A second requirement to bear in mind is the need to provide cash management procedures in writing. Such procedures may well be in place already, although not labeled as such, because they involve such matters as when payroll is handled, how vendor payments are scheduled, routine disbursement schedules, special or emergency disbursements, petty cash, and reconciliations between such items as escheated warrants and uncashed checks.

Funds control and accountability is an area well-tilled by federal auditors, and the HHS Inspector General has been one of the more active units pursuing compliance with related requirements. In the last few years, the IG has performed a few audits of state governments to check and see whether recorded obligations under awards were offset by applicable credits in the form of uncashed checks or as escheated warrants. All too frequently, they found that they were not offset, which made for some fairly fertile auditing territory.

Cash Depositories

With regard to cash depositories, the first requirement is to establish internal controls to safeguard funds and at the same time ensure their easy access. For universities, hospitals and nonprofit organizations, Circular A-110 states that they must have interest-bearing accounts. For state and local governments, though, the Circular A-102 common rule is silent on the subject, probably because state and local agencies familiar to the federal government, and the likelihood that one of them would fail to put grant funds into an interest-bearing account is slim.

CASH DEPOSITORIES

- Safeguard – "Keep and find"
- Use interest-bearing accounts
- Insured accounts

By contrast, Circular A-110 states explicitly that pending disbursement, grant funds must be placed in an interest-bearing account. One common misconception regarding this requirement is that the accounts into which federal funds are placed must be insured by the Federal Deposit Insurance Corporation. Earlier versions of circulars A-102 and A-110 did indeed refer to FDIC-insured accounts, but they never made such insurance mandatory. Later, when the circulars were revised the reference to FDIC insurance was dropped altogether. What the circulars now require is that funds be deposited in insured accounts "whenever possible."

Placing federal funds into an uninsured account calls into question safety, particularly in light of some fairly high-profile failures of certain state-chartered institutions as well as of some unfortunate investment arrangements made with federal funds. As a practical matter, the need to safeguard federal grants trumps other options and makes federal insurance necessary, even if not actually required by law.

Prompt Disbursement

The standard for prompt disbursement of federal drawdowns is to minimize the elapsed time between the transfer of funds from the U.S. Treasury and the issuance or redemptions of checks, warrants or payments by other means for program purposes. Nowhere in the federal rules is the number of days explicitly stated that a grantee is permitted to hold the cash before disbursing it, although the common misconception is to the contrary, and grantees have been known to ask about a "three-day rule."

Such a rule does appear in the instructions for Standard Form 272 (Federal Cash Transactions Report). Block 12 instructs the grantee to enter the estimated number of days that will pass before the cash on hand, shown on line 11J, will be expended. If more than three days' worth of required cash remains on hand, the grantee must explain why the drawdown was made prematurely or else offer other reasons for the excess cash. Such an explanation need not be made with regard to prescheduled or automatic advances.

The fact that the rules surrounding prompt disbursement are not hard and fast does not mean, of course, that awardees should play fast and loose. Anecdotal evidence points to payment interruptions by some of the major federal agency payment systems once they determined that certain grantees were carrying an excess cash balance. Payments remained interrupted until these grantees disbursed the cash that they had on hand or brought it down to a three-day level.

Crediting and Reporting Interest

With regard to crediting and reporting interest on federal funds that have been advanced, as well as other applicable credits, §__.41(c) of Circular A-102 and §__.52(a)2 of Circular A-110 address the responsibility for specific financial reporting on the subject of cash flow. Section 11 of Standard Form 272 addresses the gross disbursements that the grantee has made. Because such a report is made on a cash basis, the interest earnings are treated on a cash basis as well. Thus, pending disbursement, any interest accruing to the recipient belongs ultimately to the federal government, with a minor adjustment.

Questions often arise as to when the interest on federal funds begins to accrue and when it ends. Interest earned between the crediting to the account and the issuing of a payment must be refunded to the federal government. Any additional interest that accrues between the issuance of the payment check and its actual clearance apparently is claimed by some grantees. Yet the claim is dubious. The language in circulars A-102 and A-110 does not differentiate as to the time when the interest accrues. Furthermore, Standard Form 272 is a cash-basis report as opposed to an accrual report. Finally, although the Cash Management Improvement Act does not apply to all grantees, section 205.15(a) of the law describes the interest as being credited from the time the funds are credited to the accounts of the recipient and the payout of the funds. The payout of the funds is said to occur when the check is redeemed and not when it is disbursed.

To claim the interest that accrues between the issuance and the clearance of the reimbursement check is a risky proposition and creates a potential issue for audit. The more interest that a grantee earns on federal funds advanced, the more evidence there is that

---

CREDITING AND REPORTING INTEREST EARNED ON FEDERAL FUNDS ADVANCED AND OTHER APPLICABLE CREDITS

- Circular A-102 common rule §__.41(c)
- Circular A-110, §__.52(a)(2) (2 C.F.R. §215.52(a)(2))
- SF 272 Federal Cash Transactions Report
    - Line 11 (f) – Gross disbursements (cash basis)
    - Line 11 (i) – Adjustments from prior periods
    - Line 13 (a) – Advances to subgrantees and subcontractors
- SF 270 Request for Advance or Reimbursement
- Treasury requirement for EFT in grants
- Interest earnings
    - Check clearance, not check disbursement
- Interest retention
    - $100 annually for governmental entities
    - $250 annually for nongovernmental entities

---

a grantee is not minimizing the elapsed time between the transfer of funds and their disbursement.

Interest retention is addressed in OMB Circular A-102, which allows a grant recipient to retain $100 of interest annually for administrative purposes. Circular A-110 allows the retention of $250 annually. A grantee might be tempted to assert that such allowances apply per grant, and not per grantee. The regulation is not clear on this point, because it does not go into that level of detail. However, in a number of federal audits with findings of poor cash management or failure to refund interest, the dollar amount of the refund has been determined to apply on an annual basis. Although the dollar amount itself is usually relatively minor, the amount of interest that a grantee chooses to retain is easy to track and thus puts it at risk from the standpoint of a future audit.

Cash Management Requirements of Subrecipients

One area of concern involves the flow-through of cash management requirements to subrecipients. Consider first what happens when the primary recipient is a state government. The Circular A-102 common rule states that state governments must pass through advances to subgrantees in much the same way that they were received from the federal government. To some extent, this standard became another golden rule. Thus, if a state is receiving advance payment, it should turn around and offer the same to its subgrantees. Although not required to use a federal payment system for that purpose, the state would need to set up some mechanism so that advances could be made to subgrantees to finance their operations under assistance awards. OMB Circular A-110 includes similar language regarding the flow-through of cash management requirements to subrecipients that are nonprofit organizations.

States must follow special cash management requirements for a host of programs listed in the Cash Management Improvement Act. These programs are fairly large state-administered programs, such as Temporary Assistance for Needy Families, the Child Support Enforcement Program, and the Federal Aid Highway Program. Each state must handle payments for about 18 to 20 such programs under respective federal-state agreements.

SPECIAL CONCERNS

Higher education only – Student financial aid

- The "real" three-day rule – 34 C.F.R. §668.166(a)(1)
- Funds held in trust – 34 C.F.R. §668.161(b)
- Do not use as collateral – 34 C.F.R. §668.161(b)
- Direct loan funds only – keep the first $250 of interest; refund the rest by June 30 of the award year (34 C.F.R. §668.163(c)(4)
- Controls over interest earnings (34 C.F.R. §668.163 (d)(1)
- Competency and integrity/fiduciary responsibility (34 C.F.R. §668.82(a)
- Sanctions – "grounds for an emergency action against the institution, or the limitation, suspension, or termination of the institution's participation..."

For all other programs, states must minimize the time lapse between funds receipt and funds disbursement.

Another final special concern that merits discussion relates to higher education. The student financial aid programs under Title IV of the Higher Education Act and related regulations include some explicit statements about cash management. They depart a bit from the normal practices used to manage cash in other federal grants, because they introduce some notions about fiduciary responsibility and about the use of student aid funds for collateral. The regulations are intended to promote sound cash management of higher education funds and to minimize the financing cost to the federal government.

Department of Education regulations (34 C.F.R §668.161) require colleges and universities to disburse the funds within three days of receipt. Further, it says that the funds are to be held in trust on behalf of the students and are not to be used as collateral.

With respect to direct loan funds, education institutions can keep the first $250 of interest, but they must refund the remainder by June 30 of the award year. This rule is predicated primarily on the fact that the student financial aid year runs from September to June or August to May. Controls apply to interest earnings, as does a requirement for competence and integrity in upholding the fiduciary responsibility among the staff. With more rigor than set out in the general grant requirements, specific sanctions apply for failure to manage the cash properly. Those sanctions can include interruption or termination of an institution's participation in the student financial aid program.

Clearly it is important for grantees to be careful in developing and complying with sound cash management practices. Cash management is a vulnerable area, one that continues to surface as a matter of interest among the federal inspectors general. The issues and concerns involving grantees' compliance with federal cash management requirements are not likely to disappear.

Part C: Sample Subaward Agreements

FIG. C-1

Agreement #: _____

Effective Date: _____

Expiration Date: _____

COMMUNITY DEVELOPMENT BLOCK GRANT AGREEMENT
BETWEEN
STATE OF ABC
DEPARTMENT OF COMMERCE
AND
XYZ COUNTY

This Community Development Block Grant (CDBG) agreement is made by and between the STATE OF ABC, DEPARTMENT OF COMMERCE (COMMERCE), located at [address], acting pursuant to [authorizing state code section] and XYZ COUNTY, (the RECIPIENT), acting pursuant to [authorizing state code section] and Title I of the Housing and Community Development Act of 1974, as amended. The RECIPIENT'S certifications relating to Title I assistance and the provisions contained in the *Consolidated Plan, Application Handbook, Labor Standards Handbook, Environmental Handbook, Procurement and Contracting Handbook* and *Information Bulletins* are hereby incorporated by reference, together with the resolution authorizing RECIPIENT'S actions attached, and made a part of this agreement.

In consideration of the mutual representations and obligations hereunder, COMMERCE and the RECIPIENT agree as follows:

SECTION 1.   GRANT AMOUNT:

SECTION 2.   PROJECTS FOR WHICH THIS FUNDING IS PROVIDED:

Activity No. 1. Administration: _____

Activity No. 2. Housing Rehabilitation: _____

Total FY 2005 regional account award amount: _____

SECTION 3.   SCOPE OF WORK

See page _____   [Page 129]

SECTION 4.   SPECIAL CONDITIONS

See page _____   [Page 129]

SECTION 5.   REVISIONS BETWEEN AGREEMENTS

The RECIPIENT agrees that if more than one agreement is issued to it, funded from the FY 2005 regional account, all will be considered as if they were one agreement for purposes of revisions in amounts between activities. Thus, the RECIPIENT may increase or decrease funds between said agreements as long as the total of all activities does not exceed the amount indicated above as the total funds awarded to the RECIPIENT from the FY 2005 regional account. All revisions will be subject to the requirements relative to amendments and communication letter changes (CLC).

SECTION 6.   ADMINISTRATION FUNDS

The RECIPIENT agrees that it may expend Activity No. 1 Administration funds on behalf of any agreement funded with FY 2005 regional account funds, if more than one is awarded. However, all administration funds will appear in and be paid from only one regional account agreement.

FIG. C-1 (CONTINUED)

SECTION 7.   PROFESSIONAL SERVICES AGREEMENT: DIRECT PAYMENT TO A COUNCIL OF GOVERNMENT (COG)

The RECIPIENT agrees that if COMMERCE has a signed professional services agreement with the applicable COG, the following shall apply: COMMERCE shall directly pay the COG for technical assistance and application preparation (TAAP) services provided by the COG to the RECIPIENT relating to its FY 2005 regional account applications upon presentation by a bill from the COG to COMMERCE. A copy of this bill shall also be provided to the RECIPIENT. Such funds shall be subtracted from the total amount of funds identified in Activity No. 1 Administration in this or other FY 2005 regional account agreement.

SECTION 8.   DURATION

The agreement shall become effective on the date indicated on Page 125. It shall remain in force until the first of the following: l) for twenty-four (24) months from the effective date which is the expiration date shown on Page 125, 2) full completion of the scope of work, or 3) termination pursuant to the terms of this agreement.

SECTION 9.   ENVIRONMENTAL REVIEW CONDITIONS

The funding assistance authorized hereunder shall not be obligated or utilized for any activities requiring a release of funds by the state of ABC under the environmental review procedures for the CDBG program until the applicable requirements contained in the *Environmental Handbook* have been satisfied.

SECTION 10.   APPLICATION AND OTHER PRE-AWARD COSTS

In accordance with federal procedures, the RECIPIENT may use CDBG funds to reimburse itself and/or the COG for costs incurred in preparing the application. In no event shall such compensation exceed 18 percent of the total FY 2005 regional account grant amount as shown on Page 125. In addition, the RECIPIENT may use CDBG funds to reimburse itself for other pre-award costs previously approved, in writing, by COMMERCE.

SECTION 11.   RECORDS RETENTION

Pursuant to [state code section], the RECIPIENT shall retain and shall require all of its subcontractors to retain, for inspection and audit by the state of ABC, all books, accounts, reports, files and other records relating to the bidding and performance of this agreement for a period of five (5) years after its completion. Upon request by COMMERCE, the RECIPIENT shall produce a legible copy of all such records at the administrative office of COMMERCE or at the office of the auditor general. The original of all such records shall be available and produced for inspection and audit when required by COMMERCE or the auditor general.

SECTION 12.   REVISIONS

The RECIPIENT may request revisions to this agreement compliant with the requirements of Chapter 2 of the *Commerce CDBG Administration Handbook.*

SECTION 13.   CANCELLATION

The provisions of [state code section] relating to cancellation of agreements are acknowledged and are incorporated by reference.

SECTION 14.   TERMINATION FOR CAUSE

COMMERCE may terminate this agreement in whole or in part at any time whenever it determines that the RECIPIENT has failed to comply with the conditions hereof. If COMMERCE so determines, it shall notify the RECIPIENT in writing by certified mail, return receipt requested, of such termination for cause with such notification to include the reason(s) for the termination and the effective date of the termination.

FIG. C-1 (CONTINUED)

SECTION 15. TERMINATION FOR CONVENIENCE

COMMERCE or the RECIPIENT may terminate this agreement in whole or in part (one or more activities) if either party believes that continuation would not produce beneficial results. In that event, COMMERCE shall allow the RECIPIENT full credit for the CDBG share of the obligations properly incurred by the RECIPIENT prior to termination, as long as those obligations where incurred in full compliance with this agreement and with applicable laws and regulations.

SECTION 16. OBLIGATION OF STATE GENERAL APPROPRIATIONS FUNDS

Nothing herein shall be construed as obligating state general appropriation funds for payment of any debt or liability of any nature arising hereunder. The parties expressly recognize that all payments to be made by COMMERCE are solely from federal funds made available to COMMERCE for this purpose.

SECTION 17. AVAILABILITY OF FEDERAL FUNDS

Payments under this agreement are subject to the availability of the federal funds provided to the state of ABC, Department of COMMERCE for the CDBG program.

SECTION 18. ARBITRATION

This agreement is subject to arbitration only to the extent required by [state code section].

SECTION 19. INDEMNIFICATION

The RECIPIENT shall indemnify COMMERCE and the state of ABC and shall hold them, their officers, agents and employees harmless against any and all liability, loss, damages sustained by any person or property by virtue of the RECIPIENT and its subcontractor's performance under this agreement.

SECTION 20. FEDERAL GOVERNMENT LIABILITY

It is agreed by all parties that neither the federal government nor the U.S. Department of Housing and Urban Development are parties to this agreement, and that no legal liability on the part of the federal government is inferred or implied under the terms of this agreement.

SECTION 21. AUDIT EXCEPTIONS

If federal or state audit exceptions are made relating to this agreement, the RECIPIENT shall reimburse all costs incurred by the state of ABC and COMMERCE associated with defending against the audit exception or performing an audit or follow-up audit, including but not limited to: audit fees, court costs, attorneys' fees based upon a reasonable hourly amount for attorneys in the community, travel costs, penalty assessments and all other costs of whatever nature. Immediately upon notification from COMMERCE, the RECIPIENT shall reimburse the amount of the audit exception and any other related costs directly to COMMERCE as specified by COMMERCE in the notification.

SECTION 22. UNALLOWABLE USE OF FUNDS

The RECIPIENT, its officers, employees and agents, shall not utilize any federal funds provided under this agreement to solicit or influence, or attempt to solicit or influence, directly or indirectly, any member of Congress regarding pending or prospective legislation.

SECTION 23. INTEREST OF MEMBERS OF DEPARTMENT OF COMMERCE AND OTHERS

No officer or employee of COMMERCE and no public official, employee or member of the governing body of the RECIPIENT who exercises any functions or responsibilities in review or approval of the undertaking or carrying out of the agreement shall participate in any decision relating to this agreement which affects their personal interest or the interest of any corporation, partnership or association in which they are directly or indirectly interested, or have any interest, direct or indirect, in this agreement or its proceeds.

Fig. C-1 (continued)

SECTION 24. ACCESS TO RECORDS, PARTICIPANTS AND STAFF

The RECIPIENT agrees to provide COMMERCE and its representatives access at any reasonable time to all participants and staff involved in this agreement and to all records and reports involving this agreement.

SECTION 25. IDENTIFICATION OF DOCUMENTS

All reports, maps and other documents completed as a part of this agreement, other than documents exclusively for internal use by COMMERCE, shall carry the following notation on the front cover or title page, together with the date (month and year) the document was prepared:

> "Preparation of this (report, map, document, etc.) was aided through a Community Development Block Grant from the state of ABC, Department of COMMERCE and as such is not copyrightable. It may be reprinted with customary crediting of the source.

> However, any opinions, findings, conclusions or recommendations expressed are those of the authors and do not necessarily reflect the views of the Department of COMMERCE."

All reports, maps, and other documents not completed as a part of this agreement but utilizing the results of this agreement shall carry due and proper acknowledgment of support from the COMMERCE CDBG program.

SECTION 26. COPYRIGHT

No reports, maps or other documents produced in whole or in part under this agreement shall be the subject of any application for copyright or copyright registration by or on behalf of the RECIPIENT or by any employee or subcontractor of the RECIPIENT.

The RECIPIENT shall advise COMMERCE or its designee at the time of delivery of any copyrighted or copyrightable work furnished under this agreement, or any adversely held copyrighted or copyrightable material incorporated in any such work and of any invasion of the right of privacy therein contained.

SECTION 27. RIGHTS IN DATA

COMMERCE may duplicate, use and disclose in any manner and for any purpose whatsoever, within the limits established by federal and state laws and regulations, all information relating to this agreement.

SECTION 28. FUNDING CONDITIONS

COMMERCE will make the funding assistance available to the RECIPIENT upon execution of this agreement by the parties. The obligation and utilization of the funding assistance provided through this agreement are subject to the proper observation of the requirements incorporated by reference. The RECIPIENT shall require any subrecipient entities to observe and follow all provisions of this agreement.

SECTION 29. NONDISCRIMINATION

The contractor shall comply with Executive Order 75-5, which mandates that all persons, regardless of race, color, religion, sex, age, national origin or political affiliation, shall have equal access to employment opportunities, and all other applicable state and federal employment laws, rules and regulations, including the Americans With Disabilities Act. The contractor shall take affirmative action to ensure that applicants for employment and employees are not discriminated against due to race, creed, color, religion, sex, age, national origin or disability.

Fig. C-1 (continued)

IN WITNESS WHEREOF, COMMERCE and the RECIPIENT have executed this agreement.

THE STATE OF ABC,
DEPARTMENT OF COMMERCE

BY: _____

TITLE: _____

DATE: _____

RECIPIENT/GRANTEE

BY: _____

TITLE: _____

DATE: _____

SECTION 3.   SCOPE OF WORK

Activity No. 1. Administration: _____ CDBG funds

Activity No. 2. Housing Rehabilitation: _____ CDBG funds

To provide approximately 13 grants of approximately _____ each for housing rehabilitation to approximately 13 owner-occupied households in XYZ County. The county will also perform housing rehab services. This activity will meet the housing low- and moderate-income benefit national objective and serve approximately 37 persons of whom 100 percent will be low to moderate income.

SECTION 4.   SPECIAL CONDITIONS

Prior to approval of the first request for payment, RECIPIENT shall have submitted and obtained CDBG program approval for its Housing Rehab Guidelines.

FIG. C-2
(ACCOMPANIES FIG. C-1)

APPLICANT CERTIFICATIONS FOR FY 2006

The applicant hereby assures and certifies that:

1. It possesses legal authority to apply for Community Development Block Grant (CDBG) funds, and to execute the proposed program.

2. Prior to the submission of the application, the applicant's governing body has duly adopted or passed as an official act a resolution authorizing the submission of the application, including all understandings, assurances, statutes, regulations and orders contained therein, and directing and authorizing the person identified as the official representative of the applicant to act in connection with the application and to provide such additional information as may be required.

3. Its chief executive officer or other officer of the applicant approved by the state:

   a. Consents to assume the status of a responsible federal official under the National Environmental Policy Act of 1969 (NEPA) and other provisions of federal law, as specified at 24 CFR §58.1 (a)(3) and (a)(4), which further the purposes of NEPA insofar as the provisions of such federal law apply to this program.

   b. Is authorized and consents on behalf of the applicant and him(her)self to accept the jurisdiction of the federal and state courts for the purpose of enforcement of his/her responsibilities as such an official.

4. It will comply with the provisions of Executive Order 11990, relating to evaluation of flood hazards and Executive Order 11288 relating to the prevention, control and abatement of water pollution.

5. It will, in connection with its performance of environmental assessments under the NEPA, comply with Section 106 of the National Historic Preservation Act of 1966 (16 U.S.C. §470), Executive Order 11593 and the Preservation of Archeological and Historical Data Act of 1966, P.L. 93-291 (16 U.S.C. §469a-1, *et. seq.*).

6. It will administer and enforce the labor standard requirements of the Davis-Bacon Act, as amended at 40 U.S.C. §§276a-276a-5, and the Contract Work Hours and Safety Standards Act at 40 U.S.C. §§327-333.

7. It will comply with the provisions of 24 CFR Part 24 relating to the employment, engagement of services, awarding of contracts or funding of any contractors or subcontractors during any period of debarment, suspension or placement in ineligibility status.

8. It shall comply with the requirements of the Lead Based Paint Poisoning Prevention Act, 42 U.S.C. §§4821-4846 and implementing regulations at 24 CFR Part 35.

9. It will comply with the provisions of 24 CFR Part 58, "Uniform Grant Administrative Requirements" and OMB Circular A-87.

10. It will comply with the Americans With Disabilities Act and Section 504 of the Rehabilitation Act, as amended.

11. It will comply with:

    a. Title VI of the Civil Rights Act of 1964 (P.L. 88-352), and the regulations issued pursuant thereto (24 CFR Part 1).

    b. Title VIII of the Civil Rights Act of 1968 (P.L. 90-284), as amended.

    c. Section 109 of the Housing and Community Development Act of 1974.

    d. Executive Order 11063 pertaining to equal opportunity in housing and nondiscrimination in the sale or rental of housing built with federal assistance.

Fig. C-2 (continued)

    e. Executive Order 11246, and the regulations issued pursuant thereto (24 CFR Part 130 and 41 CFR Chapter 60).

    f. Section 3 of the Housing and Urban Development Act of 1968, as amended.

    g. Federal Fair Housing Act of 1988, P.L. 100-430.

    h. The prohibitions against discrimination on the basis of age under the Age Discrimination Act of 1973, 42. U.S.C. §§6101-07, and the prohibitions against discrimination against persons with handicaps under Section 504 of the Rehabilitation Act of 1973, (P.L. 93-112), as amended, and the regulations at 24 CFR Part 8.

    i. The requirements of the Architectural Barriers Act of 1966 at 42 U.S.C. §§4151-415.

12. It will comply with the Uniform Relocation Assistance and Real Property Acquisition Policies Act of 1970 and implementing regulations.

13. It will comply with applicable conflict of interest provisions, incorporate such in all contracts and establish safeguards to prohibit employees from using positions for a purpose that is or gives the appearance of being motivated by a desire for private gain for themselves or others, particularly those with whom they have family, business or other ties.

14. It will comply with the provisions of the Hatch Act, which limit the political activity of employees.

15. It will give representatives of the state, the secretary of HUD, the inspector general, and the General Accounting Office access to all books, accounts, records, reports, files and other papers, things or property belonging to it or in use by it pertaining to the administration of state CDBG assistance.

16. It will ensure that the facilities under its ownership, lease or supervision which shall be utilized in the accomplishment of the program are not listed in the Environmental Protection Agency's (EPA) list of violating facilities and that it will notify the state of the receipt of any communication from director of the EPA Office of Federal Activities indicating that a facility to be used in the project is under consideration for listing by the EPA.

17. It will comply with the flood insurance purchase requirements of Section 102(a) of the Flood Disaster Protection Act of 1973, P.L. 93-234, 87 Stat. 975, approved Dec. 31, 1973, Section 103(a) required on and after March 2, 1974.

18. It has and will comply with the provisions of the state of ABC citizen participation plan for the state of ABC CDBG program.

19. It has developed plans to minimize displacement of persons as a result of activities assisted in whole or in part with CDBG funds and to assist persons actually displaced as a result of such activities, and has provided information about such plans to the public.

20. It will not recover any capital costs of public improvements assisted in whole or in part with CDBG funds by assessing any amount against properties owned and occupied by persons of low or moderate income, including any fee charged or assessment made as a condition of obtaining access to such public improvements unless:

    a. The CDBG funds are used to pay the proportion of the fee or assessment that is financed from other revenue sources; or

    b. It will certify to the state in writing that it lacks sufficient CDBG funds to comply with (a.) but that it will not assess properties owned by very low income persons.

21. It will provide all other funds/resources identified in the application, or any additional funds/resources necessary to complete the project as described in the application as submitted, or as may be later amended.

Fig. C-2 (CONTINUED)

22. It will comply with the requirements of the Single Audit Act Amendments of 1996 and OMB Circular A-133, and if the grant is closed out prior to all funds having been audited, it shall refund to Commerce any costs disallowed as a result of an audit conducted after the date of grant closeout.

23. It hereby adopts and will enforce a policy prohibiting the use of excessive force by law enforcement agencies within its jurisdiction against any individuals engaged in nonviolent civil rights demonstrations; and will enforce applicable state and local laws against physically barring entrance to or exit from a facility or location which is the subject of such nonviolent civil rights demonstrations within its jurisdiction.

24. It will ensure that, to the best of the knowledge and belief of the undersigned:

    a. No federal appropriated funds have been paid or will be paid, by or on behalf of the undersigned, to any person for influencing or attempting to influence an officer or employee of any agency, a member of Congress, an officer or employee of Congress, or an employee of a member of Congress in connection with the awarding of any federal contract, the making of any federal grant, the making of any federal loan, the entering into of any cooperative agreement, and the extension, continuation, renewal, amendment or modification of any federal contract, grant, loan or cooperative agreement.

    b. If any funds other than federal appropriated funds have been paid or will be paid to any person for influencing or attempting to influence an officer or employee of any agency, a member of Congress, and officer or employee of Congress, or an employee of a member of Congress in connection with this federal contract, grant, loan, or cooperative agreement, the undersigned shall complete and submit Standard Form–LLL, "Disclosure Form to Report Lobbying," in accordance with its instructions.

    c. The undersigned shall require that the language of this certification be included in the award documents for all subawards at all tiers (including subcontracts, subgrants and contracts under grants, loans and cooperative agreements) and that all subrecipients shall certify and disclose accordingly.

    This certification is a material representation of fact on which reliance was placed when this transaction was made or entered into. Submission of this certification is a prerequisite for making or entering into this transaction imposed by Section 1352, Title 31, U.S. Code. Any person who fails to file the required certification shall be subject to a civil penalty of not less than $10,000 and not more than $100,000 for each such failure.

25. It shall comply with the provisions of Section 102 of the HUD Reform Act of 1989.

CERTIFIED BY:

_____

Signature of Authorized Officer of the Applicant

_____

Typed Name and Title of Authorized Officer of the Applicant

Fig. C-3
Illustrative Subaward Agreement

COMMUNITY DEVELOPMENT BLOCK GRANT AGREEMENT
BETWEEN THE CITY OF ABC AND THE XYZ CENTER

This agreement made and entered into this ___ day of _____, 20___ by and between the city of ABC, a municipal corporation, hereinafter referred to as Subgrantor, and the XYZ Center, hereinafter referred to as Provider;

Whereas, the city of ABC has received a grant from the U.S. Department of Housing and Urban Development as part of its Community Development Block Grant Program for the period _____, 20___ to _____, 20___ (hereinafter the "contract period"); and

Whereas, the primary objective of the Community Development Block Grant Program is the development of viable urban communities, including decent housing and a suitable living environment and expanding economic opportunities principally for persons of low and moderate income, and

Now, therefore, in consideration of the mutual benefits contained herein the Subgrantor and Provider do agree as follows:

1. **Contract Documents:** Contract documents shall consist of this agreement and four (4) attachments, all of which are incorporated by reference into this agreement. Attachment I contains a description of the service and goals offered by the Provider (see Page 139). Attachment II is a line item budget (see Page 140). Attachment III outlines financial management procedures for use with Community Development Block Grant funds (see Page 141). Attachment IV contains all applicable federal regulations (see Page 142).

2. **Services:** The Provider agrees to perform those services outlined in Attachment I and II.

3. **Contract Amount:** The Subgrantor agrees to make available $_____ for use by the Provider for the contract period.

4. **Alterations:** Any alterations in the work program or the budget shall be submitted to and approved in writing by the Subgrantor.

5. **Quarterly Reports:** The Provider agrees to submit quarterly program progress reports on the 15th of October, the 15th of January, the 15th of April and the 15th of July to the director of Community Development. The Provider also agrees to submit on the 15th of July a comprehensive report covering the agreed-upon objectives, activities and expenditures for the entire contract period. Such shall include performance data, including data on client feedback, with respect to the goals and objectives outlined in Attachment I.

6. **Monitoring:** The Subgrantor will schedule two (2) monitoring visits with the Provider to evaluate the progress and performance of the program and provide technical assistance.

   The subgrantor shall be provided access to all program-related records and materials at these times.

7. **City Residents Only:** The Provider agrees that Community Development Block Grant Funds shall only be used to provide services to residents of the city of ABC.

8. **Subcontract:** No part of this agreement may be assigned or subcontracted without the prior written approval of the Subgrantor.

9. **Disputes:** Except as otherwise provided in this contract, any dispute concerning a question of fact arising under this contract which is not disposed of by agreement shall be decided by the director of Planning and Community Development, who shall reduce his decision in writing and furnish a copy thereof to the city manager and the Provider. The decision of the director of Planning and Community Development shall be final and conclusive unless, within ten (10) days from the date of receipt of such copy, the Provider furnishes a written appeal to the city manager. The decision of the city manager or his duly authorized representative for the determination of such appeals shall be promptly hand delivered

---

FIG. C-3 (CONTINUED)

---

or sent by certified mail to the Provider and such decision shall be final and conclusive unless appealed to a court of competent jurisdiction within thirty (30) days of receipt of the city manager's decision, and determined by that court to have been fraudulent, capricious or arbitrary, or so grossly erroneous as necessarily to imply bad faith, or not supported by substantial evidence. In connection with any appeal proceeding under this clause, the Provider shall be afforded an opportunity to be heard, to be represented by counsel at its own expense, if it so desires, and to offer evidence in support of its appeal. Pending final decision of a dispute hereunder, the Provider shall proceed diligently with the performance of the contract and in accordance with the decision of the contracting officer.

10. **Term:** This agreement shall remain in effect through the contract period with the understanding that at the end of the first fiscal year the ABC city council has the authority to reappropriate any remaining funds.

11. **Termination of Contract for Cause:** If, through any cause, the Provider shall fail to fulfill in a timely and proper manner its obligations under the contract, or if the Provider shall violate any of the covenants, agreements or stipulations of this contract, the Subgrantor shall thereupon have the right to terminate this contract by giving written notice to the Provider of such termination and specifying, the effective date thereof at least 30 days before the effective date of such termination. In that event, all finished or unfinished documents, data, studies, surveys, drawings, maps, models, photographs and reports prepared by the Provider shall become the property of the Subgrantor.

    Notwithstanding the above, the Provider shall not be relieved of liability to the Subgrantor for damages sustained by the Subgrantor by virtue of any breach of the contract by the Provider and the Subgrantor may withhold any payments to the Provider for the purpose of setoff until such time as the exact amount of damages due to the Subgrantor from the Provider is determined.

12. **Termination for Convenience of the Subgrantor:** The Subgrantor may terminate this contract at any time giving written notice to the Provider of such termination and specifying the effective date thereof, at least 30 days before the effective date of such termination. In that event, all finished or unfinished documents and other materials shall become the property of the Subgrantor. If the contract is terminated by the Subgrantor as provided herein, the Provider will be paid an amount representative of the time the Provider has actually performed under this contract.

13. **Equal Employment Opportunities:** The Provider shall comply with equal employment opportunities as stated in Executive Order 11246, entitled "Equal Employment Opportunity" as amended by Executive Order 11375, and as supplemented in Department of Labor regulations.

14. **Program Income:** Any "Program Income" (as such term is defined under applicable federal regulations) gained from any activity of the Provider, funded by CDBG funds shall be returned to the City.

15. **Religious Organizations or Owned Property:** CDBG funds may be used by religious organizations or on property owned by religious organizations only with prior written approval from the city and only in accordance with requirements set in 24 CFR §570.200(j).

16. **Reversion of Assets:** Within 30 days of the expiration of this agreement, the Provider shall transfer to the city any CDBG funds on hand at the time of expiration and any accounts receivable attributable to the use of CDBG funds. Any real property under the Provider's control that was acquired or improved in whole or in part with CDBG funds in excess of $25,000 shall be used or disposed of in accordance with 24 CFR §570.503 (A)(8).

FIG. C-3 (CONTINUED)

17. **Conformity to HUD Regulations:** The Provider agrees to abide by guidelines set forth by the U.S. Department of Housing and Urban Development for the administration and implementation of the Community Development Block Grant Program, including applicable Uniform Administrative Requirements set forth in 24 CFR §570.502, and applicable federal laws and regulations in 24 §CFR 570.600, *et seq.*

In this regard, the Provider agrees that duly authorized representatives of the U.S. Department of Housing and Urban Development shall have access to any books, documents, papers and records of the Provider that are directly pertinent to this agreement for the purpose of making audits, examinations, excerpts and transcriptions.

18. **Examination of Records:**

(A) The Provider agrees to make available books, records, documents and other evidence pertaining to the costs and expenses of this contract (hereinafter collectively called the "records") to the extent of such detail as will properly reflect all net costs, direct and indirect labor, materials, equipment, supplies and services, and other costs and expenses of whatever nature for which reimbursement is claimed under the provisions of this contract.

(B) The Provider agrees to make available at the office of the Provider at all reasonable times during the period of this contract any books, documents, papers or records of the Provider that directly pertain to, and involve transactions relating to this contract or subcontract hereunder for inspection, audit or reproduction by an authorized representative of the Subgrantor or the Department of Housing and Urban Development.

(C) The Provider shall preserve and make available its records until expiration of three years after final payment under this contract or for such longer period, if any, as is required by applicable statute, by any other clause of this contract, or by (1) or (2) below.

   (1) If this contract is completely or partially terminated, the records relating to the work terminated shall be preserved and made available until expiration of three years from the date of the resulting final settlement.

   (2) Records that related to (i) appeals under the "Disputes" clause of this contract, (ii) litigation or the settlement of claims arising out of the performance of this contract, (iii) cost and expenses of this contract as to which exception has been taken by the auditor of the Department of Housing and Urban Development or any of its duly authorized representatives, shall be retained by the Provider under such appeals, litigation, claims, or exceptions have been disposed of.

(D) The Provider further agrees to include in each of its subcontracts hereunder, a provision to the effect that the subcontractor agrees that the auditor of the Department of Housing and Urban Development or any of its duly authorized representatives shall, until the expiration of three years after final payment under the contract, have right to examine any books, documents, papers, and records of such subcontractor that directly pertain to, and involve transactions relating to the subcontract. The term "subcontractor", as used in his paragraph only excludes
(i) purchase orders not exceeding $2,500 and (ii) subcontracts or purchase of public utility services with rates established for uniform applicability to the general public.

19. **Insurance to be Provided by Provider:** The Provider must, prior to the contract, file with the Subgrantor certificates or policies of workers' compensation, public liability, automobile liability (including non-ownership and hired vehicles) and property damage insurance satisfactory to the Subgrantor and in compliance with the law, and in form and amount sufficient to protect the Subgrantor. Each certificate or policy shall carry the provision that the insurance shall not be canceled or reduced without prior notice to the Subgrantor. All insurance required by this paragraph of the contract shall be and remain in full force and effect for the entire contract period, and the Subgrantor shall be named as an additional

Fig. C-3 (continued)

insured under such insurance contracts, which shall contain a stipulation that the insurance provided shall not terminate, lapse or otherwise expire, prior to thirty (30) days written notice to that effect, given by the insurance carrier to the Subgrantor, and that the insurance carrier will not invoke the defense of performance of a governmental function by the Provider in performing this contract.

The minimum limits of liability coverage shall be as follows:

(A) Comprehensive general liability, including premises and operations; elevator liability; providers protective liability; products liability including completed operations coverage; and contractual liability for this contract.

> Limits: $1,000,000/2,000,000
> (per occurrence/annual aggregate)

(B) Comprehensive automobile liability, including all owned automobiles; non-owned automobiles; hired car coverage.

> Limits: $500,000/I,000,000
> (per occurrence/annual aggregate)

(C) Workers' compensation, including employer's liability.

> Limits: Statutory
> Employer's Liability $100,000

This agreement, shall be binding upon all parties hereto and their respective heirs, executors, administrators, successors and assigns.

In witness thereof, the parties hereto leave executed or caused to be executed by their duly authorized officials, this agreement in five (5) copies, each of which shall be deemed an original on the date first above written.

CITY OF ABC

_____   _____

City Manager   PROVIDER AGENCY

_____   _____

SIGNATURE   TYPED NAME AND TITLE

FUNDS AVAILABLE

_____

DIRECTOR OF FINANCE

APPROVED AS TO FORM:

_____

CITY ATTORNEY

FIG. C-3 (CONTINUED)

CDBG Contract
_____, 20___ – _____, 20___

Attachment II
Budget

Block Grant Budget for 20___ – ___ Contract

Contract Amount $

	Average Cost Per Unit_____Total	
Materials:	$ _____ x	_____
Program Support:		
Crew Labor	_____	_____
Warehouse	_____	_____
Tools/Equipment	_____	_____
Vehicle Expense	_____	_____
Non-Crew Labor	_____	_____
Total Materials & Program Support:	_____	_____
Administration:	_____	_____
Indirect Costs:	_____	_____
Totals:	_____	_____

FIG. C-3 (CONTINUED)

Attachment III
Guidelines for Financial Management of CDBG-Funded Activities

To comply with federal regulations, each program must have a financial management system that provides accurate, current and complete disclosure of the financial status of the activity. This means the financial system must be capable of generating regular financial status reports which indicate the dollar amount allocated for each activity (including any budget revisions), amount obligated (i.e., for which contract exists), and the amount expended for each activity. The system must permit the comparison of actual expenditures and revenues against budgeted amounts. The city must be able to isolate and to trace every CDBG dollar received and prove where it went and for what it was used.

Accounting records must be supported by source documentation. Invoices, bills of lading, purchase vouchers, payrolls and the like must be secured and retained for four years in order to show for what purpose funds were spent. Payments should not be made without invoices and vouchers physically in hand. All vouchers/invoices should be on vendors' letterhead.

All employees paid in whole or in part from CDBG funds should prepare a time sheet indicating the hours worked on CDBG projects for each pay period. Based on these time sheets and the hourly payroll costs for each employee, a voucher statement indicating the distribution of payroll charges should be prepared and placed in the appropriate files.

The city is responsible for reviewing and certifying the financial management of any operating agency which is not a city department or bureau, in order to determine whether or not it meets all of the above requirements. If the agency's system does not meet these requirements and modifications are not possible, the city must administer the CDBG funds for the operating agency.

Financial records are to be retained for a period of four years, with access guaranteed to HUD or Treasury officials or their representative.

One copy of the vendors' audited financial statement shall be submitted to the city immediately following the end of the vendors' fiscal year(s) during which CDBG funds are received.

Payment to providers will be on a reimbursement basis to be submitted to:

_____

Grants Coordinator

_____

Street Address

_____

City, State, Zip

Requests are to be submitted on Provider's letterhead in a format consistent with the budget attachment, including an analysis of expenses to budget. A cash advance may be available upon special request.

FIG. C-3 (CONTINUED)

Attachment IV
Applicable Federal Regulations

Compliance with Section 109 of the Housing and Community Development Act of 1974

The work to be performed under this contract is subject to the requirements of Section 109 of the Housing and Community Development Act of 1974, which states that:

> "No person in the United States shall, on the ground of race, color, national origin, sex or handicap, be excluded from participation in, be denied the benefits of or be subjected to discrimination under any program or activity funded in whole or in part with funds available under this title."

Compliance with the Equal Opportunity Provisions of Executive Order No. 11246

In carrying out the contract, the contractor shall not discriminate against any employee or applicant for employment because of race, color, religion, sex, handicap or national origin. The contractor shall take affirmative action to insure that applicants for employment are employed, and that employees are treated during employment, without regard to their race, color, religion, sex, handicap or national origin. Such action shall include, but not be limited to, the following: employment, upgrading, demotion or transfer; recruitment or recruitment advertising; layoff or termination; rates of pay or other forms of compensation; and selection for training, including apprenticeship. The contractor shall post in conspicuous places, available to employees and applicants for employment, notices to be provided by the government setting forth the provisions of this nondiscrimination clause. The contractor shall state that all qualified applicants will receive consideration for employment without regard to race, color, religion, sex, handicap or national origin.

Compliance with Section 3 of the Housing and Urban Development Act of 1968

During the performance of this contract the contractor agrees as follows:

A. The work to be performed under this contract is on a project assisted under a program providing direct federal financial assistance from the Department of Housing and Urban Development and is subject to the requirements of Section 3 of the Housing and Urban Development Action of 1968, as amended, 12 U.S.C. 170 lu. Section 3 requires that, to the greatest extent feasible, opportunities for training and employment be given lower income residents of the project area and contracts for work in connection with the project be awarded to business concerns which are located in, or owned in substantial part, by persons in the area of the project.

B. The parties to this contract will comply with the provisions of said Section 3 and the regulations issued pursuant thereto by the Secretary of Housing and Urban Development set forth in 24 CFR, and all applicable rules and orders of the Department issued thereunder prior to the execution of this contract. The parties to this contract certify and agree that they are under no contractual or other disability which would prevent them from complying with these requirements.

C. The contractor will send to each labor organization or representative of workers with which he has a collective bargaining agreement or other contract or understanding, if any, a notice advising the said labor organization or workers representative of his commitments under this Section 3 clause and shall post copies of the notice in conspicuous places available to employees and applicants for employment or training.

D. The contractor will include this Section 3 clause in every subcontract for work in connection with the project and will, at the direction of the applicant for, or recipient of federal financial assistance, take appropriate action pursuant to the subcontract upon a finding that the subcontractor is in violation of regulations issued by the secretary of Housing and Urban Development, 24 CFR. The contractor will not subcontract with any subcontractor where it has notice or knowledge that the latter has been found in violation of regulations under 24 CFR and will not let any subcontract unless the subcontractor

---

FIG. C-3 (CONTINUED)

---

has first provided it with a preliminary statements of ability to comply with the requirements of these regulations.

E. Compliance with the provisions of section 3, the regulations set forth in 24 CFR, and all applicable rules and orders of the department issued thereunder prior to the execution of the contract, shall be a condition of the federal financial assistance provided to the project, binding upon the applicant or recipient of such assistance, its successors and assigns. Failure to fulfill these requirements shall subject the applicant or recipient for such assistance, its successors and assigns to those sanctions specified by the grant or loan agreement or contract through which federal assistance is provided, and to such sanctions as are specified by 24 CFR Part 135.

Conflict of Interest

No member of the governing body, or employee of the City of ABC or its designees or agents, and no other public official of such locality who exercises any functions or responsibilities with respect to the Community Development Block Grant Program, during his tenure or for one year thereafter, shall have any interest, direct or indirect, in this contract, or any subcontracts or the proceeds thereof.

Compliance with Lead-Based Paint Regulations

All construction, rehabilitation, or modernization of residential structures provided under this contract shall comply with the provisions of the Lead-Based Paint Poisoning Prevention Act (84 Stat. 2080; 42 USC 4841(3)) and the regulations thereunder (24 CFR Part 35).

Compliance with Section 504 of the Rehabilitation Act of 1973, as amended

The work to be performed under this contract is subject to the requirement of Section 504 of the Rehabilitation Act of 1973, as amended, which states that: "No otherwise qualified handicapped individual in the United States . . . shall, solely by reason of his handicap, be excluded from the participation in, be denied the benefits of, or be subjected to discrimination under any program or activity receiving federal financial assistance or under any program or activity conducted by any executive agency."

Fig. C-4

PROTOTYPE OF A FEDERAL SUBAWARD AGREEMENT

University of California, Berkeley

UCB Agreement Number _____

This Agreement is entered into by and between The Regents of the University of California, for the Berkeley campus "California" and "Institution." This agreement is for the performance of a portion of the work originally awarded to California from "Granting Agency" "grant _____" under the direction of Principal Investigator "P.I.'s Name," the parties agree to the following terms and conditions:

ARTICLE I. STATEMENT OF WORK: "Institution" shall exercise its best efforts to carry out the program indicated in Exhibit A, which is incorporated herein and made a part of this agreement.

ARTICLE II. PERIOD OF PERFORMANCE: The period of performance shall be from "begin date" to "end date." These dates are subject to "Granting Agency's" continued support of California.

ARTICLE III. CONSIDERATION: California will reimburse "Institution" actual costs for the performance of work under this agreement in the amount not to exceed $_____ which is based on the budget incorporated into this agreement as Exhibit B.

ARTICLE IV. PAYMENTS: California will reimburse "Institution" upon receipt of monthly invoices provided by "Institution." Invoices shall identify expenditures by major budget categories (i.e., salaries, fringe benefits, equipment, travel, supplies, etc.) as provided in Exhibit B. Invoices shall be dated, numbered, make reference to UCB Agreement Number _____ and be mailed to:

"Administrator's Name," "Administering Unit," "Address," University of California

ARTICLE V. PROJECT MANAGEMENT: For technical matters: California's principal investigator "P.I. name" is responsible for the overall conduct of the project. PI is responsible for technical monitoring and guidance.

"Institution's" "P.I. name" is responsible for "Institution's" portion of the project. No substitution may be made of "Institution" principal investigator without prior written approval from California.

For Business Matters:

- For California: "Senior Research Administrator," Sponsored Projects Office, UCB

- For "Institution": "Institution," Authorized Official

ARTICLE VI. REPORTS: "Institution" shall furnish California technical progress reports as required by California's P.I. Final technical report shall be submitted to California within 60 days of the project end date or within 60 days of the termination date whichever comes first. Reports are to be submitted to:

"Principal Investigator's Name," "Address"

ARTICLE VII. COPYRIGHT/PATENT: "Institution" may assert copyright on materials that it produces in the performance of the work of this agreement. California and "Agency" shall have the right to a non-transferable, irrevocable, worldwide, royalty-free, non-exclusive license to use, reproduce, publish or re-publish, or otherwise disseminate such copyrighted materials.

The standard patent rights clause found at [insert applicable federal agency regulation citation] is incorporated herein by reference.

ARTICLE VIII. RECORD RETENTION: Financial record, supporting documents and other record pertaining to this agreement shall be maintained and retained by "Institution" for a period of three years from the termination date of this agreement.

Source: University of California, Berkeley, http://www.spo.berkeley.edu/Forms/model agree/subgrant.html.

FIG. C-4 (CONTINUED)

ARTICLE IX. PUBLICATIONS: "Institution" agrees that all publications that result from work under this agreement will acknowledge that the project was supported by "Grant No. XXX" under a grant from "Granting Agency."

ARTICLE X. SUSPENSION/TERMINATION: In the event the "Granting Agency" suspends its grant to California, California shall suspend this agreement to "Institution." Notification of suspension shall be in writing from California. California will be unable to reimburse any expenses under suspension unless and until "Granting Agency" reimburses California for such costs.

Either party may terminate this agreement upon thirty days advance written notice to the other party. However, in the event that the "Granting Agency" terminates the grant to California prior to the project's end date as stated in Article II, this agreement will be immediately terminated. In the event of any form of termination, California will reimburse "Institution" for all expenses incurred through the date of termination.

ARTICLE XI. GENERAL PROVISIONS AND CERTIFICATIONS: All terms and conditions set forth in "Granting Agency's" policies "X,Y,Z" shall apply to this agreement and are incorporated herein by reference.

In addition "Institution" certifies that:

1. It is not delinquent on the repayment of any federal debt.

2. It is presently not debarred, suspended, proposed for debarment, declared ineligible, nor voluntarily excluded from covered transactions by any federal department or agency.

3. It is in compliance with the Drug-Free Work Place Act of 1988.

4. It is in compliance with P.L. 101-122, Section 1352 which covers restrictions regarding lobbying.

5. It has filed the assurances required under PHS final rule entitled "Responsibilities of Awardee and Applicant Institution for Dealing with and Reporting Possible Misconduct in Science."

6. It is in compliance with the federal financial disclosure requirements (PHS/NSF only).

ARTICLE XII. CHANGES: This agreement constitutes the entire agreement between the parties regarding the subject matter herein. Any modification to this agreement shall be made in writing and must be signed by the authorized representatives of both parties.

FOR INSTITUTION

By: _____ (signature) _____ (title)

    _____ (typed name) _____ (date signed)

FOR THE REGENTS OF THE UNIVERSITY OF CALIFORNIA

By: _____ (signature) _____ (title)

    _____ (typed name) _____ (date signed)

FIG. C-4 (CONTINUED)

Exhibit A
Scope of Work

[Insert approved scope of work proposed by "Institution"]

FIG. C-4 (CONTINUED)

Exhibit B
Budget

[Insert approved budget]

FIG. C-5

SAMPLE SUBAGREEMENT BETWEEN A UNIVERSITY AND A SUBAWARDEE

When the University has received a federal contract or grant and needs to assign work to a commercial collaborator/participant, and arrange for payment of their costs under the grant, it should use this subagreement.

This is intended as a starting draft. Not all clauses, definitions, etc. will be applicable to any specific transaction. This document MUST be tailored to the specific transaction through extensive consultation with the campus requester and interactive negotiation and understandings between the subawardee, research administrator and principle investigator.

SUBAGREEMENT NO.

between

THE REGENTS OF THE UNIVERSITY OF CALIFORNIA, BERKELEY

and

[INSERT SUBAWARDEE NAME]

THIS SUBAGREEMENT is made and entered into this _____ 2005, by and between THE REGENTS OF THE UNIVERSITY OF CALIFORNIA, BERKELEY ("California") and ("Subawardee").

WHEREAS, California has received funding from the ("Sponsor"), under (grant/contract) number _____ __ and _____

WHEREAS, California's effort requires the participation of Subawardee as set forth in the proposal which resulted in the above award;

NOW THEREFORE, in consideration of the mutual promises set forth below, California and Subawardee agree as follows:

ARTICLE I. STATEMENT OF WORK

A. INTRODUCTION: Subawardee shall exercise its best efforts to carry out the program of research described in Exhibit A, which is incorporated herein and made a part of this agreement.

B. DELIVERABLES:

ARTICLE II. PERIOD OF PERFORMANCE

The authorized period of performance of this subagreement is from _____ through _____.

Add, if appropriate: It is anticipated that this subagreement will be amended annually/periodically to add additional performance/budget periods with an ultimate end date of _____ .

ARTICLE III. COST, BILLING, AND PAYMENT

A. (i) This subagreement provides for payment on a cost-reimbursement basis. The total estimated cost shall be in general accordance with the budget attached as Exhibit B.

(ii) The amount authorized for expenditure (under this allotment) is $_____ . This amount shall not be exceeded unless this subagreement is amended to add additional funds.

Source: University of California, Berkeley, http://www.spo.berkeley.edu/Forms/model agree/industry.html.

FIG. C-5 (CONTINUED)

Add, if appropriate:

(iii) The (award under which this subagreement is written is expected to have a duration longer than that authorized in Article II above, and the) total award amount authorized is expected to be increased in accordance with the proposal and Exhibit B. Subawardee is not obligated to continue work in excess of the amount reflected in Paragraph A-ii above, and California is not obligated to reimburse costs in excess of that amount unless this subagreement is amended to increase the amount of Paragraph A-ii.

B. Subawardee may bill California monthly for reimbursement of actual costs incurred in the performance of this Subagreement. Invoices shall be numbered, dated, cite this subagreement number, show cost incurred by budget category (i.e., salaries, fringe benefits, equipment, travel, supplies, etc.) for the billing period and cumulative to date, and be submitted to: [insert address]

C. California will make provisional payment on all invoices submitted in accordance with the terms of this agreement. The final invoice, clearly marked "Final," must be submitted within 90 days after the expiration date of this agreement. The final invoice shall include the following certification: "Payment of this final invoice shall constitute complete satisfaction of all of California's obligations under this agreement and Subawardee releases and discharges California from all further claims and obligations upon payment hereof."

ARTICLE IV. RECORDS AND AUDITS

Subawardee shall maintain accurate records of all costs incurred in the performance of this work and agrees to allow representatives of California and Sponsor reasonable access to its records to verify the validity of expenses reimbursed under this subagreement. Subawardee hereby warrants that it conducts audits as required by OMB Circulars, federal cost principles, or cost accounting standards applicable to its performance as a recipient of U.S. government funds and that such audit has revealed no material findings. Subawardee shall maintain financial records, supporting documents and other records pertaining to this agreement for a period of five years from the termination date of this agreement.

ARTICLE V. PUBLICITY AND PUBLICATION

Subawardee shall not, without the prior written consent of California, issue any press releases or in any manner advertise the fact that Subawardee has entered into this subagreement. All publications resulting from the work under this agreement will acknowledge that the project was supported by the federal award identified in the recitals of this subagreement.

ARTICLE VI. SUBCONTRACTING AND ASSIGNMENT

Subawardee shall perform the work contemplated with resources available within its own organization and no portion of the work shall be subcontracted, nor shall this subagreement be assigned, without the prior written authorization of California. Nothing contained in this subagreement shall create any contractual or agency relationship between a lower tier subawardee or assignee and California.

ARTICLE VII. KEY PERSONNEL

A. California's principal investigator is Professor _____, who is responsible for the overall conduct of the project, technical monitoring, and guidance.

B. Subawardee's principal investigator is _____. No substitution may be made by Subawardee without the written consent of California.

ARTICLE VIII. TERMINATION

A. Either party may terminate this subagreement upon thirty (30) days written notice to the other party. In the event of termination, Subawardee shall be entitled to reimbursement for all costs incurred to the date of termination and for all uncancellable obligations. In no event, however, shall the termination

Fig. C-5 (continued)

settlement cause the total amount paid to Subawardee to exceed the estimated cost set forth in Paragraph A of Article III above.

B. Within 60 days of the effective date of termination, Subawardee shall submit to California a final report, a final financial report and final invoice.

ARTICLE IX. CHANGES

California, within the general scope of this subagreement, may, at any time, by written notice to Subawardee, issue additional instructions, require additional services or direct the omission of services covered by this subagreement. In such event, there will be made an equitable adjustment in price and time of performance, but any claim for such an adjustment must be made within thirty (30) days of the receipt of said written notice.

ARTICLE X. INDEMNIFICATION

A. California shall defend, indemnify and hold Subawardee, its officers, employees and agents harmless from and against any and all liability, loss, expense (including reasonable attorneys' fees) or claims for injury or damages arising out of the performance of this subagreement but only in proportion to and to the extent such liability, loss, expense, attorneys' fees or claims for injury or damages are caused by or result from the negligent or intentional acts or omissions of California, its officers, agents or employees.

B. Subawardee shall defend, indemnify and hold California, its officers, employees and agents harmless from and against any and all liability, loss, expense (including reasonable attorneys' fees), or claims for injury or damages arising out of the performance of this subagreement but only in proportion to and to the extent such liability, loss, expense, attorneys' fees or claims for injury or damages are caused by or result from the negligent or intentional acts or omissions of Subawardee, its officers, agents or employees.

ARTICLE XI. DATA RIGHTS

Subawardee holds all rights, title, and interest in the data and works it creates in the performance of this subagreement. Subawardee hereby grants to California, a royalty-free non-exclusive, irrevocable license to reproduce, translate, publish, use and dispose of, and to authorize others to do so, all data collected. As used in this clause, data collected means the original records of scientific and technical data collected during the performance of the work by the principal investigator or the project personnel. Data collected includes, but is not limited to, notebooks, drawings, lists, specifications and computations, in written, pictorial, graphic or machine form.

ARTICLE XII. PATENT RIGHTS

This subagreement is funded by an award from the U.S. Government. Subawardee is therefore granted patent rights in accordance with 37 CFR Part 401 or FAR §52.227-11, or in accordance with FAR §52.227-12 if it is a commercial entity and the prime federal sponsor is the U.S. Department of Defense or National Aeronautics and Space Administration.

ARTICLE XIII. CONFIDENTIALITY

It is expected that the work of this subagreement can be carried out without any of the parties disclosing confidential information to the other parties. However, should it become necessary to disclose confidential information, the parties will notify each other in advance of the disclosure and will negotiate in good faith with respect to protecting such confidential information.

ARTICLE XIV. DISPUTES

Any dispute arising under this subagreement which is not settled by subagreement of the parties may be settled by mediation, arbitration, or other appropriate legal proceedings. Pending any decision, appeal or judgment in such proceedings or the settlement of any dispute arising under this subagreement, Subaward-

---

FIG. C-5 (CONTINUED)

---

ee shall proceed diligently with the performance of this subagreement in accordance with the decision of California.

ARTICLE XV. INDEPENDENT CONTRACTOR

Subawardee and its employees, consultants, agents or independent contractors will perform all services under this agreement as independent contractors. Nothing in this agreement will be deemed to create an employer-employee or principal-agent relationship between California and Subawardee's employees, consultants, agents or independent contractors. Subawardee and its employees, consultants, agents and lower tier subawardees will not, by virtue of any services provided under this agreement, be entitled to participate, as an employee or otherwise, in or under any employee benefit plan of California or any other employment right or benefit available to or enjoyed by employees of California.

ARTICLE XVI. GENERAL PROVISIONS AND CERTIFICATIONS

If this subagreement is a Subaward under a federal grant or cooperative agreement, Subawardee certifies that:

1. It is not delinquent on the repayment of any federal debt.

2. It is presently not debarred, suspended, proposed for debarment, declared ineligible nor voluntarily excluded from covered transactions by any federal department or agency.

3. It is in compliance with the Drug-Free Work Place Act of 1988.

4. It is in compliance with P.L. 101-122, Section 1352, which covers restrictions regarding lobbying.

5. It has filed the assurances required under PHS final rule entitled "Responsibilities of Awardee and Applicant Institution for Dealing with and Reporting Possible Misconduct in Science."

6. It is in compliance with the federal financial disclosure requirements (PHS/NSF only).

ARTICLE XVII. PRIME AWARD PROVISIONS AND ATTACHMENTS

The following provisions of the prime award to California are incorporated by attachment, and are applicable to Subawardee and Subawardee's lower tier subagreements:

If this is written under a contract, you can use the list prepared by OP, located at (http://www.ucop.edu/matmgt/matmgt/supp5.html) and add any additional provisions from the prime award under which this is written. If using the OP list, delete FAR §52.215-26 and FAR §52.222-1 (pursuant to FAC 90-43).

ARTICLE XVIII. INTEGRATION

This subagreement states the entire contact between the parties in respect to the subject matter of the subagreement and supersedes any previous written or oral representations, statements, negotiations, or agreements. This subagreement may be modified only by written agreement executed by authorized representatives of both parties.

FIG. C-5 (CONTINUED)

IN WITNESS WHEREOF, the parties hereto have caused this subagreement to be executed by their duly authorized representatives.

FOR   THE REGENTS OF THE UNIVERSITY
                                                OF CALIFORNIA, BERKELEY
("Subawardee")   ("California")

By: _____   By: _____

Name: _____   Name: _____

Title: _____   Title: _____

Date: _____   Date: _____

FIG. C-5 (CONTINUED)

Exhibit A
Scope of Work

[Insert approved scope of work proposed by "Institution"]

Fɪɢ. C-5 (ᴄᴏɴᴛɪɴᴜᴇᴅ)

Exhibit B
Budget

[Insert approved budget]

Fig. C-6
Sample Subaward Agreement for Research Project

SUBAWARD AGREEMENT		
NPC:	SUBRECIPIENT:	
Prime Award no.	Subaward No.	
Prime Award Agency/Prime Sponsor	CFDA No./Subrecipient DUNS No.	
Subaward Period of Performance	Amount Funded this Action:	Est. Total, if incrementally funded: N/A
Project Title:		

This Subaward Agreement is entered into on this XXXX day of XXXX, 20XX to specify the terms and conditions under which **NPC** (hereinafter referred to as "**NPC**") and XXXX (hereinafter referred to as "SUBRECIPIENT"), individually and collectively hereinafter referred to as "the Parties", will participate in the conduct of a project supported by the XXXX (hereinafter referred to as "PRIME SPONSOR") entitled XXXX, grant number, XXXXX ("Prime Award").

The rules and regulations, terms and conditions governing the PRIME SPONSOR's award to **NPC** are by this reference hereby incorporated into this Subaward Agreement including but not limited to Civil Rights, Handicapped Individuals, Sex Discrimination, Debarment and Suspension, Non-Delinquency on Federal Debt, Restrictions on Lobbying (if applicable), Anti-Kickback, Conflict of Interest, and Scientific Misconduct.

1. Scope of Work

SUBRECIPIENT agrees to provide all the necessary qualified personnel, equipment, materials (except as otherwise may be provided herein), and facilities to perform the work as described in its proposal dated XXXXX which by this reference is incorporated into this Subaward Agreement at Attachment A. Any change in the scope of work requires prior written approval of **NPC**. SUBRECIPIENT agrees to use its reasonable best efforts to perform the work within the estimated cost and within the period of performance.

2. Period of Performance

The period of performance of this Subaward Agreement shall be from XXXXX through XXXX unless extended by amendment of this Agreement.

3. Estimated Cost

NPC agrees to pay SUBRECIPIENT an amount not to exceed $XX,XXX for work described in Attachment A. Funds provided may only be used for the project referenced in Attachment A. Any unexpended funds advanced shall be refunded to **NPC** with the final financial report upon termination or expiration of this Subaward Agreement.

4. Availability of Funds

Payment for all services provided pursuant to this Subaward Agreement is contingent upon the availability of funds from the PRIME SPONSOR. In the event such funds are not provided or not available to **NPC**, **NPC** may immediately terminate this Agreement for unavailability of funds. In this event, **NPC** shall inform SUBRECIPIENT of such unavailability as soon as it is known, and to the extent legally possible pay all outstanding amounts due. In the event that funds are reduced from the PRIME SPONSOR, **NPC** may unilaterally revise SUBRECIPIENT's scope of work as described in Attachment A and reduce SUBRECIPIENT's funds accordingly. **NPC** shall provide SUBRECIPIENT with notice of such reduction and change in scope of work as soon as it is known.

FIG. C-6 (CONTINUED)

---

5.   Key Personnel

The SUBRECIPIENT Principal Investigator for the performance of this subaward is Dr. XXXX. If for any reason the SUBRECIPIENT Principal Investigator cannot continue his or her duties, SUBRECIPIENT will appoint a successor, subject to the approval of **NPC**. If the Parties cannot agree on a successor, either Party may terminate this Subaward Agreement in accordance with the terms of Article 22.

All work under this Subaward Agreement shall be performed under the general guidance and technical direction of the **NPC** Principal Investigator, Dr. XXXX ("Project Director"). Such guidance and direction shall not, however, affect any change in the cost structure of this Agreement, increase its estimated cost, or extend the period of performance. Only **NPC** and SUBRECIPIENT's Authorized Official shall mutually make such changes, in writing.

The Project Director is responsible for: monitoring the SUBRECIPIENT's technical progress, including the surveillance and assessment of performance and recommending changes in requirements; interpreting the statement of work and any other technical performance requirements; performing technical evaluation as required; performing technical inspections and acceptances required by this Agreement; assisting in the resolution of technical problems encountered during performance.

6.   Authorized Representatives

The Authorized Representatives of **NPC** and SUBRECIPIENT for technical and administrative matters are listed in the Attachment B to this Subaward Agreement. Changes to the authorized representatives will be communicated in writing between Parties, without necessity of a formal amendment.

7.   Prior Approvals

The SUBRECIPIENT is hereby authorized to re-budget in accordance with the terms and conditions of the Prime Award and NIH Grants Policy Statement, unless specific prior approval restrictions are provided in this Article. SUBRECIPIENT shall obtain written approval from the **NPC** Authorized Official named in Attachment B for any actions requiring **NPC** prior approval.

The following require prior approval of **NPC**'s Authorized Official:

- Change in Key Personnel (Article 5)
- Carry-forward of unobligated balance to future budget years
- Subawards not referenced in Attachment A
- No-cost time extension
- Rebudgeting within categories of more than 25% of total costs.
- Any others required by Project Director or referenced in the Prime Award.

8.   Intellectual Property

The determination of the rights of ownership and disposition of inventions resulting from the performance of the research under this Subaward Agreement shall be in accordance with Article 31.D. SUBRECIPIENT will ensure that this policy is applicable to all persons who perform any part of the work under this Agreement and who may be reasonably expected to make inventions. Compliance with the Standard Patent Rights clauses as specified in 37 C.F.R., Part 401.14, FAR 52.227-11, or 35 U.S.C. 200 et.seq., whichever is appropriate and applicable.

9.   Reports

A. Final Technical Reports. SUBRECIPIENT shall submit a technical report to the Project Director, describing accomplishments and significant research findings derived from the work conducted under this Subaward Agreement within 45 days after the end date specified under Article 2.

Fig. C-6 (continued)

B. Property Reports. If property is acquired under this Subaward Agreement and property reports are a requirement of the Prime Award, SUBRECIPIENT shall submit a report of equipment purchased to *NPC*'s Accounting Office at *123 Address, Anywhere, State 12345* within 45 days of the Agreement end date.

C. Case Reports/Deliverables (Human Subjects/Animal Studies). If the scope of work set forth in Attachment A is being conducted under a protocol for human subjects or animals, SUBRECIPIENT agrees to timely submit all completed case report forms, questionnaires and/or records to *NPC* as required under the protocol. *NPC* reserves the right to use any data, questionnaire and/or record pursuant to the Health Insurance Portability and Accountability Act ("HIPAA") and related regulations for publication purposes or for any business, education or research purpose it deems applicable, including, without limitation, for submission to any regulatory agency, domestic or foreign.

D. Any additional reports are due as detailed in the Terms of Award from the PRIME SPONSOR and are incorporated into this Subaward Agreement at Attachment A.

10.   Data Collection

If data collection activities are being performed under this Subaward Agreement, the data collection activities are the responsibility of SUBRECIPIENT. The PRIME SPONSOR and *NPC*'s support do not constitute approval of the accuracy or content of any survey design, questionnaire content or data collection procedures.

11.   Site Visits

NPC and PRIME SPONSOR, through authorized representatives, have the right, at all reasonable times, to make site visits to review project accomplishments and to provide such technical assistance as may be required. If any site visit is made on the premises of SUBRECIPIENT, SUBRECIPIENT shall provide all reasonable facilities and assistance for the safety and convenience of *NPC* and PRIME SPONSOR's representatives in the performance of their duties. All site visits and evaluations shall be performed in such a manner as will not unduly interfere with or delay the work.

12.   Human Subjects

If the scope of work as described in Attachment A involves use of human subjects, such use will be in accordance with 45 C.F.R. 46, Subpart A "Protection of Human Subjects." As applicable, evidence of approval by the SUBRECIPIENT's Institutional Review Board shall be provided to *NPC* prior to initiating this project and annually thereafter for the duration of this Subaward Agreement.

13.   Biologic Material

SUBRECIPIENT certifies that Biologic Materials will be used or obtained solely in performance of the work set forth in Attachment A. The term "Biologic Materials" shall include the materials derived from subjects enrolled in the Study and used pursuant to the protocol, including, but not limited to, CSF, blood, bone marrow, urine, sera, tumors, and other biological materials.

SUBRECIPIENT certifies that appropriate informed consents have been obtained from its patients to allow *NPC* to use Biological Materials obtained from SUBRECIPIENT in accordance with the study protocol. It is understood by the Parties that all Biological Materials will be used in accordance with the protocol. In the event of early termination thereof or any termination or expiration of this Agreement, whichever is earliest, all unused Biologic Materials shall be destroyed or returned to SUBRECIPIENT pursuant to the terms of the protocol or direction of the Project Director.

14.   Recombinant DNA

If this Subaward Agreement involves recombinant DNA technology, SUBRECIPIENT must establish a standing Biosafety Committee as set forth in the "NIH Guidelines for Recombinant DNA Research" and the "Administrative Practices Supplement to the NIH Guidelines for Research Involving Recombinant DNA Molecules."

Fɪɢ. C-6 (ᴄᴏɴᴛɪɴᴜᴇᴅ)

15.   Allowable Costs

Allowable costs shall be determined by SUBRECIPIENT in accordance with cost principles generally accepted by, or required to be used by, like organizations in effect at the effective date of this Subaward Agreement:

1. OMB Circular A-21 – Cost Principles for Educational Institutions

2. OMB Circular A-87 – Cost Principles for State & Local Governments and Indian Tribal Governments

3. OMB Circular A-122 – Costs Principles for Non-Profit Institutions

4. 45 C.F.R. 74, Appendix E – Cost Principles for Hospitals

5. 48 C.F.R. Subpart 31.2 (FAR) – Cost Principles for Commercial Organizations

16.   Billing

For services satisfactorily rendered, and upon receipt and approval of the invoices, **NPC** agrees to compensate SUBRECIPIENT for direct and indirect costs incurred in the performance of this Subaward Agreement, provided that the total of such costs does not exceed the estimated cost as provided in Article 3 herein.

SUBRECIPIENT shall submit monthly invoices for allowable costs incurred in the performance of work under this Agreement to the following address:

NPC
123 Address
Anywhere, State 12345

Invoices should be submitted to **NPC**'s Financial Contact as indicated in Attachment B and must reference **NPC**'s Subaward Agreement number XXX. SUBRECIPIENT will be notified if additional information is required.

The final invoice, clearly marked FINAL, must be received within 60 days after the Period of Performance indicated in Article 2. **NPC**'s final payment to SUBRECIPIENT shall be forwarded upon receipt and acceptance of all required reports (as set forth in Article 9). In order to comply with its obligations to PRIME SPONSOR, **NPC** must receive SUBRECIPIENT's final invoice within 60 days after the period of performance indicated in Article 2. If the final invoice cannot be submitted within such 60-day period, SUBRECIPIENT shall notify **NPC**'s Financial Contact as indicated in Attachment B in writing within the 60-day period, indicating the reason for the delay. If **NPC** does not receive the final invoice within the 60-day period or has not been notified of any delay in the final invoice within the 60-day period, **NPC** reserves the right to refuse payment of SUBRECIPIENT's final invoice.

If this Subaward Agreement is from federal pass-through sources, including all amendments thereto, then the final voucher must be signed and marked final by the SUBRECIPIENT with the following statement:

*"The SUBRECIPIENT assures to **NPC** that all expenditures were incurred in full compliance with OMB Circular A-133 or its own applicable audit regulations. Disallowed costs if found during the retention period of this Subaward Agreement will be promptly refunded to **NPC**."*

17.   Audit

SUBRECIPIENT shall maintain and have available for audit and inspection all administrative and financial documents, and all other records, allocated to this Subaward Agreement for a period of three years following the expiration date except that, if an audit is initiated before the expiration of the three year period, the records shall be retained until audit findings have been resolved. The above records are subject to inspection and audit by **NPC**, its designated representatives, representatives of the DHHS Awarding Agency, the DHHS Inspector General or the Comptroller General of the United States or any of their duly authorized representatives at all reasonable times and upon advanced notice during the life of the Agreement and for three years thereafter, or longer if required by audit.

Fig. C-6 (CONTINUED)

Any costs paid to SUBRECIPIENT by **NPC** which are subsequently found to be disallowed under audit shall be refunded to **NPC**.

SUBRECIPIENT agrees to comply with the requirements of OMB Circular A-133.

SUBRECIPIENT further agrees to provide **NPC** with copies of its current independent auditor's report. In cases of noncompliance with federal laws and regulations, SUBRECIPIENT will also provide copies of responses to auditor's report(s) and a plan for corrective action. All records and reports prepared in accordance with the requirements of OMB Circular A-133 shall be available for inspection by **NPC**, its designated representatives, representatives of the DHHS Awarding Agency, the DHHS Inspector General or the Comptroller General of the United States or any of their duly authorized representatives at all reasonable times and upon advanced notice during the life of the Subaward Agreement and for three years thereafter, or longer if required by audit.

18. Property

Title to use and disposition of property and equipment purchased (subject to prior approval) under this agreement shall vest pursuant to OMB Circular A-110, FAR Part 45 and/or terms and conditions of the Prime Award, whichever is applicable.

19. Program Income

SUBRECIPIENT shall inform **NPC** of any program-related income resulting from this Subaward Agreement and shall maintain appropriate records for the receipt and disposition of such income to enable **NPC** to fulfill its responsibilities to PRIME SPONSOR. SUBRECIPIENT agrees to utilize any program income in accordance with the policy of PRIME SPONSOR and the Prime Award, if any.

20. Liability for Negligence

SUBRECIPIENT will be responsible for damages to the extent caused by the negligence of its officers, agents and employees arising from the performance of this Subaward Agreement. **NPC** will be responsible for all damages to the extent caused by the negligence of its officers, agents and employees arising from the performance of this Agreement.

21. Insurance

SUBRECIPIENT shall obtain and maintain comprehensive liability insurance or self-insurance sufficient to cover its responsibilities under this project. If requested, SUBRECIPIENT agrees to provide evidence of such insurance to **NPC** via Certificate of Insurance or other documentation acceptable to **NPC** within thirty (30) days of written request.

22. Termination

Either Party may terminate this Subaward Agreement upon thirty (30) days written notification to the other Party. However, in the event that **NPC**'s Sponsor terminates its award to **NPC** pursuant to Article 4, this Agreement will be immediately terminated. In the event of termination **NPC** will pay for costs incurred and noncancelable commitments through the date of termination, contingent upon **NPC** having received said funds from PRIME SPONSOR. Upon termination, SUBRECIPIENT shall make all reasonable efforts to mitigate costs. SUBRECIPIENT will furnish all necessary reports of research completed or in progress through the date of termination, as required under Article 9.

23. Publication

It is the intent of the Parties to freely publish and disseminate research results under this Subaward Agreement subject to any restrictions or requirements imposed by PRIME SPONSOR and the Prime Award. SUBRECIPIENT shall provide **NPC** the opportunity to review any proposed manuscript under this Agreement thirty (30) days prior to SUBRECIPIENT's submission for publication and will consider **NPC's** comments in good faith. A copy of the publication resulting from the work performed in whole or in part under this Agree-

---

FIG. C-6 (CONTINUED)

ment shall be submitted to **NPC** and an unrestricted, worldwide, royalty-free and other fee-free license to use or copy them shall be provided to **NPC**.

SUBRECIPIENT shall acknowledge support of the PRIME SPONSOR as follows: "*This project has been funded in whole or in part with federal funds from the NIH under Grant No. _____. The results were independently derived and do not reflect any endorsement on the part of the federal government or **NPC**.*" Any copyrighted or copyrightable materials shall be subject to a royalty-free, nonexclusive and irrevocable license to the United States Government to reproduce, publish or otherwise use and to authorize others to do so for United States Government purposes.

24. Publicity

Neither Party shall identify the other Party in any products, publicity, promotion, promotional advertising, or other promotional materials to be disseminated to the public, or use any trademark, service mark, trade name, logo, or symbol that is representative of the other Party or its entities, whether registered or not, or use the name, title, likeness, or statement of any faculty member, employee, or student, without the other Party's prior written consent. Any use of the other Party's name shall be limited to statements of fact and shall not imply endorsement by that Party to the other Party's products or services.

25. Laws and Regulations

This Subaward Agreement is governed by federal law and, to the extent not inconsistent therewith, the laws of the State of Washington. The Parties agree to comply with all applicable local, state and federal laws and regulations regarding the work conducted under this Agreement.

26. Dispute Resolution

If any dispute arises between the Parties in connection with this Subaward Agreement and it cannot be resolved by mutual agreement after meetings between the Parties, it shall be submitted to a neutral third party appointed by the American Arbitration Association or other arbitrator agreed to by the parties. Arbitration will be held in **City, State**, or at some other mutually agreeable location.

27. Assignment

Neither Party may assign this Subaward Agreement without the prior written consent of the other Party and the prior consent of PRIME SPONSOR if required.

28. Severability

If any provision of this Subaward Agreement becomes or is declared illegal, invalid, or unenforceable, the provisions will be divisible from this Agreement and deemed to be deleted from the Agreement. If the deletion substantially alters the basis of the Agreement, the Parties will negotiate in good faith to amend the provisions of the Agreement to give effect to the original intent of the Parties.

29. Independent Contractors

NPC and SUBRECIPIENT are independent contractors and neither is an agent, joint venturer, or partner of the other.

30. Amendments or Changes

Amendments or changes to this Subaward Agreement must be in writing and signed by each Party's authorized representative, with the exception of changes to Attachment B.

31. Representations & Certifications

SUBRECIPIENT agrees to exercise its reasonable efforts to ensure that compliance, assurances and certifications required by DHHS are met. Such compliance, assurances and certifications required of SUBRECiPIENT shall include but not necessarily be limited to:

Fig. C-6 (CONTINUED)

A. <u>Civil Rights.</u> Compliance with Title VI of the Civil Rights Act of 1964.

B. <u>Handicapped Individuals.</u> Compliance with Section 504 of the Rehabilitation Act of 1973 as amended.

C. <u>Sex Discrimination.</u> Compliance with Section 901 of Title IX of the Education Amendments of 1972 as amended.

D. (1) <u>Patents, Licenses, and Inventions.</u> The determination of the rights of ownership and disposition of inventions resulting from the performance of the research under this grant shall be in accordance with DHHS policy. SUBRECIPIENT will ensure that this policy is applicable to all persons who perform any part of the work under this AGREEMENT and who may be reasonably expected to make inventions. Compliance with the Standard Patent Rights clauses as specified in 37 C.F.R., Part 401.14, FAR 52.227-11, or 35 U.S.C. 200 et.seq., whichever is appropriate and applicable.

   (2) The rights in Article 8 (within) shall apply to the extent that the U.S. Department of Veterans Affairs' rights pursuant to 35 U.S.C. § 102,37 C.F.R. Part 501, and 38 C.F.R. §§ 1.650-1.663 are not applicable.

E. <u>Debarment and Suspension.</u> SUBRECEPIENT must certify that it is not presently debarred, suspended, proposed for debarment, declared ineligible, or voluntarily excluded from covered transactions by any federal department or agency of the United States of America.

F. <u>Non-Delinquency on Federal Debt.</u> SUBRECIPIENT is not delinquent on the repayment of any debt(s) to the government of the United States of America.

G. <u>Drug-Free Workplace.</u> Compliance with the Drug-Free Workplace Act of 1988, 45 C.F.R. Part 76, Subpart F.

H. <u>Restrictions on Lobbying.</u> Compliance with 101-121, Title 31, Section 1352, which prohibits the use of (federal) appropriated funds for lobbying in connection with this particular Subaward Agreement. The undersigned shall require that the language of this certification be included in the award documents of all subawards at all tiers (including subcontracts, subgrants, and contracts under grants, loans, and cooperative agreements) and that all SUBRECIPIENTS shall certify and disclose accordingly. This certification is a material representation of fact upon which reliance was placed when this transaction was made or entered into. Submission of this certification is a prerequisite for making or entering into this transaction imposed by Section 1352, Title 31, U.S.C. Any person who fails to file the required certification shall be subject to a civil penalty of not less than $10,000 and not more than $100,000 for each such failure.

I. <u>Anti-Kick Back Act of 1986.</u> SUBRECEPIENT certifies, by signing this document that to the best of its knowledge it has not received any money, fee, commission, credit, gift, gratuity, things of value, or compensation of any kind, provided directly or indirectly, for the purpose of improperly obtaining or rewarding favorable treatment in connection with the Prime Award or in connection with this Subaward Agreement relating to the Prime Award.

J. <u>Conflict of Interest.</u> Compliance with 42 C.F.R. 50, Subpart F.

K. <u>Revitalization Act.</u> Pursuant to NIH Appropriations Act (P.L.106-554, 506(12-00), when purchasing equipment or products under this assistance award, SUBRECEPIENT should, whenever possible, purchase only American-made items. (Buy American Act, 41, U.S.C. 10, and implemented by FAR Subparts 25.1 and 25.2.)

L. <u>Continued Ban on Funding of Human Embryo Research and Prohibition for Cloning of Human Embryo Research and Prohibition for Cloning of Human Beings.</u> Pursuant to Current Law or Public Law 106-113 Section 510 FY2000, the NIH is prohibited from using appropriated funds to support human embryo research. Contract funds may not be used for (1) the creation of a human embryo or embryos for research purposes; or (2) research in which a human embryo or embryos are destroyed, discarded, or knowingly subjected to risk of injury or death greater than that allowed for research on fetuses in utero under 45

FIG. C-6 (CONTINUED)

C.F.R. 46.208(a)(2) and Section 498(b) of the Public Health Service Act (42 U.S.C.289g(b)). The term "human embryo or embryos" includes any organism, not protected as a human subject under 45 C.F.R. 46 as of the date of the Act, that is derived by fertilization, parthenogenesis, cloning, or any other means from one or more human gametes or human diploid cells. Additionally, in accordance with a March 4, 1998 Presidential Memorandum, federal funds may not be used for cloning of human beings.

M. <u>Domestic Travel</u>. Pursuant to OMB Circular A-21, section J. 48, government regulations require that only the cost of the lowest available airfare may be charged directly or indirectly to government sponsored projects.

N. <u>Foreign Travel.</u> Government regulations require that U.S. carriers, economy fare, be used (1) for departure from and entry into the United States and (2) for any other portions of the trip where U.S. carriers are available.

O. SUBRECIPIENT has filed the assurance required under the PHS final rule entitled "Responsibilities of Awardee and Applicant Institutions for Dealing with and Reporting Possible Misconduct in Science." If SUBRECIPIENT does not have its own assurance, SUBRECIPIENT agrees to be bound by **NPC's**.

P. SUBRECEPIENT agrees to fulfill the requirements of any other Assurance(s) included in the NIH Grants Policy Statement (NIHGPS) (Rev.) 12/03, as may be required by DHHS for the work undertaken by SUBRECEPIENT.

By signing this Subaward Agreement, SUBRECIPIENT agrees to maintain current Representations and Certifications for the duration of the conduct of this project.

32.   Objectivity in Research/Conflict of Interest

SUBRECIPIENT certifies it has written and enforced conflict of interest policy that is consistent with the provision of 42 C.F.R. Part 50, Subpart F "Responsibility of Applicants for Promoting Objectivity in Research." If SUBRECIPIENT does not have such a policy, it agrees to abide by **NPC's** policy. SUBRECIPIENT also certifies that to the best of SUBRECIPIENT's knowledge, all financial disclosures related to the activities funded by this Subaward Agreement and required by its conflict of interest policy have been made; and that all identified conflicts of interest under this Agreement will have been satisfactorily managed, reduced or eliminated prior to the expenditures of any funds under this Agreement in accordance with SUBRECIPIENT's conflict of interest policy. SUBRECIPIENT's Administrative Contact must disclose conflicts, which cannot be satisfactorily managed, reduced or eliminated.

33.   HIPAA

In connection with research studies, SUBRECIPIENT may collect "Protected Health Information" ("PHI") as defined in 45 C.F.R. 164.501. SUBRECIPIENT shall obtain a patient authorization or informed consent from study subjects to allow SUBRECIPIENT to disclose the PHI to **NPC** and PRIME SPONSOR. If either Party de-identifies PHI in accordance with the standards as set forth in 45 C.F.R. 164.514, the Parties may use and disclose the de-identified information as allowed by law.

34.   NO WARRANTIES

NPC MAKES NO WARRANTIES, EXPRESS OR IMPLIED, AS TO ANY BIOLOGICAL MATERIAL, DATA OR RESULTS UNDER THIS SUBAWARD AGREEMENT AND SHALL NOT BE LIABLE FOR INDIRECT OR CONSEQUENTIAL DAMAGES IN CONNECTION THEREWITH. THE PROVISIONS OF THIS CLAUSE SHALL SURVIVE THE TERMINATION OF THIS AGREEMENT.

35.   Salary Limitations

None of the funds awarded under this Subaward Agreement shall be used to pay the salary of an individual at a rate in excess of the amount allowed under federal law. This limitation applies to any subcontracts under any tier under this Agreement.

Fig. C-6 (continued)

36. **Entire Agreement**

This Subaward Agreement represents the entire agreement and understandings between the Parties with respect to its subject matter. It supersedes all prior or contemporaneous discussions, representations, or agreements, whether written or oral, of the Parties regarding this subject matter.

Accepted for:

NPC   XXXXXXXXXXXXXXXXXXXXX

By: _____   By:_____

Name _____   Name: _____

Title: _____   Title:_____

Date: _____   Date _____

                                                                    EIN: _____

FIG. C-6 (CONTINUED)

ATTACHMENT A
Subrecipient Proposal and Budget

Fig. C-6 (continued)

ATTACHMENT B
Contacts

NPC Contacts	Subrecipient Contacts
Administrative Contact: Name: Address: Telephone: Fax: Email:	Administrative Contact: Name: Address: Telephone: Fax: Email:
Project Director (*NPC* Principal Investigator): Name: Address: TTelephone: Fax: Email:	SUBRECIPIENT Principal Investigator: Name: Address: Telephone: Fax: Email:
Financial Contact: Name: Address: Telephone: Fax: Email:	Financial Contact: Name: Address: Telephone: Fax: Email:
Authorized Official: Name: Address: Telephone: Fax: Email:	Authorized Official: Name: Address: Telephone: Fax: Email:

Part D: Regulatory Requirements

Excerpts from OMB Circulars

The following are excerpts of OMB circulars that are particularly relevant to subrecipient monitoring issues. They address the pass-through entity's responsibility to monitor subrecipients, prior approval provisions and related-audit requirements. There may be other provisions that affect individual subawards. Readers, therefore, may find it useful to review the circulars in their entirety. The circulars are available on the Internet at OMB's home page, http://www.whitehouse.gov/OMB/grants/index.html, or from the Government Printing Office, 202-512-1800.

OMB Circular A-110, *Uniform Administrative Requirements for Grants and Agreements With Institutions of Higher Education, Hospitals and Other Nonprofit Organizations*

General

§___.5 Subawards.

Unless sections of this circular specifically exclude subrecipients from coverage, the provisions of this circular shall be applied to subrecipients performing work under awards if such subrecipients are institutions of higher education, hospitals or other nonprofit organizations. State and local government subrecipients are subject to the provisions of regulations implementing the grants management common rule, "Uniform Administrative Requirements for Grants and Cooperative Agreements to State and Local Governments," published at 53 FR 8034 (March 11, 1988).

§___.13 Debarment and suspension.

Federal awarding agencies and recipients shall comply with the nonprocurement debarment and suspension common rule implementing Executive Orders 12549 and 12689, "Debarment and Suspension." This common rule restricts subawards and contracts with certain parties that are debarred, suspended or otherwise excluded from or ineligible for participation in federal assistance programs or activities.

§___.51 Monitoring and reporting program performance.

(a) Recipients are responsible for managing and monitoring each project, program, subaward, function or activity supported by the award. Recipients shall monitor subawards to ensure subrecipients have met the audit requirements as delineated in §___.26.

Special Conditions

§___.14 Special award conditions.

If an applicant or recipient: (a) has a history of poor performance, (b) is not financially stable, (c) has a management system that does not meet the standards prescribed in this circular, (d) has not conformed to the terms and conditions of a previous award, or (e) is not otherwise responsible, Federal awarding agencies may impose additional requirements as needed, provided that such applicant or recipient is notified in writing as to: the nature of the additional requirements, the reason why the additional requirements are being imposed, the nature of the corrective action needed, the time allowed for completing the corrective actions, and the method for requesting reconsideration of the additional requirements imposed. Any special conditions shall be promptly removed once the conditions that prompted them have been corrected.

Prior Approvals

§___.25 Revision of budget and program plans.

(a) The budget plan is the financial expression of the project or program as approved during the award process. It may include either the federal and nonfederal share, or only the federal share, depending upon federal awarding agency requirements. It shall be related to performance for program evaluation purposes whenever appropriate.

(b) Recipients are required to report deviations from budget and program plans, and request prior approvals for budget and program plan revisions, in accordance with this section.

(c) For nonconstruction awards, recipients shall request prior approvals from federal awarding agencies for one or more of the following program or budget related reasons.

(1) Change in the scope or the objective of the project or program (even if there is no associated budget revision requiring prior written approval).

(2) Change in a key person specified in the application or award document.

(3) The absence for more than three months, or a 25 percent reduction in time devoted to the project, by the approved project director or principal investigator.

(4) The need for additional federal funding.

(5) The transfer of amounts budgeted for indirect costs to absorb increases in direct costs, or vice versa, if approval is required by the federal awarding agency.

(6) The inclusion, unless waived by the federal awarding agency, of costs that require prior approval in accordance with OMB Circular A-21, "Cost Principles for Institutions of Higher Education," OMB Circular A-122, "Cost Principles for Nonprofit Organizations," or 45 CFR Part 74 Appendix E, "Principles for Determining Costs Applicable to Research and Development under Grants and Contracts with Hospitals," or 48 CFR Part 31, "Contract Cost Principles and Procedures," as applicable.

(7) The transfer of funds allotted for training allowances (direct payment to trainees) to other categories of expense.

(8) Unless described in the application and funded in the approved awards, the subaward, transfer or contract-

ing out of any work under an award. This provision does not apply to the purchase of supplies, material, equipment or general support services.

(d) No other prior approval requirements for specific items may be imposed unless a deviation has been approved by OMB.

(e) Except for requirements listed in paragraphs (c)(1) and (c)(4) of this section, federal awarding agencies are authorized, at their option, to waive cost-related and administrative prior written approvals required by this circular and OMB Circulars A-21 and A-122. Such waivers may include authorizing recipients to do any one or more of the following.

(1) Incur pre-award costs 90 calendar days prior to award or more than 90 calendar days with the prior approval of the federal awarding agency. All pre-award costs are incurred at the recipient's risk (i.e., the federal awarding agency is under no obligation to reimburse such costs if for any reason the recipient does not receive an award or if the award is less than anticipated and inadequate to cover such costs).

(2) Initiate a one-time extension of the expiration date of the award of up to 12 months unless one or more of the following conditions apply. For one-time extensions, the recipient must notify the federal awarding agency in writing with the supporting reasons and revised expiration date at least 10 days before the expiration date specified in the award. This one-time extension may not be exercised merely for the purpose of using unobligated balances.

(i) The terms and conditions of award prohibit the extension.

(ii) The extension requires additional federal funds.

(iii) The extension involves any change in the approved objectives or scope of the project.

(3) Carry forward unobligated balances to subsequent funding periods.

(4) For awards that support research, unless the federal awarding agency provides otherwise in the award or in the agency's regulations, the prior approval requirements described in paragraph (e) are automatically waived (i.e., recipients need not obtain such prior approvals) unless one of the conditions included in paragraph (e)(2) applies.

(f) The federal awarding agency may, at its option, restrict the transfer of funds among direct cost categories or programs, functions and activities for awards in which the federal share of the project exceeds $100,000 and the cumulative amount of such transfers exceeds or is expected to exceed 10 percent of the total budget as last approved by the federal awarding agency. No federal awarding agency shall permit a transfer that would cause any federal appropriation or part thereof to be used for purposes other than those consistent with the original intent of the appropriation.

(g) All other changes to nonconstruction budgets, except for the changes described in paragraph (j), do not require prior approval.

(h) For construction awards, recipients shall request prior written approval promptly from federal awarding agencies for budget revisions whenever (1), (2) or (3) apply.

(1) The revision results from changes in the scope or the objective of the project or program.

(2) The need arises for additional federal funds to complete the project.

(3) A revision is desired which involves specific costs for which prior written approval requirements may be imposed consistent with applicable OMB cost principles listed in §___.27.

(i) No other prior approval requirements for specific items may be imposed unless a deviation has been approved by OMB.

(j) When a federal awarding agency makes an award that provides support for both construction and nonconstruction work, the federal awarding agency may require the recipient to request prior approval from the federal awarding agency before making any fund or budget transfers between the two types of work supported.

(k) For both construction and nonconstruction awards, federal awarding agencies shall require recipients to notify the federal awarding agency in writing promptly whenever the amount of federal authorized funds is expected to exceed the needs of the recipient for the project period by more than $5,000 or five percent of the federal award, whichever is greater. This notification shall not be required if an application for additional funding is submitted for a continuation award.

(l) When requesting approval for budget revisions, recipients shall use the budget forms that were used in the application unless the federal awarding agency indicates a letter of request suffices.

(m) Within 30 calendar days from the date of receipt of the request for budget revisions, federal awarding agencies shall review the request and notify the recipient whether the budget revisions have been approved. If the revision is still under consideration at the end of 30 calendar days, the federal awarding agency shall inform the recipient in writing of the date when the recipient may expect the decision.

Audits

§ ___.26 Nonfederal audits.

(a) Recipients and subrecipients that are institutions of higher education or other nonprofit organizations (including hospitals) shall be subject to the audit requirements contained in the Single Audit Act Amendments of 1996 (31 U.S.C. §§7501-7507) and revised OMB Circular A-133, "Audits of States, Local Governments, and Nonprofit Organizations."

(b) State and local governments shall be subject to the audit requirements contained in the Single Audit Act Amendments of 1996 (31 U.S.C. §§7501-7507) and revised OMB Circular A-133, "Audits of States, Local Governments, and Nonprofit Organizations."

(c) For-profit hospitals not covered by the audit provisions of revised OMB Circular A-133 shall be subject to the audit requirements of the federal awarding agencies.

(d) Commercial organizations shall be subject to the audit requirements of the federal awarding agency or the prime recipient as incorporated into the award document.

Grants Management Common Rule, *Uniform Administrative Requirements for Grants and Cooperative Agreements to State and Local Governments*

General

§ ___ .35 Subawards to debarred and suspended parties.

Grantees and subgrantees must not make any award or permit any award (subgrant or contract) at any tier to any party which is debarred or suspended or is otherwise excluded from or ineligible for participation in federal assistance programs under Executive Order 12549, "Debarment and Suspension."

§ ___ .37 Subgrants.

(a) *States.* States shall follow state law and procedures when awarding and administering subgrants (whether on a cost reimbursement or fixed amount basis) of financial assistance to local and Indian tribal governments. States shall:

(1) Ensure that every subgrant includes any clauses required by federal statute and executive orders and their implementing regulations;

(2) Ensure that subgrantees are aware of requirements imposed upon them by federal statute and regulation;

(3) Ensure that a provision for compliance with Section ___ .42 is placed in every cost reimbursement subgrant; and

(4) Conform any advances of grant funds to subgrantees substantially to the same standards of timing and amount that apply to cash advances by federal agencies.

(b) *All other grantees.* All other grantees shall follow the provisions of this part which are applicable to awarding agencies when awarding and administering subgrants (whether on a cost reimbursement or fixed amount basis) of financial assistance to local and Indian tribal governments. Grantees shall:

(1) Ensure that every subgrant includes a provision for compliance with this part;

(2) Ensure that every subgrant includes any clauses required by federal statute and executive orders and their implementing regulations; and

(3) Ensure that subgrantees are aware of requirements imposed upon them by federal statutes and regulations.

(c) *Exceptions.* By their own terms, certain provisions of this part do not apply to the award and administration of subgrants:

(1) Section ___ .10;

(2) Section ___ .11;

(3) The letter-of-credit procedures specified in Treasury regulations at 31 CFR Part 205, cited in § ___ .21; and

(4) Section ___ .50.

§ ___ .40 Monitoring and reporting program performance.

(a) Monitoring by grantees. Grantees are responsible for managing the day-to-day operations of grant and subgrant supported activities. Grantees must monitor grant and subgrant supported activities to assure compliance with applicable federal requirements and that performance goals are being achieved. Grantee monitoring must cover each program, function or activity.

Special Conditions

§ ___ .12 Special grant or subgrant conditions for "high-risk" grantees.

(a) A grantee or subgrantee may be considered "high risk" if an awarding agency determines that a grantee or subgrantee:

(1) Has a history of unsatisfactory performance;

(2) Is not financially stable;

(3) Has a management system which does not meet the management standards set forth in this part;

(4) Has not conformed to terms and conditions of previous awards; or

(5) Is otherwise not responsible; and if the awarding agency determines that an award will be made, special conditions and/or restrictions shall correspond to the high risk condition and shall be included in the award.

(b) Special conditions or restrictions may include:

(1) Payment on a reimbursement basis;

(2) Withholding authority to proceed to the next phase until receipt of evidence of acceptable performance within a given funding period;

(3) Requiring additional, more detailed financial reports;

(4) Additional project monitoring;

(5) Requiring the grantee or subgrantee to obtain technical or management assistance; or

(6) Establishing additional prior approvals.

(c) If an awarding agency decides to impose such conditions, the awarding official will notify the grantee or subgrantee as early as possible, in writing, of:

(1) The nature of the special conditions/restrictions;

(2) The reason(s) for imposing them;

(3) The corrective actions which must be taken before they will be removed and the time allowed for completing the corrective actions; and

(4) The method of requesting reconsideration of the conditions/restrictions imposed.

Prior Approvals

§ ___ .30 Changes.

(a) *General.* Grantees and subgrantees are permitted to rebudget within the approved direct cost budget to meet unanticipated requirements and may make limited program changes to the approved project. However, unless waived by the awarding agency, certain types of post-award changes in budgets and projects shall require the prior written approval of the awarding agency.

(b) *Relation to cost principles.* The applicable cost principles (see § ___ .22) contain requirements for prior approval of certain types of costs. Except where waived, those requirements apply to all grants and subgrants even if paragraphs (c) through (f) of this section do not.

(c) *Budget changes.* (1) Nonconstruction projects. Except as stated in other regulations or an award document, grantees or subgrantees shall obtain the prior approval of the awarding agency whenever any of the following changes is anticipated under a nonconstruction award:

(i) Any revision which would result in the need for additional funding.

(ii) Unless waived by the awarding agency, cumulative transfers among direct cost categories, or, if applicable, among separately budgeted programs, projects, functions, or activities which exceed or are expected to exceed ten percent of the current total approved budget, whenever the awarding agency's share exceeds $100,000.

(iii) Transfer of funds allotted for training allowances (i.e., from direct payments to trainees to other expense categories).

(2) Construction projects. Grantees and subgrantees shall obtain prior written approval for any budget revision which would result in the need for additional funds.

(3) Combined construction and nonconstruction projects. When a grant or subgrant provides funding for both construction and nonconstruction activities, the grantee or subgrantee must obtain prior written approval from the awarding agency before making any fund or budget transfer from nonconstruction to construction or vice versa.

(d) *Programmatic changes.* Grantees or subgrantees must obtain the prior approval of the awarding agency whenever any of the following actions is anticipated:

(1) Any revision of the scope or objectives of the project (regardless of whether there is an associated budget revision requiring prior approval).

(2) Need to extend the period of availability of funds.

(3) Changes in key persons in cases where specified in an application or a grant award. In research projects, a change in the project director or principal investigator shall always require approval unless waived by the awarding agency.

(4) Under nonconstruction projects, contracting out, subgranting (if authorized by law) or otherwise obtaining the services of a third party to perform activities which are central to the purposes of the award. This approval requirement is in addition to the approval requirements of §____.36 but does not apply to the procurement of equipment, supplies, and general support services.

(e) *Additional prior approval requirements.* The awarding agency may not require prior approval for any budget revision which is not described in paragraph (c) of this section.

(f) *Requesting prior approval.* (1) A request for prior approval of any budget revision will be in the same budget formal the grantee used in its application and shall be accompanied by a narrative justification for the proposed revision.

(2) A request for a prior approval under the applicable federal cost principles (see §____.22) may be made by letter.

(3) A request by a subgrantee for prior approval will be addressed in writing to the grantee. The grantee will promptly review such request and shall approve or disap-prove the request in writing. A grantee will not approve any budget or project revision which is inconsistent with the purpose or terms and conditions of the federal grant to the grantee. If the revision, requested by the subgrantee would result in a change to the grantee's approved project which requires federal prior approval, the grantee will obtain the federal agency's approval before approving the subgrantee's request.

Audits

§____.26 Non-federal audit.

(a) *Basic Rule.* Grantees and subgrantees are responsible for obtaining audits in accordance with the Single Audit Act Amendments of 1996 (31 U.S.C. §§7501-7507) and revised OMB Circular A-133, "Audits of States, Local Governments, and Nonprofit Organizations." The audits shall be made by an independent auditor in accordance with generally accepted government auditing standards covering financial audits.

(b) *Subgrantees.* State or local governments, as those terms are defined for purposes of the Single Audit Act Amendments of 1996, that provide federal awards to a subgrantee, which expends $500,000 or more (or other amount as specified by OMB) in federal awards in a fiscal year, shall:

(1) Determine whether state or local subgrantees have met the audit requirements of the act and whether subgrantees covered by OMB Circular A-110, "Uniform Administrative Requirements for Grants and Agreements with Institutions of Higher Education, Hospitals, and Other Nonprofit Organizations," have met the audit requirements of the act. Commercial contractors (private for-profit and private and governmental organizations) providing goods and services to state and local governments are not required to have a single audit performed. State and local governments should use their own procedures to ensure that the contractors has complied with laws and regulations affecting the expenditure of federal funds;

(2) Determine whether the subgrantee spent federal assistance funds provided in accordance with applicable laws and regulations. This may be accomplished by reviewing an audit of the subgrantee made in accordance with the act, Circular A-110, or through other means (e.g., program reviews) if the subgrantee has not had such an audit;

(3) Ensure that appropriate corrective action is taken within six months after receipt of the audit report in instance of noncompliance with federal laws and regulations;

(4) Consider whether subgrantee audits necessitate adjustment of the grantee's own records; and

(5) Require each subgrantee to permit independent auditors to have access to the records and financial statements.

(c) *Auditor selection.* In arranging for audit services, §____.36 shall be followed.

Recordkeeping

§___.42 Retention and access requirements for records.

(a) *Applicability.*

(1) This section applies to all financial and programmatic records, supporting documents, statistical records, and other records of grantees or subgrantees which are:

(i) Required to be maintained by the terms of this part, program regulations or the grant agreement, or

(ii) Otherwise reasonably considered as pertinent to program regulations or the grant agreement.

(2) This section does not apply to records maintained by contractors or subcontractors. For a requirement to place a provision concerning records in certain kinds of contracts, see §____.36(i)(10).

(b) *Length of retention period.*

(1) Except as otherwise provided, records must be retained for three years from the starting date specified in paragraph (c) of this section.

OMB Circular A-133, *Audits of States, Local Governments and Nonprofit Organizations*

General

§____.200 Audit requirements.

(a) *Audit required.* Nonfederal entities that expend $500,000 or more in a year in federal awards shall have a single or program-specific audit conducted for that year in accordance with the provisions of this part. Guidance on determining federal awards expended is provided in §____.205.

(b) *Single audit.* Nonfederal entities that expend $500,000 or more in a year in federal awards shall have a single audit conducted in accordance with §____.500 except when they elect to have a program-specific audit conducted in accordance with paragraph (c) of this section.

(c) *Program-specific audit election.* When an auditee expends federal awards under only one federal program (excluding research and development (R&D)) and the federal program's laws, regulations, or grant agreements do not require a financial statement audit of the auditee, the auditee may elect to have a program-specific audit conducted in accordance with §____.235. A program-specific audit may not be elected for R&D unless all of the federal awards expended were received from the same federal agency, or the same federal agency and the same pass-through entity, and that federal agency, or pass-through entity in the case of a subrecipient, approves in advance a program-specific audit.

(d) *Exemption when federal awards expended are less than $500,000.* Nonfederal entities that expend less than $500,000 a year in federal awards are exempt from federal audit requirements for that year, except as noted in §____.215(a), but records must be available for review or audit by appropriate officials of the federal agency, pass-through entity and Government Accountability Office (GAO).

Pass-Through and Subrecipient Responsibilities

§____.210 Subrecipient and vendor determinations.

(a) *General.* An auditee may be a recipient, a subrecipient, and a vendor. Federal awards expended as a recipient or a subrecipient would be subject to audit under this part. The payments received for goods or services provided as a vendor would not be considered federal awards. The guidance in paragraphs (b) and (c) of this section should be considered in determining whether payments constitute a federal award or a payment for goods and services.

(b) *Federal award.* Characteristics indicative of a federal award received by a subrecipient are when the organization:

(1) Determines who is eligible to receive what federal financial assistance;

(2) Has its performance measured against whether the objectives of the federal program are met;

(3) Has responsibility for programmatic decision making;

(4) Has responsibility for adherence to applicable federal program compliance requirements; and

(5) Uses the federal funds to carry out a program of the organization as compared to providing goods or services for a program of the pass-through entity.

(c) *Payment for goods and services.* Characteristics indicative of a payment for goods and services received by a vendor are when the organization:

(1) Provides the goods and services within normal business operations;

(2) Provides similar goods or services to many different purchasers;

(3) Operates in a competitive environment;

(4) Provides goods or services that are ancillary to the operation of the federal program; and

(5) Is not subject to compliance requirements of the federal program.

(d) *Use of judgment in making determination.* There may be unusual circumstances or exceptions to the listed characteristics. In making the determination of whether a subrecipient or vendor relationship exists, the substance of the relationship is more important than the form of the agreement. It is not expected that all of the characteristics will be present and judgment should be used in determining whether an entity is a subrecipient or vendor.

(e) *For-profit subrecipient.* Since this part does not apply to for-profit subrecipients, the pass-through entity is responsible for establishing requirements, as necessary, to ensure compliance by for-profit subrecipients. The contract with the for-profit subrecipient should describe applicable compliance requirements and the for-profit subrecipient's compliance responsibility. Methods to ensure compliance for federal awards made to for-profit subrecipients may include pre-award audits, monitoring during the contract and post-award audits.

(f) *Compliance responsibility for vendors.* In most cases, the auditee's compliance responsibility for vendors is only to ensure that the procurement, receipt and payment for goods and services comply with laws, regulations and the provisions of contracts or grant agreements. Program compliance requirements normally do not pass through to vendors. However, the auditee is responsible for ensuring compliance for vendor transactions which are structured such that the vendor is responsible for program compliance or the vendor's records must be reviewed to determine program compliance. Also, when these vendor transactions relate to a major program, the scope of the audit shall include determining whether these transactions are in compliance with laws, regulations and the provisions of contracts or grant agreements.

§____.400 Responsibilities.
* * * * *

(c) Federal awarding agency responsibilities. The federal awarding agency shall perform the following for the federal awards it makes:

(1) Identify federal awards made by informing each recipient of the CFDA title and number, award name and number, award year and if the award is for R&D. When some of this information is not available, the federal

agency shall provide information necessary to clearly describe the federal award.

(2) Advise recipients of requirements imposed on them by federal laws, regulations, and the provisions of contracts or grant agreements.

(3) Ensure that audits are completed and reports are received in a timely manner and in accordance with the requirements of this part.

(4) Provide technical advice and counsel to auditees and auditors as requested.

(5) Issue a management decision on audit findings within six months after receipt of the audit report and ensure that the recipient takes appropriate and timely corrective action.

(6) Assign a person responsible for providing annual updates of the compliance supplement to OMB.

(d) Pass-through entity responsibilities. A pass-through entity shall perform the following for the federal awards it makes:

(1) Identify federal awards made by informing each subrecipient of CFDA title and number, award name and number, award year, if the award is R&D, and name of federal agency. When some of this information is not available, the pass-through entity shall provide the best information available to describe the federal award.

(2) Advise subrecipients of requirements imposed on them by federal laws, regulations, and the provisions of contracts or grant agreements as well as any supplemental requirements imposed by the pass-through entity.

(3) Monitor the activities of subrecipients as necessary to ensure that federal awards are used for authorized purposes in compliance with laws, regulations and the provisions of contracts or grant agreements and that performance goals are achieved.

(4) Ensure that subrecipients expending $500,000 or more in federal awards during the subrecipient's fiscal year have met the audit requirements of this part for that fiscal year.

(5) Issue a management decision on audit findings within six months after receipt of the subrecipient's audit report and ensure that the subrecipient takes appropriate and timely corrective action.

(6) Consider whether subrecipient audits necessitate adjustment of the pass-through entity's own records.

(7) Require each subrecipient to permit the pass-through entity and auditors to have access to the records and financial statements as necessary for the pass-through entity to comply with this part.

§ ___ .405 Management decision.

(a) *General.* The management decision shall clearly state whether or not the audit finding is sustained, the reasons for the decision and the expected auditee action to repay disallowed costs, make financial adjustments or take other action. If the auditee has not completed corrective action, a timetable for follow-up should be given. Prior to issuing the management decision, the federal agency or pass-through entity may request additional information or documentation from the auditee, including a request for auditor assurance related to the documenta-

tion, as a way of mitigating disallowed costs. The management decision should describe any appeal process available to the auditee.

(b) *Federal agency.* As provided in § ___ .400(a)(7), the cognizant agency for audit shall be responsible for coordinating a management decision for audit findings that affect the programs of more than one federal agency. As provided in § ___ .400(c)(5), a federal awarding agency is responsible for issuing a management decision for findings that relate to federal awards it makes to recipients. Alternate arrangements may be made on a case-by-case basis by agreement among the federal agencies concerned.

(c) *Pass-through entity.* As provided in § ___ .400(d)(5), the pass-through entity shall be responsible for making the management decision for audit findings that relate to federal awards it makes to subrecipients.

Costs

§ ___ .230 Audit costs.

(a) Allowable costs. Unless prohibited by law, the cost of audits made in accordance with the provisions of this part are allowable charges to federal awards. The charges may be considered a direct cost or an allocated indirect cost, as determined in accordance with the provisions of applicable OMB cost principles circulars, the Federal Acquisition Regulation (FAR) (48 CFR Parts 30 and 31) or other applicable cost principles or regulations.

(b) Unallowable costs. A nonfederal entity shall not charge the following to a federal award:

(1) The cost of any audit under the Single Audit Act Amendments of 1996 (31 U.S.C. §7501 et seq.) not conducted in accordance with this part.

(2) The cost of auditing a nonfederal entity which has federal awards expended of less than $500,000 per year and is thereby exempted under § ___ .200(d) from having an audit conducted under this part. However, this does not prohibit a pass-through entity from charging federal awards for the cost of limited scope audits to monitor its subrecipients in accordance with § ___ .400(d)(3), provided the subrecipient does not have a single audit. For purposes of this part, limited scope audits only include agreed-upon procedures engagements conducted in accordance with either the AICPA's generally accepted auditing standards or attestation standards, that are paid for and arranged by a pass-through entity and address only one or more of the following types of compliance requirements: activities allowed or unallowed; allowable costs/cost principles; eligibility; matching, level of effort and earmarking; and reporting.

Reporting

§ ___ .320 Report submission.

* * * * *

(e) Additional submission by subrecipients. (1) In addition to the requirements discussed in paragraph (d) of this section, auditees that are also subrecipients shall submit to each pass-through entity one copy of the reporting package described in paragraph (c) of this section for each pass-through entity when the schedule of findings and questioned costs disclosed audit findings relating to federal awards that the pass-through entity provided or the summary schedule of prior audit findings reported the status of any audit findings relating to federal awards that the pass-through entity provided.

(2) Instead of submitting the reporting package to a pass-through entity, when a subrecipient is not required to submit a reporting package to a pass-through entity pursuant to paragraph (e)(1) of this section, the subrecipient shall provide written notification to the pass-through entity that: an audit of the subrecipient was conducted in accordance with this part (including the period covered by the audit and the name, amount, and CFDA number of the federal award(s) provided by the pass-through entity); the schedule of findings and questioned costs disclosed no audit findings relating to the federal award(s) that the pass-through entity provided; and the summary schedule of prior audit findings did not report on the status of any audit findings relating to the federal award(s) that the pass-through entity provided. A subrecipient may submit a copy of the reporting package described in paragraph (c) of this section to a pass-through entity to comply with this notification requirement.

Excerpt from OMB *Circular A-133 Compliance Supplement*

The OMB *Circular A-133 Compliance Supplement* provides auditors performing single audits of pass-through entities that spend at least $500,000 in federal funds each year with guidance for auditing their subrecipient monitoring systems. It identifies the aspects of subrecipient monitoring that auditors should test and the procedures they should use. Pass-through entities that have single audits performed should be aware that the compliance supplement provides audit guidance for other compliance areas in addition to subrecipient monitoring, such as allowable costs or eligibility. Therefore, they may want to review the compliance supplement in its entirety, which is available on-line at: http://www.whitehouse.gov/OMB/grants/index.html.

Subrecipient Monitoring

Compliance Requirements

A pass-through entity is responsible for:

- Identifying to the subrecipient the federal award information (e.g., CFDA title and number, award name, name of federal agency) and applicable compliance requirements.
- Monitoring the subrecipient's activities to provide reasonable assurance that the subrecipient administers federal awards in compliance with federal requirements.
- Ensuring required audits are performed and requiring the subrecipient to take prompt corrective action on any audit findings.
- Evaluating the impact of subrecipient activities on the pass-through entity's ability to comply with applicable federal regulations.

Factors such as the size of awards, percentage of the total program's funds awarded to subrecipients, level of risk involved and the complexity of the compliance requirements may influence the extent of monitoring procedures.

Monitoring activities may take various forms, such as reviewing reports submitted by the subrecipient, performing site visits to the subrecipient to review financial and programmatic records and observe operations, arranging for agreed-upon procedures engagements for certain aspects of subrecipient activities, such as eligibility determinations, reviewing the subrecipient's single audit or program-specific audit results, and evaluating audit findings and the subrecipient's corrective action plan.

The requirements for subrecipient monitoring are contained in the A-102 Common Rule (§___.37 and §___.40(a)), OMB Circular A-110 (§___.51(a)), federal awarding agency program regulations, and the terms and conditions of the award.

Audit Objectives

Determine whether the pass-through entity:

1. Identified federal award information and compliance requirements to the subrecipient, and approved only allowable activities in the award documents.
2. Monitored subrecipient activities to provide reasonable assurance that the subrecipient administers federal awards in compliance with federal requirements.
3. Ensured required audits are performed and requires appropriate corrective action on monitoring and audit findings.

4. Took appropriate action using sanctions in cases where the subrecipient continued to show inability or unwillingness to have the required audits.
5. Evaluates the impact of subrecipient activities on the pass-through entity.

Suggested Audit Procedures

(Note: The auditor may consider coordinating the tests related to subrecipients performed as part of cash management (tests of cash reports submitted by subrecipients), eligibility (tests that subawards were made only to eligible subrecipients), and procurement (tests of suspension and debarment certifications) with the testing of subrecipient monitoring.)

1. Discuss subrecipient monitoring with the pass-through entity's staff to gain an understanding of the scope of monitoring activities, including the number, size and complexity of awards to subrecipients.

2. Test award documents and/or approved agreements to ascertain if the pass-through entity made subrecipients aware of the award information (e.g., CFDA title and number, award name, name of federal agency) and requirements imposed by laws, regulations and the provisions of contract or grant agreements, and to verify that the activities approved in the award documents were allowable. This testing should include procedures to verify that the pass-through entity required subrecipients expending $500,000 or more in federal awards during the subrecipient's fiscal year to have audits made in accordance with OMB Circular A-133.

3. Review the pass-through entity's documentation of subrecipient monitoring to ascertain if the pass-through entity monitored that subrecipients used federal funds for authorized purposes and takes actions in response to monitoring findings. This review should include procedures to verify that the pass-through entity monitored the activities of subrecipients not subject to OMB Circular A-133, using techniques such as those discussed in the compliance requirements provisions of this section.

4. Verify that the pass-through entity receives audit reports from subrecipients required to have an audit in accordance with OMB Circular A-133, issues timely management decisions on audit and monitoring findings, and requires subrecipients to take timely corrective action on deficiencies identified in audits and subrecipient monitoring.

5. Verify that the effects of subrecipient noncompliance are properly reflected in the pass-through entity's records.

Glossary

These definitions are drawn from several sources including circulars A-110 and A-133, the grants management common rule and the *Webster's New World Dictionary, Second College Edition.*

Administrative requirements – areas common to grants in general, such as financial management, types and frequency of reports, and retention of records. These are distinguished from programmatic requirements, which are unique to each program or grant, such as activities that can be supported by grants under a particular program.

Auditor – an auditor, that is a public accountant or a federal, state or local government audit organization, which meets the general standards specified in *Government Auditing Standards.* The term does not include internal auditors of nonprofit organizations.

Award – financial assistance that provides support to accomplish a public purpose. Awards include grants and other agreements in the form of money, or property in lieu of money, to an eligible recipient. The term does not include: technical assistance, loans, loan guarantees, interest subsidies, insurance and direct payments to individuals. The term excludes contracts entered into and administered under procurement laws and regulations. See "Grant."

Awarding agency – a federal agency (with respect to a grant) or a pass-through entity (with respect to a subgrant). See "Federal awarding agency."

CFDA number – the number assigned to a federal program in the *Catalog of Federal Domestic Assistance* (CFDA).

Contract – a procurement contract under an award or subaward, and a procurement subcontract under a recipient's or subrecipient's contract.

Corrective action – action taken by the auditee that corrects identified deficiencies, produces recommended improvements or demonstrates that audit findings are either invalid or do not warrant auditee action.

Federal award – federal financial assistance and federal cost-reimbursement contracts that nonfederal entities receive directly from federal awarding agencies or indirectly from pass-through entities. It does not include procurement contracts (under grants or contracts) used to buy goods or services from vendors. Any audits of such vendors shall be covered by the terms and conditions of the contract.

Federal awarding agency – the federal agency that provides an award to the recipient. See "Awarding agency."

Federal financial assistance – assistance that nonfederal entities receive or administer in the form of grants, loans, loan guarantees, property (including donated surplus property), cooperative agreements, interest subsidies, insurance, food commodities, direct appropriations and other assistance. The term does not include amounts received as reimbursement for services rendered to individuals under Medicare and Medicaid.

Federal program – a federal agency function, activity, service or project that is created to implement a public policy or initiative and authorized by statute, regulation or other legal authority.

Grant – an award of financial assistance (including cooperative agreements) in the form of money, or property in lieu of money, provided to an eligible grantee. The term does not include technical assistance, loans, loan guarantees, interest subsidies, insurance or direct appropriations. Also, the term does not include grants to individuals, such as fellowships or other lump sum awards. See "Award."

Grantee – a state or local government, nonprofit organization, college, or university to which a grant is awarded and which is accountable for the use of the funds provided. The grantee is the entire legal entity even if only a particular component of the entity is designated in the grant award document. See "Recipient."

Indian tribe – any Indian tribe, band, nation or other organized group or community, including any Alaskan Native village or regional or village corporation (as defined in, or established under, the Alaskan Native Claims Settlement Act), that is recognized by the United States as eligible for the special programs and services provided by the United States to Indians because of their status as Indians.

Internal control – a process designed to provide reasonable assurance that the objectives in the following categories are achieved: effectiveness and efficiency of operations, reliability of financial reporting, and compliance with applicable laws and regulations.

Local government – any unit of local government within a state, including a county, borough, municipality, city, town, township, parish, local public authority, special district, school district, intrastate district, council of governments and any other instrumentality of local government.

Management decision – the evaluation by the federal awarding agency or pass-through entity of the audit findings and corrective action plan and the issuance of a written decision as to what corrective action is necessary.

Material weakness – a significant deficiency, or combination of significant deficiencies, that results in more than a remote likelihood that material noncompliance with a type of compliance requirement of a federal program will not be prevented or detected. A material weakness is more severe than a significant deficiency.

Monitor – to check or regulate the performance of.

Nonfederal entity – a state, local government or nonprofit organization.

Nonprofit organization – any corporation, trust, association, cooperative, or other organization that is operated primarily for scientific, educational, service, charitable or similar purposes in the public interest; is not organized primarily for profit; and uses its net proceeds to maintain, improve or expand its operations. The term nonprofit organization includes nonprofit institutions of higher education and hospitals.

OMB – the U.S. Office of Management and Budget.

Pass-through entity – a nonfederal entity that provides a federal award to a subrecipient to carry out a federal program.

Primary recipient. See "Pass-through entity."

Prior approval – written approval by an authorized official evidencing prior consent.

Recipient – a nonfederal entity that expends federal awards received directly from a federal awarding agency to carry out a federal program.

Reportable conditions – significant deficiencies in the design or operation of internal control that could adversely affect the entity's ability to record, process, summarize and report financial data consistent with the assertions of management in the financial statements.

Significant deficiency – a control deficiency, or combination of control deficiencies, that adversely affects the entity's ability to administer a federal program such that there is more than a remote likelihood that noncompliance with a type of compliance requirement of a federal program that is more than inconsequential will not be prevented or detected.

State – any state of the United States, the District of Columbia, the Commonwealth of Puerto Rico, the Virgin Islands, Guam, American Samoa, the Commonwealth of the Northern Mariana Islands, and the Trust Territory of the Pacific Islands, any instrumentality thereof, any multistate, regional, or interstate entity that has governmental functions, and any Indian tribe.

Subaward – an award of financial assistance in the form of money, or property, made under an award by a recipient to an eligible subrecipient or by a subrecipient to a lower tier subrecipient. The term includes financial assistance when provided by any legal agreement, even if the agreement is called a contract, but does not include procurement of goods and services or any form of assistance that is excluded from the definition of award.

Subgrant. See "Subaward."

Subgrantee. See "Subrecipient."

Subrecipient – a nonfederal entity that expends federal awards received from a pass-through entity to carry out a federal program. It does not include an individual that is a beneficiary of such a program. A subrecipient may also be a recipient of other federal awards directly from a federal awarding agency. Guidance on distinguishing between a subrecipient and a vendor is provided in Chapter 2 of this manual.

Vendor – a dealer, distributor, merchant or other provider of goods or services that are needed to administer a federal program. These goods or services may be for an organization's own use or for the use of beneficiaries of the federal program. Guidance on distinguishing between a subrecipient and a vendor is provided in Chapter 2 of this manual.

Index

This Page
Intentionally Left Blank

Practical, Time-Tested Guidance
For Grant Professionals

Federal Education Grants Management: What Administrators Need to Know

Federal Education Grants Management: What Administrators Need to Know is the only resource that focuses specifically on the unique compliance requirements associated with grants from the U.S. Department of Education. *You'll find:* A clear explanation – finally – of the Education Department's General Administrative Regulations and what they mean to you; How to find out which expenditures are allowable under federal grants; The ins-and-outs of key requirements like supplement-not-supplant and maintenance of effort; How to use the A-133 Single Audit Compliance Supplement to pinpoint the government's current audit priorities and avoid audit traps; Why understanding indirect costs can save you thousands of dollars; How to make sure your internal controls pass the government's tough tests; Understand the timeline for obligating funds and make sure you use every nickel by the deadline, and much more!

Federal Grants Management Handbook

The *Federal Grants Management Handbook* is the most comprehensive and trusted source for administering federal program funds – from submitting grant proposals to setting up financial management systems for payment and reporting… initiating audits and grant closeout to searching for best practices and procedures. Also available online.

Single Audit Information Service

The *Single Audit Information Service* is a comprehensive guide to all of the steps federal grantees and auditors must follow to ensure Single Audit Act compliance. From soliciting bids for audit services to preparing audit reports to resolving audit findings with federal officials, the *Service* provides detailed analyses of every aspect of single audit law and policy. It provides cost-effective and practical guidance on preparing for and performing single audits. All of the primary source documents grantees and auditors need are included –OMB circulars, GAO standards and federal agency regulations and guidance. Throughout the *Service*, you'll find helpful compliance tools such as checklists, sample reports and proven methods of single audit compliance. Regular *Service* updates provide up-to-date news and analysis.

GrantsWire

Created with the busy grant writer in mind, GrantsWire is a new tool to get reliable information on federal as well as private foundation grants. It provides just-released details on grant opportunities from federal agencies and private foundations on a weekly basis delivered via e-mail. Our GrantsWire Research Team zeros in on the latest funding opportunities and regulatory changes to deliver: one, compact, easy to scan e-mail filled with summaries of all the recently announced federal, private and corporate grant opportunities; just-announced rules that affect how you operate your grant-funded programs; summaries that include all of the pertinent intelligence you need to find grant funding and manage your federally funded programs – complete with a direct link to the actual rule or grant opportunity and direct links to new grant opportunities – not available from any of our competitors! Go to: **www.grantswire.com**.

Local/State Funding Report

Since 1972, Local/State Funding Report has detailed the latest federal funding programs, offering must-have intelligence and concise, comprehensive coverage of available dollars in rural development… healthcare… law enforcement… housing… juvenile justice… energy… emergency and disaster aid… transportation… the list goes on.

Guide to Federal Funding for Governments and Nonprofits

The *Guide to Federal Funding for Government and Nonprofits* offers fast, easy access to current, precise funding information on more than 750 federal grant-making programs – all grouped by function, not by agency. Thousands of your colleagues in local governments and in nonprofit agencies use the *Guide* to discover federal grant money every day.

Techniques for Monitoring Federal Subawards

This softbound book, written by the editors of the *Federal Grants Management Handbook* and *Single Audit Information Service*, explains grantees' and subrecipients' responsibilities, how to structure subaward agreements – and what provisions to include in those agreements, how to determine the most cost-effective monitoring methods, and details what auditors will look for in grantees' monitoring activities. Techniques include sample subaward agreements, checklists and excerpts from OMB circulars.

This Page
Intentionally Left Blank

This Page
Intentionally Left Blank

This Page
Intentionally Left Blank